Zora Neale Hurston

Recent Titles in Black History Lives

W.E.B. Du Bois: A Life in American History
Charisse Burden-Stelly and Gerald Horne

Thurgood Marshall: A Life in American History
Spencer R. Crew

Barack Obama: A Life in American History
F. Erik Brooks and MaCherie M. Placide

Harriet Tubman: A Life in American History
Kerry Walters

Zora Neale Hurston

A LIFE IN AMERICAN HISTORY

Stephanie Li

Black History Lives

BLOOMSBURY ACADEMIC
NEW YORK • LONDON • OXFORD • NEW DELHI • SYDNEY

BLOOMSBURY ACADEMIC
Bloomsbury Publishing Inc
1385 Broadway, New York, NY 10018, USA
50 Bedford Square, London, WC1B 3DP, UK
29 Earlsfort Terrace, Dublin 2, Ireland

BLOOMSBURY, BLOOMSBURY ACADEMIC and the Diana logo
are trademarks of Bloomsbury Publishing Plc

First published in the United States of America by ABC-CLIO 2020
Paperback edition published by Bloomsbury Academic 2025

Copyright © Stephanie Li, 2025

Cover photo: Zora Neale Hurston, ca. 1935-43. (Photo Researchers/Alamy)

All rights reserved. No part of this publication may be reproduced or transmitted in any form or by any means, electronic or mechanical, including photocopying, recording, or any information storage or retrieval system, without prior permission in writing from the publishers.

Bloomsbury Publishing Inc does not have any control over, or responsibility for, any third-party websites referred to or in this book. All internet addresses given in this book were correct at the time of going to press. The author and publisher regret any inconvenience caused if addresses have changed or sites have ceased to exist, but can accept no responsibility for any such changes.

Library of Congress Cataloging-in-Publication Data
Names: Li, Stephanie, 1977–
Title: Zora Neale Hurston : a life in American history / Stephanie Li.
Description: Santa Barbara : ABC-CLIO, 2020. | Series: Black history lives | Includes bibliographical references and index.
Identifiers: LCCN 2019040841 (print) | LCCN 2019040842 (ebook) | ISBN 9781440866548 (print) | ISBN 9781440866555 (ebook)
Subjects: LCSH: Hurston, Zora Neale. | Authors, American—20th century—Biography. | African American women authors—20th century—Biography. | Folklorists—United States—Biography. | Novelists, American—20th century—Biography. | African American novelists—20th century—Biography. | Hurston, Zora Neale—Criticism and interpretation.
Classification: LCC PS3515.U789 Z76325 2020 (print) | LCC PS3515.U789 (ebook) | DDC 813/.52—dc23
LC record available at https://lccn.loc.gov/2019040841
LC ebook record available at https://lccn.loc.gov/2019040842

ISBN: HB: 978-1-4408-6654-8
PB: 979-8-2161-9519-1
ePDF: 978-1-4408-6655-5
eBook: 979-8-2161-6971-0

Series: Black History Lives

To find out more about our authors and books visit www.bloomsbury.com and sign up for our newsletters.

Contents

Series Foreword vii

Preface ix

CHAPTER 1
Origins and Childhood *1*

CHAPTER 2
Exile and Instability *13*

CHAPTER 3
Education—Howard and Harlem *23*

CHAPTER 4
The Young Anthropologist *51*

CHAPTER 5
Mule Bone *73*

CHAPTER 6
Independence and *Jonah's Gourd Vine* *83*

CHAPTER 7
Jamaica, Haiti, and *Their Eyes Were Watching God* *99*

CHAPTER 8
Wanderings and Fame *117*

CHAPTER 9
Nightmare and Recovery *149*

CHAPTER 10
The Final Years *167*

Why Zora Neale Hurston Matters *189*

Timeline *201*

Bibliography *207*

Index *213*

Series Foreword

The Black History Lives biography series explores and examines the lives of the most iconic figures in African American history, with supplementary material that highlights the subject's significance in our contemporary world. Volumes in this series offer far more than a simple retelling of a subject's life by providing readers with a greater understanding of the outside events and influences that shaped each subject's world, from familial relationships to political and cultural developments.

Each volume includes chronological chapters that detail events of the subject's life. The final chapter explores the cultural and historical significance of the individual and places their actions and beliefs within an overall historical context. Books in the series highlight important information about the individual through sidebars that connect readers to the larger context of social, political, intellectual, and pop culture in American history; a timeline listing significant events; and a comprehensive bibliography for further research.

Preface

The purpose of this book is to introduce students and general readers to the life, work, and genius of Zora Neale Hurston. Despite Hurston being one of the most important writers of the twentieth century, there are few comprehensive biographies of her life. The most thorough of these, Robert Hemenway's *Zora Neale Hurston: A Literary Biography* (1977) and Valerie Boyd's *Wrapped in Rainbows: The Life of Zora Neale Hurston* (2003), are written for an audience already familiar with Hurston's signal achievements. By contrast, this biography does not assume any prior knowledge of Hurston or her writings but instead welcomes readers who have little understanding of Hurston's place in the American literary canon. My hope is that this volume will serve as a point of departure for future study of Hurston's work.

This biography is indebted to Hemenway and Boyd's extensive research and consideration of Hurston's life. It also relies heavily on Carla Kaplan's *Zora Neale Hurston: A Life in Letters* (2003). This collection, while not comprehensive, is the best source for understanding Hurston's playful, often changeable self and the concerns most dear to her heart. As with all of Hurston's work, these letters require readers to be sensitive to the ways in which she performs for an audience. However, taken together, they capture the range of her desires, interests, and political commitments.

Ultimately, however, the principal source for this biography is Hurston's own published work: her novels, short stories, essays, anthropological studies, plays, and journalistic pieces. As the recently published *Barracoon: The Story of the Last "Black Cargo"* (2018) demonstrates, we are still catching up with the totality of Hurston's writings and the range of her interests. Collections such as *Go Gator and Muddy the Water: Writings by Zora Neale Hurston from the Federal Writers' Project* (1999), *Mule Bone: A Comedy of Negro Life* by Langston Hughes and Zora Neale Hurston (1991), and *The Complete Stories* (1995) have helped make Hurston's less famous work more accessible to a broad audience. However, many key pieces, including her journalistic essays and later political articles, have yet to be published in book form. My hope is that increased interest in Hurston's work will encourage the publication of her complete writings.

Finally, I owe a special thanks to Sandra Carpenter and Beth Bevis for their research assistance. I am also grateful for ABC-CLIO and Kim Kennedy-White for providing me with the opportunity to write this biography.

1

Origins and Childhood

During her lifetime, Zora Neale Hurston gave at least three different dates for the day she was born. Her first biographer, Robert E. Hemenway, stated that she was probably born in 1901 in Eatonville, Florida. In fact, she was born ten years earlier, on January 7, 1891, and over four hundred miles away in Notasulga, Alabama. Hurston lied for a variety of reasons about her age. When she was in her twenties, she posed as a teenager hoping to complete her high school education. Later, she slashed a decade off her age in order to act as a young ingénue eager for the guidance and patronage of wealthy mentors in 1920s Harlem. From the very start of her life, Hurston mixed fact and fantasy, myth and history to create a truth that is less concerned with accuracy than with her own desires and belief in self-creation. There are fewer biographies of Hurston than would be expected of a writer of her stature, but unlike such male counterparts as Richard Wright and James Baldwin, she presents unique challenges to delineating a factual representation of her life. With Hurston, there are truths in her lies and fantasies in her history. Teasing these apart reveals the complexities of a creative trickster who fashioned art out of her life. A literary genius and an anthropological visionary, Hurston remains one of the most fascinating figures in American letters because she refuses to be contained by simplistic definitions. A feminist who never seems to have used the word, a black writer who at times both essentialized and spurned race, Hurston seems to multiply the closer we look, inhabiting and performing various selves that reflect a transcendent artistic vision.

> **EATONVILLE**
>
> Eatonville was initially founded by three former Union officers, Captain Josiah Eaton, Captain Lewis Lawrence, and another officer whose name has been lost to history. After the Civil War, they traveled as far as South America in search of a new home but at last returned to Florida, where the land was more hospitable. Eventually, Captain Eaton sold the land to Lawrence, who then sold it to Joseph Clarke. Eaton never saw the town that bears his name prosper into a flourishing municipality.
>
> Eatonville continues to be inhabited primarily by African Americans. The 2010 census reports that just under 85 percent of the population is black. The town remains quite small, with slightly more than 2,000 residents. Nonetheless, it remains fiercely dedicated to its most famous daughter. In 1990, the town established the Zora Neale Hurston Museum of Fine Arts, locally known as The Hurston. The free museum regularly showcases the work of emerging artists of the wide African diaspora and also manages the Zora Neale Hurston Trail, which includes numerous stops throughout town that were significant to her life. The museum is also at the center of the Zora Neale Hurston Festival, which is held every year in the town.

The paradoxes of Hurston's life are on full display in one of the resources most critical to this biography, her collected letters. Edited by Carla Kaplan, the over six hundred letters published in a single volume in 2003 provide a wealth of information and insight into one of the greatest American writers of the twentieth century. However, as Kaplan cautions, they complicate our understanding of Hurston as much as they clarify who she was. Ever attuned to her audience and her own ambitions, Hurston presented herself in often-varied guises. Kaplan observes, "She performed such different selves for her various correspondents that her letters sometimes seem written by different people" (Kaplan 2003, 21). What emerges from her life and letters is a woman who continually reinvented herself to adapt to changing circumstances. Even as she reigned as queen of the Harlem Renaissance, hosting late-night parties and dancing until the wee hours of the morning, she also insisted that the rural backcountry of Florida was her true home. There she traded in her ostrich hats and gilded scarves for a pair of overalls to reap her own vegetables and grow lustrous gardens. Hurston railed against white supremacy but denounced the Supreme Court decision in *Brown v. Board of Education*, which outlawed segregated schools. To understand Hurston's life is to confront her at times contradictory passions and her keen awareness of her own persona. Hurston was a consummate performer who knew how to charm people of many backgrounds, and yet her letters, which remain incomplete, affirm a number of abiding passions: her adoration of black folk culture, her exuberant love of language and writing, as well as her deep commitment to nurturing individual relationships. These themes prove constant in a life marked by personal upheaval, financial instability, and a changing social landscape that began with the Progressive Era and ended just as the civil rights movement was gaining national force.

Notasulga, Alabama, Hurston's true birthplace, was the home of her formerly enslaved grandparents and a place where her ambitious "over the creek" (Southern speak for "from the other side of the tracks") father was looked down upon by her mother's more prosperous family. Hurston described the town as located "in an outlying district of landless Negroes, and Whites not too much better off" (Hurston 1942, 7). By contrast, Eatonville, an all-black town in Florida first incorporated in 1887, promised a new, independent path for the young family. In her autobiography, Hurston identified Eatonville as the first "Negro town" not just in America, but "perhaps in the world" (Hurston 1942, 6). Such a claim ignores early nineteenth-century all-black towns like Wilberforce, Ohio and New Philadelphia, Illinois, but more egregiously disregards every town and city in Africa. However, such historical realities were of little value to the monumental weight of Hurston's characterization of Eatonville as a place defined by its pioneering self-creation and racial independence. Presumably, only such a mythical place could have birthed a woman of her vision and artistry. As with so much of Hurston's sense of self, the legend is appealing even if it is untrue. However, Hurston's emphasis on Eatonville is not without merit. She spent her formative years in Eatonville and likely had no memories of her birthplace. If we understand the birth of Hurston as tied to the birth of her consciousness, then Eatonville is very much her hometown.

Hurston's father, John, first came across Eatonville while working as a traveling carpenter. Physically strong and handsome, he was eager to escape the rumors of Notasulga, which suggested that his especially light skin and green eyes were the result of his being born to a mother who had been involved with a white supervisor. At the Macedonia Baptist Church, he spied Lucy Ann Potts, who sang treble in the choir, and he began slipping love notes into her hymnal. The youngest child of a land-owning family, Lucy was a slight, dark-skinned girl. She married John against the wishes of her family in 1882. According to the Pottses, John's people were "regular hand-to-mouth folks. Didn't own pots to pee in, nor beds to push them under. Don't have no more pride than to let themselves be hired by poor white trash" (Hurston 1942, 8). Lucy's mother was so aghast at the prospect of John Hurston as her son-in-law that she refused to attend the marriage of her sixteen-year-old daughter. Still, Lucy loved John fiercely, and he in turn resolved to give her the best life he could. The twenty-one-year-old groom took his new wife to a cabin on a white man's plantation, where they initially worked as sharecroppers. By the end of the year, the couple welcomed their first child, Hezekiah Robert, commonly known as Bob. Their second child died prematurely but was soon followed by two more sons, John Cornelius and Richard William, and then a girl, Sarah Emmeline.

John adored his first daughter; he bestowed special attention on her, changing her diapers, tickling her chubby cheeks, and indulging her every wish. However, while Sarah was her father's favorite child, his second daughter, Zora Neal Lee Hurston, proved to be her only sister's very opposite. While her sister bore a conventional name, not even Hurston knew the origin of the unusual "Zora." She speculated that a friend of Lucy, Mrs. Neal, may have contributed her own name to the child. Or perhaps her mother "had read it somewhere or somebody back in those woods was smoking Turkish cigarettes" (Hurston 1942, 21). Consistent with her habit of making everything her own, Hurston disregarded the name "Lee" entirely and at some point in her life added an *e* to "Neal."

John was away working when his youngest daughter was born, and according to Hurston, he threatened to cut his own throat upon returning home to the news of her birth. Even as he adored Sarah, he wanted more boys to increase the family's holdings. In *Dust Tracks on a Road*, Hurston writes that when Lucy's water broke, she was alone because it was hog-killing time and friends and neighbors were off enjoying the butchering. Too weak to move, Lucy lay down on the floor. She was surprised and relieved by the arrival of a white man who had finished his own butchering and brought supplies for the family, since he knew John was not at home. The elderly white man helped with the birth and, according to Hurston's autobiography, became an informal mentor to the young writer. He repeatedly warned her "don't be a nigger" because "niggers lie and lie!" (Hurston 1942, 30). The story is impossible to corroborate, though it does neatly position Hurston as a child of both black and white worlds. Her father, who would later become a significant source of tension and strife, is replaced in this account by a nameless white man who counsels her to rise above stereotypes and instead live truthfully. While Hurston was in many ways true to herself, it is ironic that the story's factual truth remains uncertain. As with so much of her life, legend proves more salient than historical accuracy.

Soon after Hurston's birth, John began looking for another place for the family to live. With five children to care for, he was eager to provide more opportunities and resources for his growing family. Though he had steady work as a carpenter, he longed for a better life and an escape from his own personal and family history. Eatonville, a town composed entirely of African Americans in central Florida, seemed like an ideal place to make a new life. Stunned by the very existence of such a town, John sought to learn more. Eatonville wasn't even a decade old when John moved his entire family there in 1893. The town was built on land purchased by white philanthropist Lewis Lawrence, who lived in nearby Maitland, and developed under the guidance of Tony Taylor, its first mayor, and Joe Clarke, its first marshal. Clarke sold 4,000-square-foot parcels to black settlers who transformed the land into homes, gardens, and orange groves. Under the stewardship of Eatonville's mayor, Columbus H. Boger, the town developed its own post office, general store, school, library, and newspaper, *The Eatonville Speaker*, as well as two churches. Most of the town residents worked in the orange groves or served as hired help for the white families of Maitland. Struck by the opportunities offered by Eatonville and the town's embodiment of black self-sufficiency, John spent a year there preparing for the arrival of his family. By the time they arrived in 1894, he had purchased a five-acre plot in the center of town and had begun work on what would become a two-story eight-room house.

Hurston took her first steps in this house surrounded by chinaberry trees and jasmine bushes. She writes in her autobiography that as a child she was slow to walk. She explains that she was only inspired to get on her feet when one day, left alone in the kitchen, a hog entered the house. When Lucy returned, she found the hog scouring for crumbs on the floor and her daughter toddling about. Reflecting on the story, Hurston muses, "The strangest thing about it was that once I found the use of my feet, they took to wandering. I always wanted to go. I would wander off in the woods all alone, following some inside urge to go places" (Hurston 1942, 22). The story is classic Hurston. Its accuracy is, of course, impossible to verify, but even if entirely fabricated, the anecdote demonstrates a deeper truth about Hurston's sense of self. She is a woman who even as a child did everything on her own time and who delighted in both solitude and the discovery of new places. The story, whether factually true or not, affirms her fundamental spirit and desire to make her own way.

As an adult, Hurston never spoke of her Alabama roots but instead identified Eatonville as her home. It influenced all aspects of her growing sense of self and the diversity inherent to black life. The town leaders and teachers were all black, as were the people she observed throughout her childhood and adolescence engaged in petty fights and domestic dramas. Without a meaningful racial distinction among the residents, Hurston understood blackness to be the foundation of all life, from choir practice to fruit picking, from newspaper editing to medical practices. She came to understand that there was no limit to the possibilities of black life. This vision influenced her later reluctance to embrace racialized categories even as she continually affirmed the wisdom and genius of African American culture. She instead preferred to view people as a collection of individuals, marked by both triumph and failure.

Hurston's mother, Lucy, especially encouraged such an expansive view of the world. She raised her children to "jump at de sun," because even if they didn't grasp the sun, they would at least get off the ground (Hurston 1942, 13). Lucy was resolved that her children would fly. She worked as a seamstress and taught Sunday school at the Macedonia Baptist Church, but perhaps most importantly, she was the engine behind her husband's growing ambitions. She urged him to follow his passion for preaching, and in 1893, John became the pastor of Zion Hope Baptist Church in Sanford, a town twenty miles east of Eatonville. John's commanding voice helped grow the church's membership and inspired his nickname, "God's Battle-Axe." In 1912, John was elected mayor of Eatonville. In his three terms, he built the town's first jail and wrote many of its municipal laws.

At home, the Hurston family also continued to grow. Over the next five years, Lucy birthed three additional sons, Clifford Joel, Benjamin Franklin, and Everett Edward. The Hurstons tended a large vegetable garden next to their house and made frequent use of the town's three lakes, which offered a variety of fresh fish. The children often feasted on oranges, grapefruits, tangerines, guavas, and other fruits that grew in the yard. Amid this bounty, Hurston recalls eating hard-boiled eggs until she was stuffed and then using the extras as missiles. Their home regularly hosted lively games for the children and a steady stream of visitors who delighted in the family's bounty. Despite the boisterous tumult of a full house, Lucy always insisted that the children tend nightly to their homework. She instructed them all in math up to long division and in English to diagramming sentences. When her children progressed beyond her limited education, she turned them over to her eldest son, Bob, and watched carefully to see that attention was paid by all.

John shared his wife's belief in education, but he was far more circumspect in encouraging his children's ambitions. This attitude may have contributed to his difficulty with Hurston, whose rambunctious temperament and sassy retorts often garnered her father's ire. In particular, he was concerned that her sharp tongue would lead to problems with white people. Though John was hardly a meek man, he worried that Hurston's Eatonville upbringing had not properly equipped her with the deference often necessary to navigate a virulently racist country. The freedom and pride engendered by Hurston's all-black environment was anomalous in a historical period defined by deep racial divides. Jim Crow laws, which mandated segregation across the South as well as engrained social norms that demanded black submissiveness, remained commonplace well into the civil rights era. John was right to worry that his daughter's sassy tongue might lead to a violent encounter outside the haven of Eatonville. Lucy, however, continued to encourage her daughter's independent spirit while John indulged the mild-mannered Sarah. Despite witnessing this overt favoritism,

> ## JIM CROW LAWS
>
> Jim Crow laws were developed in the late nineteenth century after Reconstruction as a way to enforce racial segregation in the South. With the Supreme Court's "separate but equal" decision in the case of *Plessy v. Ferguson*, segregation became the norm in public facilities and transportation. However, restrooms, schools, and other public resources for African Americans were invariably inferior to those offered to whites. Segregation also extended to restaurants, hotels, and other areas of social life.
>
> The name "Jim Crow" refers to an 1830s song and dance routine by white actor Thomas D. Rice in which he dressed in blackface and performed racist stereotypes. By midcentury, "Jim Crow" became a demeaning term applied to African Americans, and in the 1890s, *The New York Times* used the phrase "Jim Crow laws" to apply to statutes that barred blacks from participating equally in public life.
>
> Jim Crow laws began to be dismantled with the civil rights movement of the 1950s and 1960s. The 1955 Montgomery bus boycott, which began with Rosa Parks refusing to give up her seat, lasted over a year and finally ended in the desegregation of privately run buses. Such acts of civil disobedience and the leadership of Martin Luther King Jr., among others, galvanized President Lyndon B. Johnson to sign the Civil Rights Act of 1964, which outlawed discrimination in all public accommodations, schools, and workplaces.

Hurston appears not to have developed any resentment toward her older sister. Instead, she learned to use her father's adoration of Sarah for her own purposes. By including Sarah in her routine mischief, she discovered that she could count on a lighter punishment if they got caught.

John often brought special dresses and ribbons home for Sarah, but such gifts were of little interest to Hurston, who preferred the company of boys. More interested in the roughhousing of her male peers than in the dolls that fascinated the neighborhood girls, Hurston learned that she was physically strong and quite capable of holding her own in a fight. The boys tolerated her presence because she never ran home to tell after a "good pummeling." Both John and Lucy frowned upon this play, forcing Hurston to find satisfaction in solitude. She later reflected, "I was driven inward. I lived an exciting life unseen," even as she "wanted action." In this invisible life, Hurston developed dramatic stories for invented personalities like Miss Corn-Shuck or Mr. Sweet Smell. Store-bought dolls were of little interest to the imaginative Hurston, who found that

> dolls caught the devil around me. They got into fights and leaked sawdust before New Year's. They jumped off the barn and tried to drown themselves in the lake. Perhaps, the dolls bought for me looked too different from the

ones I made up for myself. The dolls I made up in my mind, did everything. Those store-bought things had to be toted and helped around. (Hurston 1942, 30)

Hurston's early play with dolls affirms her lifelong passion for imaginative drama as well as her supreme self-confidence that her creations were invariably more interesting than anything handed down to her.

The intricate dynamics of her large family would certainly have provided ample fodder for Hurston's early imaginative life. John and Lucy were prominent townspeople with a complicated relationship. Though John did not physically abuse Lucy, Hurston recalls that he seriously threatened her twice. In the first instance, Lucy noted that if he failed to provide for his family, "there was another man over the fence waiting for his job" (Hurston 1942, 10). John immediately made clear that this common expression was something Lucy should never say. The second time involved John pulling out his Winchester rifle after a party. Though John had suggested that he and Lucy switch partners for the evening, when she went home with another man, he led her inside their home with his gun's muzzle at her back.

In fact, John had little reason to doubt his wife's love and affection for him. Rather, he was the one with the roving eye, and, over time, he indulged in a number of affairs. While Lucy tended to the house and cared for their children, John often spent weekends in Sanford, preaching and overseeing his parishioners or assisting with revival meetings throughout the state. These visits offered opportunities for the popular preacher to become especially intimate with some of his faithful. Lucy was well aware of her husband's adultery and was not afraid to confront him. According to Hurston, she once even "rode herd on one woman with a horse whip about Papa, and 'spoke out' another one" (Hurston 1942, 11). John was delighted with his wife's gumption, but none of these fights did anything to change his behavior. Nonetheless, the couple stayed together, remaining pillars of their community. Hurston recognized the sharp contrast between the esteemed public reputation of "God's Battle-Axe" and his hard-working wife and the private conflicts she observed at home. In her autobiography, she surmised that John's evolution from an impoverished sharecropper to a celebrated pastor was at the root of her parents' struggle:

> My mother took her over-the-creek man and bare-knuckled him from brogans to broadcloth, and I am certain that he was proud of the change, in public. But in the house, he might have always felt over-the-creek, and because that was not the statue he made for himself to look at, he resented it. But then, you cannot blame my mother too much if she did not see him as his entranced congregations did. The one who makes the idols never worships them, however tenderly he might have molded the clay. You cannot have knowledge and worship at the same time. Mystery is the essence of divinity. (Hurston 1942, 69)

This remarkable passage highlights the tension of John's position as well as her mother's struggle to love and accept her husband. John's local prominence as a municipal and religious leader fulfilled his early desire for a better life, but Lucy knew all too well his human failings—the insecurities that led him to infidelity and a history that hardly promised such a fulfilling life.

Despite the difficulties between her parents, Hurston had an often-idyllic childhood. One of her favorite activities involved sitting atop the gatepost in front of her home where the road to Orlando ran past. She often waved and spoke to white travelers, unusual sights in Eatonville. On occasion, Hurston would ride along with them for a little while before walking back home. Although her parents reprimanded her for these adventures, Hurston was eager to learn more about white people and their response to her. She writes of her emerging understanding of racial difference in the 1928 essay "How It Feels to Be Colored Me":

> During this period, white people differed from colored to me only in that they rode through town and never lived there. They liked to hear me "speak pieces" and sing and wanted to see me dance the parse-me-la, and gave me generously of their small silver for doing these things, which seemed strange to me for I wanted to do them so much that I needed bribing to stop. Only they didn't know it. The colored people gave me no dimes. They deplored any joyful tendencies in me, but I was their Zora nevertheless. (Hurston 1979, 152–153)

Although contemporary readers may find the image of young Hurston singing and dancing for coins offered by white travelers a troubling affirmation of stereotypical behavior, Hurston delights in the memory. She presents herself as not only happy to perform for the strangers, but almost needing to do so, as if her bodily exuberance must be expressed. Hurston suggests, then, that performance is not something to be avoided but rather is an occasion for joy. By contrast, her fellow African Americans don't reward her with money and instead "deplored any joyful tendencies." Despite their insistence on more restrained behavior, Hurston understands that she belongs to them and not to the white spectators. This short passage highlights the complexity of Hurston's approach to race. There is no simple delineation between evil, exploitative whites and good, nurturing blacks. Instead, she presents us with affection on both sides, even as neither group reflects her own unique position.

Growing up, Hurston had little contact with nonblacks except for the occasional visitor to the Robert Hungerford Industrial and Normal School. The first and only school for black children in the area, Hungerford emphasized self-reliance and achievement: "Inspiration, motivation, and the development of a positive self image were the driving forces of all students who attended the school. The insistence on excellence was paramount"

(Otey 1989, 11). The school's philosophy was consistent with the vision of famed educator and author Booker T. Washington, whose own Tuskegee Institute was grounded in the belief that hard work would lead to self-sufficiency and, in turn, racial equality. These ideas would prove foundational to Hurston's developing sense of identity and racial progress.

The school's founders, Russell and Mary Calhoun, often hosted white educators and missionaries in hopes of finding new patrons for their work. When Hurston was in the fifth grade, her class was visited by two white women who singled her out for questioning. Responding that she loved school after an inspired reading of the myth of Persephone, Hurston was then invited to visit the women at the Park House Hotel in Maitland. Lucy scrubbed her youngest daughter well and dressed her in a red-and-white dress before sending her off to the nearby town accompanied by her brother John. Hurston delighted in the occasion to explore the world beyond Eatonville and to stand on her own for the first time. The women fed her fancy snacks like stuffed dates and preserved ginger while praising Hurston for her advanced reading skills. They then sent her home with a mysterious cylinder wrapped in paper and ribbon. Once back with her family, Hurston opened the package to discover one hundred gold pennies. Hurston recalled this as one of the most joyful moments of her life: "It was not avarice that moved me. It was the beauty of the thing. I stood on the mountain" (Hurston 1942, 38).

The women continued to send Hurston presents, including fairy tales, Greek and Roman myths, copies of *The Swiss Family Robinson* and *Gulliver's Travels*, as well as a collection of Norse tales. These texts supplemented Hurston's varied readings from the Bible (she was especially drawn to parts of the New Testament and the section in Leviticus in which Moses instructs the Hebrews on what not to do). She admired Odin for plucking out his own eye to drink from the well of knowledge and Hercules for his many noble adventures. With such heroes as models, Hurston longed to escape her mundane chores and provincial lifestyle. She later noted, "In a way this early reading gave me great anguish through all my childhood and adolescence. My soul was with the gods and my body in the village" (Hurston 1942, 41).

However, there was one center of knowledge in her village that equaled any book for its vivid storytelling and insights into human nature: the porch of Joe Clarke's store. Immortalized in Hurston's most famous novel, *Their Eyes Were Watching God* (1937), this public site of talk, story, and casual philosophizing was crucial to Hurston's conception of black life. Although children were not permitted to sit around the porch and listen to what was often adult conversation about matters of love and sex, Hurston learned to make errands to the store last long enough to catch a bit of the stories and gossip under discussion. Such "adult double talk" shaped

Hurston's own writing voice, which delights in vivid metaphors to describe personal dramas and intimate forces. She came to understand the porch as "the heart and spring of the town" where all manner of emotions and human desires were displayed (Hurston 1942, 45). In addition to chronicling the lives of Eatonville residents, porch talk also included "lying sessions" in which folktales about "God, Devil, Brer Rabbit, Brer Fox, Sis Cat, Brer Bear, Lion, Tiger, Buzzard, and all the wood folk" took center stage (Hurston 1942, 48). These stories would later constitute much of the folklore Hurston returned to Florida to collect as a budding anthropologist.

Such folktales involved stories about how black people became colored, as well as why God bestowed men and women with different qualities. The tales confirmed essential truths for Hurston and inspired new imaginative possibilities: "Many of them stirred up fancies in me. It did not surprise me at all to hear that the animals talked. I had suspected it all along. Or let us say, that I wanted to suspect it. Life took on a bigger perimeter by expanding on these things" (Hurston 1942, 52). These vivid narratives or, as some called them, "lies," supplied the young writer with a series of indelible phrases like "My heart was beneath my knees, and my knees in some lonesome valley" and "slave ships in shoes," which captured both the vitality of her imagination and her upbringing. Just as it is sometimes impossible to draw clear distinctions between the fact and fantasy of Hurston's life, it can be fruitless to distinguish Hurston's singular voice and perspective from the collective voice of Eatonville. The self and community merge such that the artistry of Hurston's writings is inextricable from a more ancient wisdom and spirit. Hurston admitted as much in her autobiography, observing of her early attention to black folktales and stories, "I picked up glints and gleams out of what I heard and stored it away to turn to my own uses" (Hurston 1942, 52).

These stories also expanded the limit of what was possible in her immediate world. She recalled telling her mother one afternoon how a nearby lake welcomed her to take a walk: "Well, I stepped out on the lake and walked all over it. It didn't even wet my feet. I could see all the fish and things swimming around under me, and they all said hello, but none of them bothered me" (Hurston 1942, 53). While Lucy was delighted with her daughter's story, her grandmother, Sarah Potts, was infuriated by such flagrant lies. The older woman could only see her upstart son-in-law in Hurston's deceptions and seeming disrespect. Ironically, Sarah Potts's disapproval of Hurston was the one sentiment she shared with John, who also despised his daughter's fanciful storytelling. Although Lucy always enjoyed Hurston's imagination, the young writer learned to keep many of her thoughts and narratives to herself. This protective strategy may explain the onset of powerful visions Hurston experienced sometime in her childhood as her imaginative life turned inward.

In her autobiography, Hurston estimates that she was about seven years old when the visions began. One afternoon, she fell into a restless sleep after fleeing from a spanking. She describes seeing a series of twelve scenes depicting her future. The images were disconnected but united by her conviction in their absolute truth. Awakening from these visions, Hurston experienced a profound if intangible change: "I had knowledge before its time. I knew my fate. I knew that I would be an orphan and homeless, I knew that while I was still helpless, that the comforting circle of my family would be broken and that I would have to wander cold and friendless until I had served my time" (Hurston 1942, 42). Some of the visions involved more precise images—a train, a shotgun house, two women arranging flowers—which correlated to more specific episodes in her later life. However, scholars and biographers continue to be at pains to decipher their meaning. The visions returned at uneven intervals throughout Hurston's life, sometimes repeating night after night, then ceasing for weeks if not months at a time. They only completely stopped when the visions came to pass in her actual life and she moved closer to the final image of the women with the flowers. Hurston kept her visions a secret, afraid of what others might say about these disturbing scenes. Yet they had a deep impact on her, fostering a loneliness that stayed with her all her life. For Hurston, the visions signaled the end of her childhood and the beginning of darker times.

2

Exile and Instability

Hurston's ominous visions were followed by the first significant trauma of her life: the death of her mother. After returning from a visit to Alabama where she tended to her dying sister, Lucy exhibited troubling signs of depression and exhaustion. Her trip back home reignited old conflicts about her marriage to John, and she was reminded of the mysterious death of her favorite nephew, Jimmie. After attending a party, the boy was found headless next to the railroad track. Known for his good looks, he may have been the victim of a jealous rival, or it is possible there was a racial motive for the attack. Either way, Lucy's grief returned, and her despair was exacerbated by the strain of raising eight children, then ranging in age from five to twenty-one, as well as the humiliations of an unfaithful husband. Though only thirty-nine years old, she took to her bed.

One September day in 1904, Lucy called her youngest daughter to her and told her to obey her carefully. Lucy's requests centered on rejecting a series of superstitious customs usually followed among the dying. She did not want a clock or mirror to be covered, nor was her pillow to be removed from her head as she passed. Though Hurston promised her mother not to follow these customs, she had not expected Lucy to pass so quickly. She was playing outside before she at last joined the commotion in her mother's room and found neighborhood women performing the very acts Lucy had hoped to evade. Though Hurston tried to stop the adults, she was only a child and was unable to prevent the will of others, including her father, who physically restrained her from interfering with the customary death rites. Hurston bore a tremendous sense of failure for her inability to honor her mother's dying wishes. This frustration combined with an awareness that, with Lucy's passing, her entire world had changed. Home would no longer be the home she once knew.

All of Lucy's children suffered as a result of her death. Bob was anguished that he arrived too late to witness his mother's final moments, and Sarah became the primary caretaker of little Everett. John too was left bereft, saying again and again, "Poor thing! She suffered so much." Hurston was puzzled by this statement and wondered if his love was also mixed with remorse and relief. She later reflected that she wished to look into her father's heart at this important moment: "I was Mama's child. I knew that she had not always been happy, and I wanted to know just how sad he was that night" (Hurston 1942, 68). Though she loved her father deeply, she was uncertain as to the depth of his love and commitment to Lucy. A firmer trust in John would have helped all the Hurston children weather the changes that soon befell the family.

The day after Lucy's burial, Bob and Sarah returned to school in Jacksonville. John, so frequently away from home, was unable to care for all the children. As a result, Hurston was sent to join her older siblings at the Florida Baptist Academy. As her older brother Dick drove her to Maitland to catch the train to Jacksonville, Hurston saw the first image in her childhood visions come to fruition. She had seen herself on a curved road leaving home and overcome with sorrow: "I had seen myself upon that curve at night leaving the village home, bowed with grief that was more than common. As it all flashed back to me, I started violently for a minute, then I moved closer beside Dick as if he could shield me from those others that were to come. . . . I was on my way from the village, never to return to it as a real part of the town" (Hurston 1942, 69–70). Lucy's death marked the beginning of Hurston's independence, an independence born as much of self-will as basic need.

Jacksonville proved to be a world apart from her Eatonville home. She writes that the city "made me know that I was a little colored girl" (Hurston 1942, 70). The white people who surrounded her were neither welcoming nor amused by her antics. Here she was stripped of both her individuality and her safe, affirming environs. Without the casual familiarity that had marked her relationship to the world, Hurston struggled to understand her place. At school, she found that she did not easily fit in with the other girls. Careless with her dress and general presentation, she was always more interested in listening in on adult talk than finding matching stockings or tending to her hair. She fared far better in the classroom, though she quickly became infamous for her sassy back talk. She also missed the bountiful natural world of Eatonville as well as the camaraderie of her brothers and their friends.

Two months after Lucy's death, Hurston's sister, Sarah, decided to return home. Accustomed to her father's special attention and beloved by their youngest brother, she preferred life with her family to the loneliness of Jacksonville. A few weeks later, she wrote to her siblings with surprising news: John had married again. His wedding to Mattie Moge, who at twenty-two was only six years older than Hurston, took place on February 12, 1905. Born in Oviedo, a nearby town, Mattie was younger than John's eldest son. The speed of the marriage led many to wonder if John had become involved with Mattie while Lucy was still alive. Sarah, once the apple of her father's eye, soon became an object of scorn and envy for the new Mrs. Hurston, who soon insisted that John throw his daughter out of the house. Shortly after her return to Eatonville, Sarah married John Robert Mack, a Baptist minister who was almost ten years her senior, and took her youngest brother Everett with her to her new home.

Hurston remained relatively isolated from her family's conflicts while she was at school in Jacksonville. However, one day, a school administrator notified her that her room and board had not been paid. This news was followed by a lengthy attack on her father's reputation. Though John did not pay the outstanding bill, Hurston was able to stay through the end of the year by scrubbing the school stairs every Saturday, cleaning up the pantry, and helping in the kitchen after her classes. Despite these hardships, she continued to excel academically. She placed first in a citywide spelling bee that involved all the local African American schools. The grand prize was a world atlas and a Bible, in addition to all the lemonade and cake Hurston could eat. This success attracted the attention of the school's president, N. W. Collier, about whom she writes lovingly in her autobiography: "He had such a big laugh that I made up my mind to hurry up and get grown and marry him" (Hurston 1942, 79). Hurston biographer Valerie Boyd identifies this girlhood crush as evidence of the writer's "first romantic longings" (Boyd 2003, 53). Hurston was so taken with the disciplinarian that she wrote letters to herself from Collier and then answered them with her own passionate notes. However, this fantasy affair came to a rude end after he spanked her for putting a wet brick at the foot of a teacher's bed. Stinging from this insult, Hurston resolved not to marry him and to instead let "him starve for my love." She declared, "I was going off and [would] die in a pitiful way. Very lonely and dramatic at the same time" (Hurston 1942, 81). She recounts the story with humorous self-righteousness and the same dramatic flair that would later appear in her fiction.

Although Hurston hoped that her father would retrieve her at the end of the academic year, John instead wrote that the school should adopt her. However, no one was interested in caring for a young girl on her own. The same administrator who reminded Hurston of her father's failures at last took pity and paid for a boat ticket to take her home. The trip was at least a delight, as Hurston, suffocated by city living during the school year, luxuriated in the natural beauty on display as she traveled down the St. Johns River on a side-wheeler known as *City of Jacksonville*. She mused, "The wild thing was back in the jungle" (Hurston 1942, 82). Peering inside the first-class dining room, Hurston enjoyed the spectacle of the dapper waiters and sumptuous dishes. Though she had not packed a lunch of her own, a kind, one-eyed waiter slipped her pieces of cake and pie as well as bits of chicken and steak sandwiches. The boat ride offered many luscious sights of people waving from docks, wild hogs running on shore, and a group of turpentine workers who ate out of shoeboxes and sang along to a guitar as a bottle passed between them. The following day, the boat arrived at Sanford, where Hurston then took a train to Maitland.

The trip back to Eatonville proved far more enjoyable than her actual arrival, upon which she immediately recognized that "my father's house was no longer home. The very walls were gummy with gloom" (Hurston 1942, 84). Her younger siblings were ill-fed and clad in dirty rags. They proved too much for their new stepmother, and John was too distracted to see to their care. The younger children were eventually dispersed to the homes of family friends, but even with this change, resentments continued to fester for Hurston. She was especially outraged by Mattie Moge's usurpation of Lucy's old feather bed. This was the one object Hurston's mother had brought from her family home in Alabama, and it thus held special resonance for her. Hurston convinced her brothers to help her rescue the bed, but Mattie, who she later named "The Black Anne Boleyn," called upon John to discipline his unruly daughter. Hurston and her brother John Cornelius confronted their father, who grabbed a knife, and the three faced off until their father dropped the knife in his hand and told his son to leave home. Although Hurston succeeded in retrieving her mother's bed, she saw a beaten man in her father. Diminished by the loss of Lucy and the frustrations of Mattie, he was no longer the bold and domineering presence of her childhood. Though only one of her parents had died, Hurston pictured herself as "homeless and uncared for," a sentiment that fulfilled the second image of her visions: "There was a chill about that picture which used to take me up shivering. I had always thought I would be in some lone, arctic wasteland with no one under the sound of my voice. I found the cold, the desolate solitude, and earless silences, but I discovered that all that geography was within me" (Hurston 1942, 85).

Boyd describes the time immediately following Hurston's departure from home as "The Wander Years." Hurston was reluctant to speak about this period of her life, and Boyd notes that the writer's comments "seemed contrived to conceal rather to reveal" (Boyd 2003, 57). There are no witnesses who might confirm or elaborate upon Hurston's own vague account of these years, and only a few brief public records exist to guide our understanding of her activities and whereabouts. Following the fight with Mattie over the feather bed, Hurston left her father's house toward the end of 1905. In *Dust Tracks on a Road*, she explains that she initially lived with various relatives and friends. They offered little comfort to the still grieving teenager. Although she never lost her passion for books and reading, her education was uneven due to her frequent relocations and the need to contribute to household expenses. It proved to be a luxury she could not easily afford. Hurston admits to having been a difficult houseguest at this time, too frustrated and miserable for those who took her in.

She thus resolved to support herself, an empowering ambition but one not easily fulfilled. At sixteen, Hurston was quite inexperienced in domestic duties, and her youthful appearance put off potential employers. A few times she was offered work, Hurston lost the job by focusing more on her employer's library than the task at hand. She cobbled together a meager existence by cleaning and caring for young children for roughly two dollars a week. Much of her personal sustenance came from reading books, in particular Milton's *Paradise Lost*, which she claims to have discovered in a pile of garbage. Over the years, Hurston slowly migrated up the St. Johns River, away from Eatonville and back to Jacksonville, where two of her brothers lived. John Cornelius worked as a foreman in a fish house, and Bob was a nurse at a Negro hospital. The comfort of family would have been especially appealing for Hurston following some difficult episodes with various employers. While working as a maid during this period for a sick woman named Mrs. Moncrief, Hurston was propositioned by the man of the house. Mr. Moncrief promised to take Hurston to Canada, and though she was eager for another life, she had no interest in a future with this "chuckle-headed" man (Hurston 1942, 95). Hurston spoke to Mrs. Moncrief about her husband's unwanted attention, and the two women cried over their misfortune. Even when Mr. Moncrief learned what Hurston had told his wife, he still insisted she accompany him to Canada. Finally, she lied to appease him and then ran away without ever receiving her final pay. She eventually heard that Mr. Moncrief had abandoned his wife and left town accompanied by another young black woman.

Longing for home, family, and the opportunity to pursue her education, Hurston was heartened by an invitation from her brother Dick to join him and his family in Sanford. John soon heard about Hurston's return, and he asked that she come back to him in Eatonville. Despite all their previous conflicts, she could not deny her father, and she obeyed his request. Upon returning, she found that the public scorn of Mattie had taken its toll, and John, "dragging like a stepped-on worm," had become too weak to defend her against his longtime friends and parishioners (Hurston 1942, 98). Unable to defy the judgment of the townspeople, Mattie focused her ire on

John's children. Within a month of Hurston's return, a massive fight developed between her and her stepmother. In her autobiography, Hurston claims that Mattie started things off by calling her "a sassy, impudent heifer" and throwing a bottle at her head. Mattie missed, and Hurston took the advantage, pushing her stepmother against the wall and pummeling her in the face:

> The feelings of all those six years were pressing inside me like steam under a valve. I didn't have any thoughts to speak of. Just the fierce instinct of flesh on flesh—me kicking and beating on her pudgy self—those two ugly false teeth in front—her dead on the floor—grinning like a dead dog in the sun. Consequences be damned! (Hurston 1942, 76)

Although Mattie outweighed Hurston, she was no match for the younger woman's fury, and soon Mattie could do little more than spit in her stepdaughter's face. John watched from the doorway, too stunned to do anything else but observe the spectacle before him. Only a neighboring friend of Mattie's tried to intervene, but Hurston responded by throwing a hatchet at the woman's head. The neighbor ran away screaming that Hurston had gone crazy. Hurston became more infuriated when she saw her stepmother collapse to the floor, claiming that she "had not beaten more than two years out of her yet" (Hurston 1942, 77). At last John stepped in, pulling his daughter away and likely saving both her life and that of his wife.

Mattie was severely bruised, while Hurston found that she had a few scratches, though her rage was hardly quelled. She vowed to make her stepmother pay in full for the grief and hurt she suffered. However, when she again visited Mattie years after graduating from Barnard, Hurston found not a seething rival but a pathetic invalid. Mattie came to suffer from a persistent sore on her neck, and Hurston left her unharmed—if still wishing that there was more of her stepmother's neck to rot. In *Dust Tracks on a Road*, Hurston states that her fight with Mattie exacerbated the tension between her stepmother and her father. Mattie demanded that John have Hurston arrested, and when he demurred, she asked for help from the church. There she found even less sympathy and soon became the object of scorn for many of Lucy's old friends. Once again, John was reluctant to defend his wife, and it appears the relationship eventually deteriorated.

Despite Hurston's physical victory over Mattie, the fight led to her exile from her family's home and the death of her relationship with her father. Boyd reports that in leaving Eatonville in 1911, Hurston also effectively vanished from the public record. In the years that follow, she appears in no census listing, city directory, school file, or hospital report. From her autobiography, she seems to have stayed in Florida, and for a time she worked in a doctor's office. Hurston excelled at the work and was encouraged by her boss to become a nurse, but she decided to move in with her brother Bob, who was studying at the Meharry Medical College in Nashville,

> ### THE BLACK CHURCH
>
> The black church has a long history in the United States. After the end of slavery, African Americans were often discouraged if not actually prevented from attending the same churches as whites. Many newly emancipated slaves joined churches originally formed by free blacks or began new parishes of their own. These Protestant churches, which often drew upon African spiritual traditions, became the center of black communities throughout the North and South. Many of these churches offered more than just Sunday services. They provided care and support for the poor, literacy programs for the young and uneducated, as well as homes for the orphaned and indigent. The black church was instrumental in the development of the civil rights movement and the practice of peaceful protest.
>
> The black church also fostered unique forms of preaching and worship that welcome and encourage a more participatory role for parishioners. Laypeople are invited to call out and respond to the words of the preacher in a dynamic exchange that makes for an especially robust and energizing form of worship. Black preaching also frequently relies upon vivid storytelling to illustrate doctrine and belief. Biblical tales become vivid adventures, while real life experiences take on the urgency of divine significance. Although Hurston never identified herself as religious, she clearly derived much of her flair for language and storytelling from her father's pulpit.

Tennessee. Founded in 1876, Meharry was one of two medical schools open to black students. Bob was married with three children, and he was eager for help around the house while he finished his studies.

Hurston was thrilled with Bob's invitation; at last she would have a home and family to support her. She imagined that her life of loneliness and poverty was finally behind her. However, Hurston soon discovered that Bob ran a strict household. He and his wife, Wilhelmina, lived with their young children, George, Wilhelmina, and infant Hezekiah Robert Jr., in the Black Bottom neighborhood of Nashville. A 1912 portrait of the family (and the first known photograph of Hurston) depicts a somber group. While Bob's right hand rests gently on his seated wife's shoulder, Hurston stands with her arms behind her and her face downcast. She looks less like a family member than a much-needed servant. Although Hurston hoped that she would at last be able to return to school, Bob soon explained that his wife would frown upon such a frivolous pursuit. He insisted that she begin by working around the house and suggested that eventually the situation would change. Hurston soon became frustrated with the arrangement as she realized that she was not even paid for her labor. She found some solace in the joy offered by her niece and nephews, but the situation was not tenable in the long term.

Bob graduated in 1913 and then moved his family, along with Hurston, to Memphis. He set up a medical practice in a storefront office and bought a two-story house in the Scott Street neighborhood. Although Bob provided a comfortable home for his sister, Hurston soon chafed against the constant housework and caretaking. The following year, with the help of a white friend who sometimes gave her small gifts, including a pair of gloves, Hurston got a job as a personal attendant to the lead singer of a Gilbert and Sullivan repertoire company. Identified only as "Miss M-----" in *Dust Tracks on a Road*, Hurston's boss assumed her new maid was a young teenager when in fact she was well into her twenties. Hurston did nothing to clarify the truth. In fact, she was relieved that Miss M----- didn't ask anything about her family, and she happily accepted the weekly wage of ten dollars.

The work was light, amusing, and ideal for a budding artist eager to learn more about the world. Hurston tended to Miss M-----'s clothes and makeup and helped her dress for performances. However, the most exciting aspect of her job was the dynamic group of artists she joined. Although she was the only African American among the company members, she was embraced as a wide-eyed ingénue. She was a favorite target for practical jokes, and though many proved to be racial in nature, Hurston took them with good-humored pragmatism. Being especially sensitive would do nothing to increase her standing among this creative crowd: "The whole experience on that job gave me an approach to racial understanding . . . it discouraged any sensitiveness on my part, so that I am still not conscious of my race no matter where I may go. I found out too that you are bound to be jostled in the 'crowded street of life'" (Hurston 1942, 118). Although it may be an overstatement to say that Hurston lost an awareness of her race by working with the troupe, she did discover that focusing on racial slights limited her ability to engage with the world. She learned to put aside what she considered her personal vanity and become a prankster of her own. The traveling troupe was mostly composed of Northerners who delighted in her Southern slang. With "the map of Dixie on my tongue," Hurston showed them how, as a Southern child, she was "raised on simile and invective." As she explained, "It is an every day affair to hear somebody called a mullet-headed, mule-eared, wall-eyed, hog-nosed, gator-faced, shad-mouthed, screw-necked, goat-bellied, puzzle-gutted, camel-backed, butt-sprung, battle-hammed, knock-kneed, razor-legged, box-ankled, shovel-footed, unmated so and so!" (Hurston 1942, 104). Members of the group often teased her just to hear her sassy retorts. Hurston was also an easy object of fun because she was so new to the life of the company and thus easily shocked by their antics. Still, it was an exciting life and always full of ice cream sodas and all the Coca-Cola she could drink.

Miss M----- also paid for Hurston to take a manicuring class. She honed her skills on the group and soon became quite adept at the practice.

Although Hurston was arguably, as Boyd suggests, a kind of "pet Negro" to the troupe, she made the most of the experience (Boyd 2003, 71). She often borrowed books from the Harvard-educated tenor in the group, and by observing closely the troupe's performances, she became well versed in light opera and the operations of the theater as a whole. The time that she spent with the company also exposed her to a broad range of white people, including Anglo-Saxons, Irish, and Jews. Living and working with them in such close proximity proved that whites were not so different from the black men and women she grew up with in Eatonville. She marveled at their ability to come together in times of crisis: "I saw thirty-odd people made up of all classes and races living a communal life. There were little touches of professional jealousy and a catty crack now and then, but let sickness or trouble touch any member and the whole cast rallied around to help out" (Hurston 1942, 117–118). Over the year and a half that Hurston spent with the company, she traveled through most of New England and along the Eastern seaboard.

Although Hurston enjoyed her experiences with the group, she was ready to move on when Miss M----- suddenly decided that she was going to get married to a wealthy businessman and would leave the theater. She urged Hurston to return to school. At a stop in Baltimore, Miss M----- gave Hurston some money and they parted ways. Although her salary with the troupe had been irregular, she had always had food and shelter as well as the comfort of the group. Still, Hurston decided to take this opportunity to begin anew. She resolved that she would continue her education, though she recognized as well that throughout her time with Miss M-----, she "had been in school all that time. I had loosened up in every joint and expanded in every direction" (Hurston 1942, 116). The loneliness that had previously haunted her had at last faded, and she learned that she need not depend on family alone to find happiness and fulfillment. She had also seen seven of her visions come to pass and emerged both stronger and more hopeful for the future.

Just as she had during her earlier attempt at self-support, Hurston quickly realized that what she most needed was money. While traveling with the troupe, she had not been able to save enough to reenroll in school. Her first steady job was as a waitress in a restaurant where she was frequently left a nickel tip for a meal that cost a quarter. Many of her male customers made clear their interest in her, but though Hurston was unconcerned about virtue, she found there was neither love nor significant material advantage in these offers.

Around this time, Hurston became sick and needed to have her appendix removed. Unable to pay for any medical expenses, she became a patient at the free ward of the Maryland General Hospital. Hurston did not fear death and was convinced that no one would miss her if she died, but the procedure shook her so intensely that she made a wager with God: "I bet God that if I lived, I would try to find out the vague directions whispered in my ears and find the road it seemed that I must follow" (Hurston 1942, 122). Hurston underwent the procedure alone, and upon waking late that night, she resolved to fulfill her bargain with God.

Hurston found another waitressing job, but it was difficult to save money. Moreover, she kept feeling like "I was only jumping up and down in my own foot-tracks" (Hurston 1942, 122). For a time, she worked with her housemate, Martha Tucker, to sell cigarettes, soft drinks, and other items from their home on Pennsylvania Avenue. The confectionary is listed in the 1917 Baltimore City Directory. Her sister, Sarah, also operated a business in the same neighborhood, running a restaurant out of her home. Despite the close proximity of the sisters, Hurston kept her distance because she disliked Sarah's husband, John Mack, and in particular how he treated his wife. Nonetheless, a genuine affinity thrived between the sisters, and years later, Sarah named her daughter after Hurston.

Not content to focus only on work, Hurston managed to begin attending night high school in Baltimore and again found relief and purpose in pursuing her education. Unmentioned in her autobiography is how she was able to make this happen. The State of Maryland provided free education for all African Americans between the ages of six and twenty. In 1917, Hurston was twenty-six, but by taking ten years off her birth date, she easily qualified for the free classes. By posing as a sixteen-year-old, Hurston wisely allowed for four more years to finish school, and due to her youthful looks, no one questioned her subterfuge. Boyd notes that from this time forward, Hurston almost always lied about her age, shaving at least a decade off the true date: "Thus 1917, the year she went back to school, marked Hurston's rebirth—the moment she was reborn, by her own imaginative labor, as the woman she was to become" (Boyd 2003, 75). This deception seemed a small price to pay to honor her wager with God and become the dream-chasing daughter her mother had raised.

3

Education—Howard and Harlem

While enrolled in night school, Hurston met Dwight O. W. Holmes, an especially inspirational teacher whom she described as "a pilgrim to the horizon," whose "face killed the drabness and discouragement in me" (Hurston 1942, 123). Holmes complimented Hurston on her writing one day after class and never asked about her past. She understood this disregard for her personal history as an indication that all that mattered were the choices and actions she took now. Education provided a way for her to leave the past behind and indulge in a world made new by poets, writers, and her own ambitions. Unsurprisingly, Hurston's most powerful memory of Holmes is not of a personal exchange between them but instead his introduction of an especially moving piece of literature. While listening to Holmes recite Samuel Taylor Coleridge's poem "Kubla Khan" to the class one evening, Hurston believed that he directed the poem specifically to her. That night she was possessed by images stirred by his words. This profound experience convinced her that she "was not of the work-a-day world" but was instead a part of a larger poetic vision: "This was my world, I said to myself, and I shall be in it, and surrounded by it, if it is the last thing I do on God's green dirt-ball" (Hurston 1942, 123). Hurston had discovered the direction she had longed for before her appendicitis. Without even alerting Holmes, the following week she went to Morgan Academy, an elite black prep school, to register for classes.

At Morgan Academy, the high school division of Morgan College (now Morgan State University), Hurston took an exam and received two years of high school credit for her previous courses. She was placed in the class of 1920 by the dean, William Pickens. Hurston had previously written to Pickens expressing her deep desire to attend Morgan: "I want to get all that Morgan has to give. I feel that I will have done something equal to the course at Morgan, if I have really known you and Mrs. Pickens" (Kaplan 2003, 54, letter from Hurston to William Pickens in 1917/1918). For Hurston, befriending the intellectual couple was just as important as studying at Morgan. She understood her education as emanating in part from her personal relationships. Understanding the trajectory of others' success would be key to charting her own. The letter, which is the first record of her written correspondence with others, represents an especially bold approach for a young woman who owned little more than a dress, a pair of shoes, and one change of underwear.

Aware of Hurston's financial difficulties as well as her natural talents, Pickens consulted his wife, who found Hurston a job at the home of Dr. Baldwin, a white clergyman and one of the trustees at the school. His wife had recently broken her hip and needed someone to help dress and care for her. The arrangement provided Hurston with two dollars a week as well as a place to stay. Because she was primarily needed in the mornings and evenings, Hurston was free to take classes in the day and to make use of the family library. She recalls committing Thomas Gray's *Elegy Written in a Country Churchyard* to memory in a single night because she was afraid she might not have the chance to read it again. She then moved on to the *Ballad of Reading Gaol* and the *Rubaiyat*. These lofty texts posed a striking contrast to the dime novelists she had grown accustomed to. However, Hurston came to value texts of all kinds and believed that developing the habit of reading was most essential, as matters of taste would naturally evolve on their own.

Aware that she was making up for lost time at Morgan Academy, Hurston committed herself fully to her studies. Her classmates came from some of the most elite African American families in Baltimore. They were well dressed and heir to the fortunes and reputations of their parents. Hurston believed she couldn't compare to their bright, attractive faces, but she held her own with her single change of clothes and her tan oxfords. Though Hurston was shy among her peers, she made friends with Mary Jane Watkins, a future dentist, when she sneezed on the second day of school and had nothing to wipe her nose. Watkins passed her a handkerchief without a word, and the two began a longtime bond. Another classmate, Bernice Hughes, the daughter of a school trustee, named Hurston the "old Knowledge Bug" and vowed to sit close to her in class so the future writer could "study for both of us" (Hurston 1942, 126). Hurston quickly became a favorite of the entire Hughes family.

With her charm and intellect, Hurston soon found that her lack of clothes was no obstacle to finding friends. Classmates would occasionally tease her and ask what she would wear to school tomorrow. However, she turned such questions into offers to borrow clothes from others. Her peers may have poked fun at her, but when it came to academics, they deeply respected her. Hurston recalls that whenever her English teacher was absent, she was asked to lead the class, sometimes for an entire week. She noted that her classmates were always obedient until the bell rang. Only then would they laugh about her serious teaching face.

Hurston excelled in a variety of ways at Morgan Academy. With the help of Dean Pickens, she placed second in the school's oratorical contest. She also credits the school with her first publication—an allegory involving the faculty members—which she printed on the blackboard of the assembly hall early one morning. She imagined Dr. Spencer, the school's president, as the "Great Grey Bear" and Dean Pickens as the "Ferocious Pick" (Hurston 1942, 128). Though Dr. Spencer was initially embarrassed by the story, after the service was over, he burst out laughing, freeing everyone else to join in.

Hurston was delighted with the two years she spent at Morgan: "The atmosphere made me feel right. I was at last doing the things I wanted to do. Every new thing I learned in school made me happy" (Hurston 1942, 129). She was a model student in English and history. For the 1917–1918 academic year, her scores in science and music were satisfactory at eighty-one and seventy-nine, respectively. Only math proved to be a significant challenge. She received a seventy-four and later admitted that the professor passed her only because he knew that she did well in all her other subjects.

That summer, however, Hurston received some unsettling news: her father had died in Memphis after a train collided with his car. John had recently moved to Memphis and there maintained closer contact with his eldest son, Bob. Biographer Valerie Boyd notes that in the documents related to his move, he was not listed as married, suggesting that at some point he had left Mattie behind. At the time of his death, he was fifty-seven years old. After years of separation and lingering resentments, it is no surprise that Hurston chose not to attend his funeral. John had long ceased to be a meaningful figure in her life, and by 1918, she had new plans of her own. However, his memory would endure, becoming the central focus of her first novel, *Jonah's Gourd Vine* (1934).

Initially, Hurston planned on staying on at Morgan for college. However, one weekend at the Hughes household, she met Mae Miller, the daughter of Howard University dean Dr. Kelly Miller and cousin to Bernice. After only a few hours together, Mae concluded, "Zora, you are

> ### HOWARD UNIVERSITY
>
> Founded in 1867 under a federal charter, Howard University remains the most prestigious historically black university in the United States. It includes thirteen schools and colleges, including top-rated programs in business, law, and medicine, and it produces more black doctorate recipients than any other university. Located in Washington, D.C., Howard has long affirmed a fierce commitment to social change. Throughout the 1940s, students were especially active in protest movements. They regularly organized sit-ins and strikes against establishments that refused to serve African American clientele. Howard alumnus Stokely Carmichael coined the term "Black Power," launching one of the most important social movements of the twentieth century. In 1965, President Lyndon B. Johnson used his commencement address at Howard to describe his vision of civil rights and argued forcefully for the implementation of affirmative action to counter the effects of slavery's long legacy on African American opportunities for success. More recently, President Barack Obama spoke to Howard's graduates in 2016 to reflect upon the state of American democracy and celebrate the totality of black life.

Howard material. Why don't you come to Howard?" (Hurston 1942, 129). Hurston describes Howard as "the capstone of Negro education in the world. There gather Negro, money, and prestige. It is to the Negro what Harvard is to the whites," and indeed it remains the most esteemed historically black university in the country (Hurston 1942, 129). Founded in 1867 in Washington, D.C., Howard aims to provide exceptional education to African American students to prepare them to be model leaders and citizens. Having heard of the elite Howard fraternities and sororities, Hurston believed she could never become part of such a rarefied world. But Mae dismissed her concerns and offered her family home to Hurston. There she would have free room and board and the influence of a powerful family to help her find a job to pay for tuition.

Hurston moved to Washington, D.C., that summer. She first found a job waitressing at the Cosmos Club, a downtown venue that only served white men. Women and people of color were only allowed entrance if they came as servants. Later, Hurston became a manicurist in Mr. George Robinson's G Street shop and soon amassed enough money for the first quarter's tuition. Unfortunately, when Hurston registered, she discovered that she would have to first make up some classes before she could enroll at the college level. Dismayed with this news, Hurston again doubted whether she could really succeed at Howard. However, she was soon convinced otherwise after running into her former teacher, Dwight O. W. Holmes, who now worked at Howard. He promised she could take classes at

Howard Academy that would prepare her for college-level work. That December, she began taking courses in history, Latin, English, and physical geography. The following May, in 1919, she at last earned her high school diploma from Howard Academy. She enrolled at Howard University that fall.

Hurston fondly remembered her first college assembly. She felt a swell of exaltation listening to the school's alma mater and gazing at the hundreds of students and faculty members. She felt a grave responsibility to live up to Howard's prestigious legacy: "My soul stood on tiptoe and stretched up to take in all that it meant. So I was careful to do my class work and be worthy to stand there under the shadow of the hovering spirit of Howard. I felt the ladder under my feet" (Hurston 1942, 131). Though dedicated to her studies, Hurston found that her grades were not as strong at Howard as they had been at Morgan. In her first quarter, she earned Bs in English and Spanish and a D in Greek. The following quarter showed some improvement; she returned to an A in English and received a B in public speaking and two Cs in Greek and Spanish. By the next year, Hurston succeeded in keeping her grades entirely to As and Bs.

The academic rigor of Howard was compounded by Hurston's need to work long hours to pay for her tuition and other expenses. She struggled to balance her studies with her job. She worked for George Robinson from 3:30 to 8:30 so that she had time in the morning and early afternoon to attend her classes. Robinson was a black entrepreneur who owned a number of barbershops in the city. The one at 1410 G Street, where Hurston worked, catered to a white clientele. Though Robinson was not educated, he employed many Howard students. Moreover, once her customers learned that she was a student, they tipped her generously, and soon she averaged between twelve to fifteen dollars a week. The G Street shop was a favorite of many prominent Washingtonians. Hurston claims to have worked on the hands of senators, congressmen, cabinet officials, and members of the National Press Club, located only a block away. She listened intently to their talk of world affairs and national politics, learning about events or developments in the Senate and White House before they appeared in the newspapers. She discovered that she was a safe confidante because no one would believe the claims of a working-class black woman. Hurston became known for her discretion, though she saw the matter differently; these important men needed someone to tell their intimate stories to. She recalled, "Soon they took me for granted and would say, 'Zora knows how to keep a secret. She's all right.' Now, I know that my discretion really didn't matter. They were relieving their pent-up feeling where it could do no harm" (Hurston 1942, 131). The very invisibility that marginalized African Americans became here a tool to discover elite information.

Hurston also listened closely to the talk among the shop's ten African American barbers and three porters. Though they lacked the social power of her white customers, they also had strong political opinions, engaging stories, and amusing secrets of their own. The barbershop proved to be an urban version of Joe Clarke's porch from Eatonville. Though the tales told here were far removed from those about Brer Rabbit and Brer Bear, the same vivid language and sharp insight into the human condition was evident in the nation's capital. The atmosphere at the barbershop may have inspired one of Hurston's first works, a poem written in 1919 that recalls the comfort and joy of Eatonville:

> I know a place that is full of light,
> That is full of dreams and visions bright;
> Where pleasing fancy loves to roam
> And picture me once more at home.

Beneath the typed poem is the scrawled note of a writer concerned that she has veered into sentimentality: "Just a bubbling over of a melancholy heart—momentarily" (Hurston 1919).

At Howard, Hurston declared English as her major and began trying her hand at crafting literary works of her own. Like many young writers, her style veered dramatically from the maudlin to the parodic. In "Twas the Night after Lobster," she satirized Edgar Allen Poe's "The Raven." Her early poems demonstrate a delight in experimentation. She sometimes approached a single topic from a variety of approaches. "Longin'" uses an exaggerated Negro dialect to reflect on love, while "Thou Art Mine" offers a more classically rendered meditation on the subject. These unpublished poems lack the wit, elegance, and maturity of her later work and often seem at pains to fill a specific rhyme scheme, as in the lines of this untitled poem:

> Who has not felt the fire of youth?
> Nor heard the call of spring?
> Nor read the lines of love and truth
> In arms and lips that cling? (Hurston 1919)

Hurston's preoccupation with love may be explained by her introduction to Herbert Arnold Sheen in 1920. The son of a Methodist minister from Decatur, Illinois, Sheen was twenty-three when the two first met. Hurston was six years older but still posing as a decade younger. Sheen had been a member of the Students Army Training Corps in World War I before coming to Howard. Like Hurston, he too worked to pay his tuition, though he also made time for plenty of pool and music; she observed, "He could stomp a piano out of this world, sing a fair baritone and dance beautifully" (Hurston 1942, 204). Though both the children of preachers, neither was especially religious. Hurston was impressed by his ability to sing and dance and soon found that she "was carried away. For the first time since my mother's death, there was someone who felt really close and warm to me" (Hurston 1942, 204). He appreciated her open-minded approach to the world, and soon they became a regular couple.

With money in her pocket and a handsome man on her arm, Hurston invested in more stylish clothes. Photographs of the period show her in tasteful hats, long dresses, and vivid colors. She faces the camera with a wide, roguish smile and a confident angle to her head. Her newfound self-assurance and flair were critical to her introduction to Greek life at Howard. Black sororities and fraternities were foundational to the university's social scene. They offered friendship and camaraderie as well as key professional opportunities. Though Mae Miller was a member of the Alpha Kappa Alpha sorority, the oldest Greek organization for black women, Hurston opted for the newly formed Zeta Phi Beta sorority. An old acquaintance of Hurston's from Howard, Ophelia Settle Egypt, recalls that there were three sororities at the university. The AKAs were known as the best dressed, the Deltas characterized by their light skin, and the Zetas renowned for their intelligence. With these descriptions in mind, Hurston was destined for the Zetas, but Egypt remembers that even among her talented sorority sisters, Hurston was exceptional; she was a brilliant loner who "was just too brainy for us" (Boyd 2003, 84).

Hurston worked with Mae Miller on Howard's annual literary journal, *The Stylus*. The publication was issued by the university's literary club, which had been founded in 1915 by English and drama professor Montgomery Gregory and famed philosophy professor Alain Locke, who would become a major figure in Hurston's literary career. To become a member of the elite club, students had to submit manuscripts to semiannual competitions. Only those identified as having produced the best writing would be invited to join the club. Due to their work with *The Stylus*, Hurston and Miller were welcome at the literary salon of Washington poet Georgia Douglas Johnson. At these events, the self-identified "Saturday Nighters" discussed developments in black art and culture. The rotating guests included poets Sterling Brown and Angelina Grime and writers like Jean Toomer and Richard Bruce Nugent, as well as James Weldon Johnson, the executive secretary of the NAACP, and W. E. B. Du Bois, the most famous black intellectual of the early twentieth century and the editor of *The Crisis*. Nearly all of these celebrities would become close personal friends and colleagues of Hurston.

Amid these many artistic luminaries, Hurston identified Dr. Lorenzo Dow Turner, the head of Howard's English department, as the teacher who most influenced her. Educated at Harvard, Turner was especially handsome and looked to be no more than thirty years old. He held his students

> ### NAACP/*The Crisis*
>
> The National Association for the Advancement of Colored People (NAACP) was founded in 1909 to promote justice and equality. It is the oldest and largest civil rights organization in the United States. Headquartered in Baltimore, though with many regional offices throughout the country, the NAACP aims "to ensure the political, educational, social, and economic equality of rights of all persons and to eliminate race-based discrimination."[1] The organization continues to support the vision of cofounder W. E. B. Du Bois through its commitment to health care for all Americans, equal justice, the protection of voting rights, educational opportunities, and youth engagement. In 1910, Du Bois founded *The Crisis*, the official publication of the NAACP and a magazine that quickly became the leading champion of civil rights in the country. *The Crisis* is now published quarterly and addresses issues of race and inequality across politics, economics, education, and culture. The NAACP also supports a powerful legal department that works on a variety of civil rights cases, often in conjunction with other organizations. The most famous lawyer to work for the NAACP is Thurgood Marshall, who successfully argued for the desegregation of public schools in *Brown v. Board of Education* and went on to become the first African American Supreme Court justice.
>
> ---
>
> 1. https://www.naacp.org/about-us.

rapt, especially the female ones, and Hurston in particular: "Listening to him, I decided that I must be an English teacher and lean over my desk and discourse on the 18th-Century poets, and explain the roots of the modern novel . . . with just that suspicion of a smile now and then before I returned to my notes" (Hurston 1942, 137). Already Hurston had come to see that texts were enlivened by a charismatic presence and that to captivate future students and readers, she would have to project charm as much as mastery.

Even as Hurston imagined a life of teaching, she began to take her own literary aspirations more seriously. In 1921, she published a poem, "O Night," in *The Stylus*, along with her first short story, "John Redding Goes to Sea." The quaint tale reflects much of Hurston's childhood and past longings. It is set in an unnamed Florida town that bears a strong resemblance to Eatonville, and the protagonist is a loner who imagines taking off down the St. Johns River to the horizon. John is described as "a queer child" who is "puzzling to the simple folk there in the Florida woods for he was an imaginative child and fond of day-dreams." John's mother wonders if her son is under the influence of "travel dust" left by an enemy when he was first born (Hurston 1995, 3). This description aligns precisely with

Lucy Hurston's belief that someone had also sprinkled "travel dust" on the doorstep the day Hurston was born (Hurston 1995, 23). John remains in his village, although his desire to escape and see the world only grows. Both his wife and mother refuse to let him go until one evening he is called to fortify the St. Johns bridge against an impending storm. The river rises to the bridge while the men struggle to complete their work. Three broken pine trees crash into the bridge, killing John. His body is carried by a log off to the sea he dreamed of seeing.

Although John Redding shares Hurston's own wanderlust and penchant for daydreaming, his name suggests that the story may also have been an homage to her father. He too exhibited an intense curiosity about the world and boldly left his own home to discover new opportunities for his family. John Redding's hectoring mother is named Matty, suggesting that Hurston understood her stepmother to be an obstacle to her protagonist's—and arguably her father's—happiness. Despite this negative association, there are aspects of the fictional Matty's character that Hurston takes quite seriously. Matty believes in superstitions and omens. Rather than mock such notions, Hurston presents a belief in the supernatural as credible and instructive. The story also highlights one of the essential qualities of Hurston's later work: the rich dialect of its main characters. John, Matty, and others do not come off as uneducated rubes but instead as eloquent orators of a vivid, poetic language.

Shortly after the publication of "John Redding Goes to Sea," Herbert Sheen left for the summer to work as a waiter in Seabright, New Jersey, a resort town. Among the affluent clientele, Sheen met a doctor from New York who suggested he become a live-in manservant while he completed his coursework at Columbia University. Sheen seized the opportunity and even asked his sister Genevieve to move with him from Washington to work as the family's cook. However, the plan ended in tragedy. On the first day of 1922, Genevieve was killed by her husband. Sheen escorted his sister's body back to their family home in Decatur. Hurston immediately offered her help and managed the legal issues in Washington. Genevieve's death was the city's first murder of the year.

Amid these tumultuous events, Hurston wrote three poems for *Negro World*, a newspaper issued by the Universal Negro Improvement Association. "Night," "Journey's End," and "Passion" were the only poems Hurston ever published in a national venue. Two of Hurston's short writings also appear in the 1923 Howard University yearbook. "A Chapter from the Book of Life" and "An Academic Nightmare" are humorous reflections on her time at school. In the yearbook, she is identified as a member of *The Stylus*, Zeta Phi Beta, and the Howard Players, a theatrical company that often traveled to different parts of the country. According to the yearbook, "Zora's greatest ambition is to establish herself in Greenwich Village where she may write stories and poems and live an unrestrained Bohemian." Her class photo is captioned with a quotation she selected: "I have a heart with room for every joy" (Howard University 1923). Though she was not yet done with her schooling, she was already looking ahead to other experiences and opportunities.

Hurston completed only one more quarter at Howard in the fall of 1923. Though she had earned an A in geology in the spring, her grade fell to a D, and she failed physical education. She only excelled in the classes that were of interest to her. Following the winter break, Hurston did not register for classes. She had been sick and did not have enough money to pay her tuition. The 1924 Washington City Directory lists Zora as a student, which suggests that she aimed to return to school, though by this time she was beginning to think of herself as a writer. Through her work at *The Stylus*, Hurston met Charles S. Johnson, the founding editor of *Opportunity: A Journal of Negro Life*. After reading "John Redding Goes to Sea" and in search of new black talent, he asked her to submit something to his magazine. She sent him the short stories "Drenched in Light" and "Spunk," both of which he published.

"Drenched in Light" was the first story by Hurston to enjoy a national audience. Published in 1924, it develops the complex use of humor and metaphor evident in "John Redding Goes to Sea." The story more obviously borrows from Hurston's own experiences by focusing on a day in the life of young Isis Watts. Like her creator, Isis enjoys sitting on top of the gatepost at the front of her Eatonville home and waving to passing travelers. She too has petty battles with her strict grandmother, who scolds her for talking to strangers, playing with boys, and worst of all, whistling. This merry prankster attempts to shave her grandmother while she sleeps but scrambles under the house when the older woman begins to stir. The enticing sounds of a marching band lure Isis from her hiding place, but she first runs home so that she can adorn herself with her grandmother's new red tablecloth as she then dances with the marching musicians. When her grandmother finds her performing before a crowd, Isis runs again and resolves to kill herself in the creek. However, a car of white people who saw her dancing stop and pick her up. Though the men are unmoved by her charms, Isis enchants a white woman who wants to keep her when they arrive at the girl's home. Confronted by Isis's angry grandmother, the white woman calms her by offering five dollars for the tablecloth and expressing her delight in the exuberant child: "I want brightness and this Isis is joy itself, why she's drenched in light!" (Hurston 1995, 25). The grandmother is moved to pride by the white woman's words, while Isis savors her first experience of joy and appreciation.

"Drenched in Light" reads almost like an excerpt from Hurston's own childhood. Isis's curiosity and liveliness are reflected in every account of

Hurston's early life. The story dispenses with the expectations of plot and conflict to develop a vivid portrait of an indelible character. In this way, it represents a remarkable evolution from "John Redding Goes to Sea." Hurston trusts in the strength of Isis as a character to propel the story forward. She also takes for granted the power and significance of her female characters. Men are incidental to "Drenched in Light"; the women are invested with all the action and charisma. If we read the story as a kind of literary introduction, we see the promise of a bold female voice that finds intimacy and joy in interracial relations without ignoring the realities of a still deeply segregated country.

"Drenched in Light" was well placed in *Opportunity*, a magazine created with the goal of exploring "Negro life as it is" (Huggins 1971, 28). It aimed to offer a more introspective and creative perspective than the other two major black publications of the time, *The Crisis* and *The Messenger*. While Du Bois's *The Crisis*, a product of the National Association for the Advancement of Colored People, was committed to documenting and decrying racial discrimination and violence, *The Messenger* characterized itself as "The Only Radical Negro Magazine in America." Its founders, A. Philip Randolph and Chandler Owen, offered a more militant alternative to Du Bois's integrationist aims. By contrast, Johnson envisioned *Opportunity* as invested in celebrating and understanding African American experience more broadly. Its motto, "Not Alms but Opportunity," speaks to his desire to recognize the challenges and multiple pathways to African American success. The magazine's early issues reflect Johnson's training as a sociologist, with essays by Ralph Bunche, E. Franklin Frazier, Melville Herskovits, and Franz Boas. By *Opportunity*'s second year, Johnson hoped to reorient the magazine toward artistic work. Although *The Crisis* had published work by Langston Hughes and *The Messenger* included Claude McKay in its pages, *Opportunity*'s deliberate commitment to the arts was foundational to fostering the talent and direction of the Harlem Renaissance.

Many scholars date the beginning of the Harlem Renaissance to March 21, 1924. That was the evening that Johnson hosted a dinner at the New York Civic Club to celebrate the recent publication of Jessie Fauset's novel *There Is Confusion* (1924). Although the invitees included Eugene O'Neill and H. L. Mencken, an exciting group of young black writers, including Langston Hughes, Countee Cullen, Jean Toomer, and Gwendolyn Bennett, quickly became the center of attention. Du Bois addressed these new voices as someone who consciously represented an older generation looking ahead to promising horizons, while James Weldon Johnson named the master of ceremonies, Alain Locke, as head of the New Negro movement. The dinner led to the development of a Black Writers' Guild, which included Fauset and Cullen. Both Hughes and Hurston, the biggest stars of the Harlem Renaissance, credited Johnson as a primary force behind the artistic movement. Hurston wrote, "Dr. Johnson was the root of the so-called Negro renaissance. It was his work, and only his hush-mouth nature has caused it to be attributed to so many others" (Hurston 1942, 138). Hughes concurred, noting that the editor "did more to encourage and develop Negro writers during the 1920s than anyone else in America" (Lewis 1979, 125).

In part because Johnson had "said something about New York" in one of his letters to Hurston, the budding writer decided to move there: "So the first week of January, 1925, found me in New York with $1.50, no job, no friends, and a lot of hope" (Hurston 1942, 138). Hurston arrived with the hope of completing her studies in the city, though not to the neglect of her budding writing career. With a number of short stories and plays in mind, she went to the office of the National Urban League to track down Johnson. The famed editor had a history of taking in young writers. He helped settle Hurston into Harlem, while his wife offered carfare and homemade meals. At thirty-four, Hurston was two years older than Johnson, but she welcomed his paternal bearing and counsel.

Unlike most of the United States, Harlem was a place where African American life and identity were celebrated. Hurston delighted in the hope and energy of her neighbors, the thrill of the area's late-night clubs, and the vision of other young artists, writers, and performers. In one of her most famous essays, "How It Feels to Be Colored Me," first published in 1928, Hurston described the essential me-ness that a place like Harlem inspired in her: "At certain times I have no race, I am *me*. When I set my hat at a certain angle and saunter down Seventh Avenue, Harlem City, feeling as snooty as the lions in front of the Forty-Second Street Library, for instance" (Hurston 1979, 154). And yet this seemingly race-transcendent self emerged from a place where almost all the people were black. For race to disappear, Hurston had to return to conditions that reflected her Eatonville childhood and celebrated the broad spectrum of black life.

Harlem in the 1920s was alive with the most cutting-edge thinkers and performers of the day. James Weldon Johnson lived next to the famed pianist Fats Waller. At 131st Street and Seventh Avenue, jazz musicians gathered in the open-air site of "The Corner" to experiment with new sounds and rhythms. Nearly every night, there were poetry readings, book discussions, lectures, and performances at the Lincoln and Lafayette theaters. But none of these events compared to the raucous rent parties usually held on Saturday and Thursday nights, the evenings that domestics typically had off. Rent parties were so named because attendees had to pay a few coins to cover the host's rent, which in Harlem ran up to thirty dollars higher than other parts of the city. Although African Americans made significantly lower salaries than their white counterparts, they paid between

40 to 60 percent higher rents. This inequity was exacerbated by the difficulty blacks faced in moving out of Harlem to more affordable (and inevitably, whiter) neighborhoods. David Levering Lewis reports that the average Harlem resident could expect to pay 40 percent of his or her income on rent alone (Lewis 1979, 107–111). While rent parties were thus rooted in fundamentally racist housing practices, they evolved into a quintessential Harlem experience.

Rent parties often featured amateur singers and dancers. However, professional musicians like Duke Ellington and Fats Waller might also appear, to the delight of crowds that featured people from all walks of life—elite socialites danced the Charleston alongside construction workers and painters. All feasted on hearty dishes of soul food that included fried chicken, hoppin' john, collard greens, corn bread, and potato salad. Although Hurston continued a long-distance romance with Sheen, she made the most of these wild events. Sterling Brown notes that "When Zora was there, she *was* the party" (Hemenway 1977, 61). Hurston was known for her love of dancing but more often became the life of the party due to her flair for storytelling. The tales from Joe Clarke's porch tumbled easily from her lips along with the escapades and jokes she picked up along the way with the Gilbert and Sullivan troupe, as well as her own clever asides. Late Saturday nights did not stop her from attending services at one of Harlem's many storefront churches the following morning. Though Hurston was hardly religious in any traditional sense, something about the exuberant worship at these black churches called her back.

Rent parties and church services fueled Hurston's literary ambitions. In the fall of 1924, Johnson announced a writing contest through *Opportunity* for the best short stories, plays, poems, and essays. He received over 700 submissions, including a collection of pieces by Hurston. The following spring, the magazine hosted a dinner with hundreds of people at the Fifth Avenue Restaurant. With over $800 to give away in prize money, Johnson assembled a prestigious group of judges that included Fannie Hurst, Eugene O'Neill, Alain Locke, and James Weldon Johnson. The dinner was thick with Harlem notables like the rising singer Paul Robeson and white patron and future longtime friend to Hurston, Carl Van Vechten. The awards went to the young stars of the Harlem Renaissance: Hughes and Cullen took first and second place in poetry and shared third place. E. Franklin Frazier and Sterling Brown were recognized in the essay category. Though she did not claim any first-place prizes, Hurston took the most awards home that night. "Spunk" came in second for short stories, and her play *Color Struck* won second prize in drama. She also received two honorable mentions for the story "Black Death" and the play *Spears*. The two second-place prizes were accompanied by thirty-five dollars each, a significant windfall at the time. Mae Miller remembers that the following evening, Hurston arrived at a party full of artists and their patrons with a brightly colored scarf. She threw the scarf around her neck and exclaimed, "*Coloooooor Struckkkk?*" (Miller 1971, interview notes). Everyone fell silent at her dramatic entrance. The stage was all hers.

This story added to a collection of anecdotes told by her friends that emphasized Hurston's flair, inventiveness, and daring. Soon, writers like Hughes were eager to make her acquaintance even as others frowned upon her temerity. Arna Bontemps characterized her as the star of any group but noted, "She really was not a showoff but she just drew attention in that way" (Bontemps December 1970, interview by Robert E. Hemenway). She compelled others more with her charisma, wit, and storytelling than with her physical beauty. Her power lay in her voice and its ability to command the curiosity of whites and blacks alike. After interviewing many of her friends and associates, Robert E. Hemenway noted that Hurston's "friends were often incapable of reconciling the polarities of her personal style. Aware of this, she came to delight in the chaos she sometimes left behind" (Hemenway 1977, 5–6). The evening of the *Opportunity* awards dinner, Hurston made a strong impression upon a collection of especially influential white people. First among them was Annie Nathan Meyer, the founder of Barnard College. Meyer invited Hurston to register for classes at the Columbia-affiliated women's college. In addition to serving on the board of trustees at the school, Meyer supported a variety of African American organizations and causes. She was eager to diversify the Barnard student body and hoped Hurston, with her talent and outgoing personality, would help integrate the school.

Hurston seized upon the opportunity to complete her degree and largely dismissed the challenges of becoming its only African American student. She wrote back to Meyer quickly, conveying her tremendous enthusiasm and her hope not to disappoint her new white patron. Hurston's correspondence with Meyer conveys what may be read as a somewhat exaggerated sense of connection between them: "It is mighty cold comfort to do things if nobody cares whether you succeed or not. It is terribly delightful to me to have someone fearing with me and hoping for me let alone working to make some of my dreams come true" (Kaplan 2003, 55, letter from Hurston to Meyer in 1925). Hurston implies that only Meyer detected Hurston's talents and only Meyer supported her career. Such a description discounts the resources offered by Johnson and his wife as well as the earlier teachers who encouraged her studies. Hurston's letters to Meyer portray the influential philanthropist as her sole salvation, a flattering if not entirely accurate depiction. Ultimately, sincerity was less important here than the final effect of Hurston's words: Meyer spent the summer months gathering the funds to pay for her new protégé's tuition.

This victory was especially important because Barnard's dean, Virginia Gildersleeve, was less impressed by Hurston than Meyer. She admitted the budding writer after a promising interview but could not justify applying scholarship funds to her case given her uneven transcript from Howard. Meyer then turned to Carl Van Vechten, another person Hurston had encountered at the *Opportunity* awards dinner. He too was interested in supporting young black talent. Hurston dubbed such rich whites "Negrotarians," a term that highlights the tensions at work between the wealthy elite and their black beneficiaries (Lewis 1979, 98). Hurston soon went beyond casting Meyer as her financial savior, adopting racialized language that fed into the racial division between the two women. She ended letters with the phrase "your humble and obedient servant" and even referred to herself as "your little pickaninny" (Kaplan 2003, 60–63, letter from Hurston to Meyer in 1925). Such descriptions reified Meyer's power as a specifically white woman over the ever grateful and submissive Hurston. While it is impossible to know what Meyer thought of these characterizations, they did lead to the precise outcome Hurston wanted: in the fall of 1925, Hurston enrolled at Barnard with her tuition covered. As ever when reviewing Hurston's letters, we must be sensitive to her financial concerns as well as her talent for assessing and then fulfilling the expectations of others. This was true even when it came to the matter of her age; though Meyer and others believed her to be twenty-six years old, she was in fact thirty-four. Hurston was nobody's servant, but she was not above performing the roles that would get her what she wanted. It is worth noting that once established at Barnard, Hurston left off the cloying sign-off "your most humble and obedient servant" and instead ended her letters with the more formal "most cordially yours" (Kaplan 2003, 73, letter from Hurston to Meyer in 1925/1926).

Hurston described herself as "Barnard's sacred black cow," though she added that she had "no lurid tales to tell of race discrimination" (Hurston 1942, 139). Hurston was unique among her classmates, but, as she recounts of her time there, this did nothing to limit her studies or social activities. She stated in an occupational interest form for the school that she anticipated continuing to work as she took classes, "either as a manicurist, social worker or writer. Perhaps sell a manuscript or two." Asked about her future ambitions, she wrote, "I have had some small success as a writer and wish above all to succeed at it. Either teaching or social work will be interesting but consolation prizes" (Boyd 2003, 103). She made no mention of the fact that she was on track to become the first black graduate of the school. Her attitude was the same as if she were still among an all-black student body: "I had the same feeling at Barnard that I did at Howard only more so. I felt that I was highly privileged and determined to make the most of it. I did not resolve to be a grind, however, to show the white folks that I had brains.

I took for granted that they knew that. Else, why was I at Barnard?" (Hurston 1942, 140). Assuming that she was as entitled to her education as every other student there, Hurston found friends who added to her understanding of elite society. One friend from an economics class instructed her on which fork to use for various dishes and other details about proper behavior among the upper class.

Hurston's successes may have been "small," but they were accumulating with significant force. The summer before she enrolled at Barnard, she published "Magnolia Flower," a fable-like short story in the *Spokesman*, and that September, "The Hue and Cry about Howard University" appeared in *The Messenger*. That essay took on the protests by Howard students against the singing of Negro spirituals to the university's white president. Students decried the songs as embarrassing relics of the slave past, but Hurston argued that the songs were powerful examples of black folklore. "Magnolia Flower" is told from the perspective of a river but involves a very human dynamic. The ex-slave Bentley, strict with his black employees, builds a schoolhouse so that his beloved daughter, Magnolia, and other local children can learn to read. There she falls in love with the light-skinned teacher John. Enraged by their plans to marry because he wants Magnolia to wed a dark-skinned man, Bentley locks them up. The couple escapes, and Bentley dies of his rage. The river reflects on the affairs of humanity from a distance, aware of the long passage of time.

Most significant, however, was the publication of "Spunk," the story that brought her to the attention of Meyer and others through the *Opportunity* awards dinner. "Spunk" exhibits many of the qualities most distinctive about Hurston's work: a loving description of black life, broad use of humor and dialect, and the assumption that belief in the supernatural is not misguided but consistent with the workings of nature and the human condition. The story centers on Spunk Banks, a charming but conceited sawmill worker who takes up with a married woman. Joe Kanty, the spurned husband, confronts Spunk but is killed in the tussle that follows. Spunk believes that Joe's spirit returns to haunt him in the form of a black bobcat. He dies mysteriously, and the men on the store porch conclude that Joe caused Spunk's death. The story was later reprinted in *The New Negro: An Interpretation* (1925), a collection that was edited by Alain Locke and became one of the foundational texts of the Harlem Renaissance.

Hurston received her second-place award for "Spunk" from Fannie Hurst, a best-selling author whose novel *Imitation of Life* (1933) was later made into a hit movie starring Lana Turner. Hurst approached Hurston through Carl Van Vechten and invited her to tea that fall. At the time of the invitation, Hurston was more concerned about money than the famous writer's possible influence on her future career. In her first semester at Barnard, Hurston was overwhelmed with the additional expenses required to be an active student there: she needed not only books and new clothes, but items like a tennis racquet, golf outfit, and bathing suit. The situation was compounded by the fact that Hurston had recently been fired after her boss insisted that she arrive at 3:00 even though she could not begin work until after 5:00 p.m. Meyer suggested that she intercede on Hurston's behalf and ask Hurst for additional funds to help pay her tuition. In letters to Meyer, Hurston appears quite desperate, concerned both about her ability to stay at Barnard and the resources to feed herself:

> I've taken some tremendous loss and survived terrific shocks. I am not telling you this in search of sympathy. No melodrama. If I am losing my capacity for shock absorbing, if privation is beginning to terrify me, you will appreciate the situation and see that it isn't cowardice, but that by being pounded so often on the anvil of life I am growing less resilient. physical suffering unnerves me now. (Kaplan 2003, 67, letter from Hurston to Meyer in 1925)

Despite the attention Hurston had garnered from a collection of wealthy and influential patrons, she was in many ways on her own. Her family did not have the resources to help her, and she had no savings to rely on.

Fortunately, Hurst was quite taken by Hurston at their conversation over tea and offered to help cover her tuition fees. She even offered Hurston a job as her personal secretary and welcomed her into her West Sixty-Seventh Street apartment. The position proved advantageous in a number of ways. Dean Gildersleeve reevaluated Hurston in light of Hurst's interest in her and made available new loan opportunities. Suddenly, Hurston's classmates at Barnard who had previously kept some distance showed newfound interest in her. Hurst was one of the most widely read female authors of the early twentieth century, and the attention she bestowed upon Hurston was the envy of her peers. With greater financial stability, Hurston was able to dedicate more time to the seven classes she took her first semester at Barnard. She earned Bs in English and history and Cs in all her other classes.

Although Hurston's live-in relationship with Hurst lasted only a few weeks, it brought a degree of stability to her time at Barnard. The precise financial relationship between the two women has never been brought to light, but it certainly was beneficial to Hurston. Like Meyer and Van Vechten, Hurst was a noted "Negrotarian" who funded such organizations as the National Health Circle for Colored People and promoted artists associated with the New Negro movement. Supporting an up-and-coming writer like Hurston was a natural fit for Hurst. Moreover, the older writer saw in her new protégé a unique passion and charm worth cultivating. Soon she was sharing drafts of her next novel, *Appassionata*, and reading through Hurston's latest projects.

As she had with Meyer, Hurston clearly saw exciting opportunities opening through her relationship with Hurst. Hurst had connections from New York to Hollywood. She was a screenwriter, columnist, and bestselling author with a sense of style that even Hurston appreciated: "I doubt if any woman on earth has gotten better effects than she has with black, white and red. Not only that, she knows how to parade it when she gets it on. She will never be jailed for uglying up a town" (Hurston 1942, 197). Despite the mutual admiration between the two women, they quickly discovered that a working relationship strained their affection. Hurst was frustrated by Hurston's spotty secretarial abilities: "Her shorthand was short on legibility, her typing hit-or-miss, mostly the latter, her filing a game of find-the-thimble." As Hurst soon noted, Hurston had little patience for aiding anyone's literary project but her own: "Her mind ran ahead of my thoughts and she would interject with an impatient suggestion or clarification of what I wanted to say" (Hurst 1960, 17).

A month after Hurston moved in with Hurst, she left for a room on West 131st Street in Harlem. Despite this abrupt shift in their relationship, the writers remained on good terms. In fact, Hurst seemed to gain greater respect for Hurston in recognizing that she was "the world's worst secretary." The elder writer later quipped, "As a matter of fact, I think I should be your secretary" (Hurst 1960, 18). Hurston recognized that the older woman was instrumental to her social success among both her peers and professors at Barnard, writing to her, "Partly because you took me under your shelter, I have had no trouble in making friends. Your friendship was a tremendous help to me at a critical time. It made both faculty and students see me when I needed seeing" (Kaplan 2003, 85, letter from Hurston to Hurst in 1926). Hurst also promoted Hurston's work among magazine editors and offered her protégé feedback on her stories, even if such feedback was rarely incorporated into her revisions. Hurst introduced Hurston to many of her celebrity friends, but Hurston was generally wary of these new acquaintances, who seemed to treat her more as a fashionable item than as a serious writer. During this time, she was developing deeper relationships with other black writers like Cullen and Hughes, who shared a stronger understanding of her artistic aims.

Because she was no longer formally employed by Hurst, once again Hurston had to find a job to help pay for her tuition and living expenses. She worked part-time as a waitress and did some housekeeping for people Meyer knew. These dynamics underscore the ways in which Hurston was never on an equal footing with her Negrotarian patrons. Even as she shared her writing and aspects of her personal struggles with Hurst and Meyer, Hurston always operated at a significant remove from their wealth and entitlement. She continued to apply for scholarships to cover her tuition fees, and at last in February 1926, she received one. Despite her success,

Dean Gildersleeve continued to voice doubts that Hurston was a good fit at Barnard. She had missed one of her exams, and there had been difficulty in registering for her second semester. Though Hurston valued her coursework, she was also drawn to the social events at Harlem and was eager to cultivate closer relationships with people like Hurst and Van Vechten. And, of course, writing remained her top priority. Hemenway observes that these multiple concerns led to a kind of "vocational schizophrenia" for Hurston with Barnard's "scientific discipline and academic responsibility" posed against the "imaginative freedom, social progress and liberating iconoclasm" of Harlem (Hemenway 1977, 63–64). While many might find tension in these polarized worlds, Hurston seemed to delight in their oppositions and the ways they fostered new perspectives and insights.

To someone like Gildersleeve, however, such various commitments could only lead to distraction and possibly failure. However, her assessment also ignored the continual financial instability that would characterize most of Hurston's life. Meyer cautioned Hurston to dedicate herself to her studies, but for Hurston the issue was about staying true to herself and her dreams. She wrote back to her mentor, "But, Oh, if you knew my dreams! my vaulting ambition! How I constantly live in fancy in seven league boots, taking mighty strides across the world, but conscious all the time of being a mouse on a treadmill. Madness ensues" (Kaplan 2003, 77, letter from Hurston to Meyer in 1926). Hurston had grander plans than a degree from Barnard. Her goal was to experience the whole world and to learn far more than any university class could teach her.

While Hurston was a student at Barnard, she effectively straddled two worlds: the elite society of a women's college and 1920s Harlem, or what Arna Bontemps would call "a foretaste of heaven" (Watson 1995, 66). These two worlds began to converge when, in her second term at Barnard, she took a course in anthropology at Columbia University. The anthropology department was the first of its kind in the United States. Founded in 1899 by the German émigré Franz Boas, it remained the most prestigious department in the country, largely due to the tremendous vision and influence of Boas. Often called the Father of American Anthropology, Boas opposed scientific racism and the notion that racial difference has a biological explanation. Instead he argued for cultural relativism and the study of human difference through an understanding of specific social influences. According to Boas, no culture was greater than another, but rather all were equally profound manifestations of the broad range of human diversity.

Papa Franz, as Hurston and other students referred to him, sent Hurston to collect her first anthropological data. She measured the skulls of Harlem residents in order to disprove any racially determined difference in head size. Hurston approached the task with alacrity and her usual charm.

Langton Hughes recalled, "Almost nobody else could stop the average Harlemite on Lenox Avenue and measure his head with a strange-looking, anthropological device and not get bawled out for the attempt, except Zora, who used to stop anyone whose head looked interesting and measure it" (Hughes 1986, 235). Boas was impressed with Hurston's aptitude for cultural anthropology and encouraged her to continue her training. Hurston was quite taken with Boas or as she later called him "the King of Kings." She admired his humor and insistence that all claims be rigorously supported by data. Once, when Hurston greeted him with his nickname Papa Franz, he replied with a sly smile, "Of course, Zora is my daughter. Certainly! . . . Just one of my missteps, that's all" (Hurston 1942, 140).

With Boas, Hurston discovered a new way to understand and approach the world. Anthropology gave her some distance from the language, culture, and stories of Harlem and Eatonville. As she set out to study black folklore, she recognized that "when I pitched headforemost into the world I landed in the crib of negroism." However, "it was fitting like a tight chemise. I couldn't see it for wearing it. It was only when I was off in college, away from my native surroundings that I could see myself like somebody else and stand off and look at my garment. Then I had to have the spyglass of Anthropology to look through at that" (Hurston 1935, 1). From this perspective, Hurston recognized the tales from Joe Clarke's front porch and Harlem's vibrant parties as part of a coherent narrative attesting to the cultural diversity of black life. Folklore was something to be studied and analyzed, not just enjoyed for its humor and metaphor. However, it is important to note that Hurston ultimately differed from Boas in key ways once she headed into the field. While Boas and other anthropologists were careful not to disrupt the cultures they studied, Hurston was uninterested in acting as a clinical observer of black folklife. Instead, she actively participated in the rituals she recorded, eventually dancing along with Bahamian performers and mastering voodoo ceremonies in New Orleans and Haiti. Moreover, though Hurston held to anti-racist beliefs, at times she promoted essentialist notions of blackness that contradicted Boas's rejection of biological determinism.

While Hurston pursued her studies with Boas, she continued to be a fixture of the Harlem literati or, as Hurston dubbed them, the Niggerati. This group included Langston Hughes, Wallace Thurman, Gwendolyn Bennett, and Richard Bruce Nugent, as well as artist Aaron Douglas and sculptor Augusta Savage. Among this talented collection, Hurston was known for her assertive style and blunt wit. She was the self-proclaimed "Queen of the Niggerati" who held court on issues of politics, art, literature, and gossip. With her growing influence, Hurston was eager to help establish the Little Negro Theater through the Krigwa Players, a group founded by W. E. B. Du Bois. Hurston hoped that the new theater would showcase some of her work, but Du Bois was wary of performing plays written by its principal organizers. The Little Negro Theater put on three plays in 1926, which Du Bois highlighted in a *Crisis* editorial that defined four criteria of black theater. According to him, African American theatrical work must be about blacks, by blacks, for blacks, and performed near or in black neighborhoods.

These stringent requirements reflect Du Bois's essential belief that art is and must be propaganda. For him, the aesthetic and the political are necessarily united. By contrast, Hurston and other members of the Harlem Renaissance had more complex views on the purpose of art. They rejected Du Bois's often elitist and generally Western standards to explore other ways of imparting meaning and beauty. Opposing the rigid uplift of Du Bois's "talented Tenth," Hurston and her companions sought inspiration among "the Negro farthest down," in those who lacked university education and elite manners but instead represented a centuries-old vitality (Du Bois 2014; Hurston 1942, 145). Hughes countered Du Bois's call for propagandistic art with the now-canonical essay, "The Negro Artist and the Racial Mountain," which uses jazz and the blues as a template for a more invigorating black art. Where Du Bois threatened to deny the beauty of folk culture, Hughes celebrated the freedom and diversity of a new black art.

> We younger Negro artists who create now intend to express our individual dark-skinned selves without fear or shame. If white people are pleased we are glad. If they are not, it doesn't matter. We know we are beautiful. And ugly too. The tom-tom cries and the tom-tom laughs. If colored people are pleased we are glad. If they are not, their displeasure doesn't matter either. We build our temples for tomorrow, strong as we know how, and we stand on top of the mountain, free within ourselves. (Hughes 2014, 1324)

Hughes's bold call expressed the sentiment of a whole generation eager to break the shackles of white expectation and respectability politics. Hughes, Hurston, and others sought a creative liberation that might give voice to the full complexity of black life, from the tales of Brer Rabbit to the poetry of Bessie Smith.

Free from coursework in the summer of 1926, Hurston turned her attention more fully to her life among the "Niggerati." After finishing the semester with Bs in anthropology, English, and physical education and Cs in economics, classical civilizations, and French, she moved to an apartment at 43 West Sixty-Sixth Street. Though Hurston had enough to cover rent, she threw a "furniture party" to help transform her new place into a home. She hoped for more couches and chairs than lamps and decorative items, but since most of her Harlem friends lacked cars, larger pieces of furniture were nearly impossible to carry. Hurston fed the group what

Hughes remembered as "a *hand*-chicken dinner" since there were no forks in the apartment (Hughes 1986, 239). In part because of her culinary talents, Hurston's apartment became a central meeting point for her friends and their friends. She might serve fried shrimp and okra or just a pan of gingerbread and a bottle of buttermilk. Perhaps because of her own struggles with poverty, Hurston was particularly sensitive to hungry guests and sought to satisfy visitors with whatever she had on hand. She even at times offered others a place to stay. Artists and friends were always welcome, and while typically Hurston took part in the laughter and storytelling, at times she worked alone in her bedroom to finish a certain piece of writing.

Though Hurston's apartment was a favored location, the most boisterous action took place at 267 West 136th Street, where free rooms were available for artists. In the summer of 1926, Thurman and his white male lover lived there, as did Nugent and Hughes. Hurston and Thurman soon dubbed the rooming house "Niggerati Manor." Thurman decorated the walls with colorful phalluses while gin was said to pour from the water taps. Despite its reputation for sexual hedonism, Niggerati Manor generated numerous artistic partnerships. Finding commonality in their mutual esteem for black folk culture, Hurston and Hughes envisioned a black opera using jazz and the blues. Their project combined their distinctive talents and backgrounds; Hughes was adept at song writing, and Hurston had experience in the theater. Though the two most prominent writers of the Harlem Renaissance would later pursue this collaboration, they were first absorbed by a more ambitious project.

Hughes followed the success of "The Negro Artist and the Racial Mountain" with the suggestion that a magazine be formed that demonstrated the central tenets of his cultural manifesto. Hurston, along with Thurman, Nugent, Bennett, John P. Davis, and Aaron Douglas, urged the idea forward. They envisioned a magazine untethered by sociological or propagandistic concerns, one that gave voice to the African American masses, not the elite establishment. Unlike the other leading black magazines of the day, their journal, *Fire!!*, would be entirely literary in nature. As the most brash and independent artist of the group, Thurman was selected as the editor. Best known for his novel *The Blacker the Berry* (1929), Thurman had exceptionally dark skin and a flair for the outrageous; he was notorious for his wild nights and binge drinking. Hughes described him as "a strangely brilliant black boy, who had read everything, and whose critical mind could find something wrong with everything he read" (Hughes 1986, 234). But even with his all-nighters and sexual escapades, Thurman was committed to representing the folk and rejecting Du Bois's elitist expectations of black art. He hoped to create such a scandal with the first issue of *Fire!!* that the magazine would be banned in Boston. Such a response would no doubt boost sales. To this end, Thurman decided to write about a teenaged prostitute while Nugent focused on a homosexual. They would reveal black life as never before.

Among the collection of patrons supporting *Fire!!* was Carl Van Vechten, Hurston's longtime friend and correspondent, who would become one of the most important figures of the Harlem Renaissance. She reputedly said of him, "If Carl was a people instead of a person, I could then say, these are my people" (Hurst 1960, 19). While many white writers and thinkers came to Harlem in the 1920s, including William Faulkner and Charlie Chaplin, to gawk at black performers and indulge in the pleasures of its nightlife, Van Vechten was unique in his adulation of all things Negro and his attempts, though often misguided, to break through the color line. Known as a trendsetter and cultural impresario (he is thought to be the first man in New York to don a wristwatch), he often hosted mixed-race parties and introduced other whites to the delights of Harlem. Many were wary of his overly enthusiastic championing of black art and culture and suspected that his real interest lay in his sexual taste for black men; though his marriage to actress Fania Marinoff lasted over fifty years, he was well known as a homosexual. Others, like Nugent, described Van Vechten as "a sincere friend of the Negro," and he did much to champion the careers of Paul Robeson, Bessie Smith, and many others (Nugent 1970, interview by Robert E. Hemenway).

However, even with the support of James Weldon Johnson and Walter White of the NAACP and writers like Hurston, Hughes, and Thurman, Van Vechten seriously risked his reputation with the publication of his highly controversial novel *Nigger Heaven* in 1926. The title riffed off the term used to describe a theater's segregated balcony, but few saw much humor in the use of the most fraught word in American English. The book was nonetheless an instant best seller and revelatory for its account of Harlem life from the perspective of a white observer. Many African American intellectuals, including Du Bois, condemned the book as effectively a slap in the face, but Hurston and other members of the "Niggerati" conceded that its descriptions were accurate and if anything too admiring of black life. Van Vechten portrayed Harlem as a place of sexual transgression. What may now be understood as various forms of erotic experimentation was then read as clear evidence of perversity. Parties where sexual pleasures of all kinds were offered cafeteria-style were known as "buffet flats" and available to anyone who could pay the minor price of admission. Van Vechten wrote of the sexually liberal nightclubs and the cross-dressing performers that delighted crowds of all kinds. These depictions along with the novel's offensive title upset many black Harlemites, who felt that the book did more to indulge stereotypes than to resist them. The managers of one of Van Vechten's favorite nightclubs banned him from the premises, and other black-owned establishments soon did the same. Van Vechten was appalled by this response and sought Hurston's company to return to his beloved hot spots.

Attuned to the publicity he could garner in defending the author of *Nigger Heaven*, Thurman penned an editorial for the first issue of *Fire!!* in which he renounced the popular call to burn Van Vechten in effigy and instead insisted that a statue be built on 135th Street and Seventh Avenue to commemorate him. Despite its talented writers and influential supporters, the magazine barely made it to press. By the fall of 1926, many of its contributors and editorial members were on their way back to school or looking to begin other jobs. Hughes returned to Lincoln University in Pennsylvania, Davis left for Harvard, and Hurston was about to begin her next academic year at Barnard. Moreover, days before its publication in November, Hurston's younger brother Everett accidentally fed key manuscripts for the journal, including one by Nugent, into a fire at his sister's apartment. Despite his fury with Everett's mistake, Nugent rewrote his story on the subway, and the magazine at last appeared in print with a striking black and red cover by Aaron Douglas.

The magazine was a bold declaration and demonstration of artistic independence. In forty-eight pages, the contributors praised the beauty of jazz, the pathos of the blues, the wisdom of the folk, and the pleasures of sexual freedom. The collected works represented a wide spectrum of black life, from lynching to expatriate life, without attempting to be comprehensive. Hurston included two of her works in the issue, her play *Color Struck* and one of her finest short stories, "Sweat." As expected, reviewers seized upon the most controversial selections, Thurman's "Cordelia the Crude" and Nugent's "Smoke, Lilies and Jade," to dismiss it as little more than trash. Though one white reviewer praised its originality, most establishment black writers scorned the publication. Du Bois made no public statement about the journal but was privately pained by its content.

Thurman did not win the attention of censors with his scandalous writing, only the ire of reviewers and even some Harlem businesses. The staff of Craig's restaurant on 135th Street, a popular meeting place for the editorial board, snubbed the magazine's founders. These responses exacerbated the basic fact that few people wanted to buy the magazine. Many Harlemites could not afford the one-dollar cover price, and the editorial board neglected to establish clear channels of delivery. Though endowed with great literary talent, the founders of *Fire!!* had little savvy about marketing and distribution. Nugent resorted to hand-delivering it to bookshops and inevitably spent whatever proceeds he gathered before he even made it back to Harlem.

The only issue of *Fire!!* ever published cost almost a thousand dollars to produce. Although the seven founders each promised to contribute fifty dollars as seed money, only three actually did so; unsurprisingly, Hurston was among those who failed to pay their share. Thurman was able to get the magazine to press only by signing a promissory note, thus leaving him with a tremendous debt. Hurston and others sent him money when they could, but for years later, Thurman's wages were garnished. In an especially ironic turn, hundreds of unsold copies burned in a fire that swept through the basement of a Harlem apartment house.

Though the magazine proved devastating in many ways, Hurston remained convinced that its basic idea was both sound and necessary. The publication was a success for her in that it made her award-winning play more widely available and demonstrated that she was a writer of the first rank with "Sweat." *Color Struck* is ultimately a minor work in Hurston's oeuvre but remains significant for its subject matter. It focuses on a group of dancers on their way to a cakewalk, a contest in which the best performers will take home the largest cake ever baked in Florida. Though generally light in tone, the play finds its depth with a dark-skinned woman who is so convinced of her ugliness that she believes no one can ever love her.

"Sweat," however, represents the height of Hurston's creative powers during this time period. "Sweat" tells the story of Delia, an Eatonville woman who washes clothes, and her struggles with her abusive husband, Sykes. While Delia works incessantly, Sykes mocks her emaciated body and takes up with another woman. A group of men assemble on the porch of Joe Clarke's store and decry Sykes's ill treatment of Delia; they even consider killing him. Sykes threatens Delia with a snake in an attempt to move her out of the house that her work purchased. However, the snake ultimately bites him, and as Sykes crawls to his wife for help, she gazes upon him with rage that transforms to pity when she sees "his one open eye shining with hope." Delia knows that medical help is too far away to save Sykes, and the story ends with an ambiguous sense of the knowledge shared between the couple: "She could scarcely reach the Chinaberry tree, where she waited in the growing heat while inside she knew the cold river was creeping up and up to extinguish that eye which must know by now that she knew" (Hurston 1995, 85). While retaining the distinctive language and setting of her earlier fiction, "Sweat" represents a significant literary development for Hurston. The strength of her characters, Delia and Sykes, both complex, deeply flawed individuals, replaces the simplistic plots of her previous stories and brings depth to the musings about gender relations expressed on Joe Clarke's porch. Here, superstition and folk practices are secondary to the communal wisdom of the town and the elegant articulation of how and why men mistreat women.

"Sweat" was soon followed with the short story "Muttsy" in 1926. Published in *Opportunity*, it won second prize that year and follows the journey of Pinkie, an Eatonville ingénue, to Harlem, where she becomes absorbed in the dancing and fighting of Ma Turner's back parlor. There

Pinkie meets Muttsy, known for his "characteristic pose of indifference to the female" (Hurston 1995, 41). A noted womanizer and gambler, Muttsy promises to reform his ways if she will marry him. She agrees, though Muttsy soon resorts to his previous lifestyle, convinced that he can both please his wife and satisfy his taste for vice. That same year, Hurston also published "'Possum or Pig?" in *Forum*. This story retells a well-known tale involving John and Master and thus is less fictional than an attempt to present black folklore to a literate audience. "'Possum or Pig?" anticipates the series "The Eatonville Anthology," which was published over three months in the fall of 1926 in *Messenger*. Made up of fourteen short works, "The Eatonville Anthology" features episodes of dialogue that one might hear on the porch of Joe Clarke's store. While some of the numbered sections involve well-known folktales, others derive from Hurston's childhood memories or her observations of life in her hometown. The language is rich with vivid images like the following: "Mrs. Clarke is Joe Clarke's wife. She is a soft-looking, middle-aged woman, whose bust and stomach are always holding a get-together" (Hurston 1995, 64). Many of the stories involve difficult marriages and the consequences of poverty, highlighting the resilience of the black townspeople and their pragmatic approach to dealing with life's challenges. The collection is also important for featuring a number of recurring characters in Hurston's later fiction, including Joe Clarke and Jim Merchant.

"The Eatonville Anthology" confirmed Hurston's reputation as an engaging storyteller and demonstrates the blurred line in her work between oral and print narratives. Some of her closest associates, like Nugent and Thurman, admired her ability to keep a crowd riveted at a party with her folktales and memories of Eatonville but expressed concern that translating such stories to the page did not always lead to serious literature. Thurman's character Sweetie Mar Carr from his novel *Infants of the Spring* (1932) reflects many of Hurston's talents, as well as his doubt that mastery of Southern dialect and a flair for telling anecdotes at parties can amount to meaningful art. He describes Sweetie as "a short story writer, more noted for her ribald wit and personal effervescence than for any actual literary work" (Thurman 2013, 141–142). But for Hurston, sharing stories with others on a front porch or at a rent party was part of the very beauty of any narrative; she understood that stories are meant to be heard, laughed at, and transformed by the response of the group.

Arnold Rampersad has observed that Hurston's passion for her own cultural background "set her apart from virtually all other writers, black and white" (Rampersad 2008, xvii). "Sweat" and "The Eatonville Anthology" demonstrate this commitment to black folklife and show the evolving spectrum of Hurston's writing. True to her growing passion for anthropology, Hurston was concerned with documenting and preserving the stories she had known as a child as much as she was with giving creative expression to her own artistic voice. "The Eatonville Anthology" provides a window into black life; it is less fiction than the work of an attentive listener committed to honoring the cultural practices and beliefs of her subject. By contrast, "Sweat" takes for granted the setting and social life depicted in "The Eatonville Anthology" to explore the more intimate struggles of some of its residents. It combines an appreciation and knowledge of black folklife with a curiosity about the complexities of the human psyche. These two texts may be understood as points of departure for the rest of her literary career, which took off in the 1930s with the publication of her novels and book-length anthropological studies. Although Hurston's creative output during the Harlem Renaissance was actually quite limited, the artistic movement was foundational to her work, nurturing the writer she would eventually become.

4

The Young Anthropologist

Hurston left New York in February 1927, two years before the Harlem Renaissance effectively ended with the stock market crash of 1929. Eager to see what his protégé could accomplish out in the field before she graduated, Franz Boas had spent the previous fall looking for fellowship opportunities for Hurston. He contacted Carter G. Woodson, the director of the Association for the Study of Negro Life and the founder of *The Journal of Negro History*, about Hurston's promising abilities. The Harvard-educated historian agreed to offer $700. This sum was then matched by Elsie Clews Parsons of the American Folklore Society, providing Hurston with enough money to finance a six-month tour through the South. Boas instructed her to collect recordings of stories, songs, jokes, dances, idioms, and other cultural practices of black folklife. She suggested that she focus only on her home state, reasoning that Florida's diversity would offer a rough sample of life throughout the South. Boas agreed to a travel itinerary that would begin in Jacksonville and then move south through St. Augustine, Palatka, Sanford, and Eatonville, among other towns. Though Boas was concerned that Hurston's literary success may have fostered a degree of arrogance that might be off-putting to the people she would encounter, she approached the task with great enthusiasm. She viewed research as a formalized method of unlocking "the cosmic secrets of the world," or, as she put it more simply, anthropology was "poking and prying with a purpose" (Hurston 1942, 143). Boas chose Hurston for this project in part because she was an insider to the life he wanted to learn more about. He hoped that

> ### CARTER G. WOODSON
>
> The son of former slaves, Carter G. Woodson is the reason February is known as Black History Month. The famed historian cofounded in 1915 the Association for the Study of Negro Life and History, as well as the quarterly *The Journal of Negro History* one year later. In 1926, he initiated observance of "Negro History Week" as a way to honor African American contributions to American life and culture. Five decades later, a week became Black History Month. February was selected because the month includes Abraham Lincoln's birthday as well as the accepted birthday of Frederick Douglass.
>
> A Harvard graduate, Woodson wrote more than thirty books in his lifetime. He is best known for *The Mis-Education of the Negro* (1933), which argues that African Americans are not educated in American schools but rather indoctrinated with beliefs that instill quiescence and doubts about their intellectual abilities. Woodson argues that only by claiming their independence and becoming free of false ideas rooted in white supremacy can African Americans embrace their education. He dedicated much of his life to chronicling and preserving black history, developing an archival legacy that has inspired countless other students and scholars.

she could move past the performative facade he observed blacks don when speaking to whites and thereby record a more authentic set of cultural beliefs and practices.

Hurston welcomed the warmth and sun of Florida and took the opportunity to visit with some of her relatives. In Jacksonville, her brother John Cornelius helped her buy a used car, which would spare her from the hassle and humiliation of traveling on segregated trains. John convinced Hurston not to indulge in a sleekly outfitted Oakland Coupe and instead invest in a more practical and much less expensive Ford. Hurston conceded only with the hope that she would eventually buy the fancier car in a few months. She paid $300 for a car she dubbed "Sassy Susie."

Hurston decided to start her work in Eatonville, as she knew the town and felt confident that she could easily gather material. The town proved unchanged from her memory, and she quickly joined a group on the porch of Joe Clarke's store. Many familiar faces welcomed her back, admiring her car as well as her Barnard credentials. However, she struggled to move from long overdue social visits to anthropological fieldwork. Buttermilk and gingerbread did not elicit the material she hoped to document because, as she recalled, she addressed her subjects in "carefully accented Barnardese, 'Pardon me, but do you know any folk tales or folk songs?' The men and women who had whole treasuries of material just seeping through their pores, looked at me and shook their heads. No, they had never heard of anything like that around there. Maybe it was over in the next county." Her distinguished academic credentials held no sway among the people she was most interested in understanding. Hurston left her hometown discouraged, "my heart beneath my knees and my knees in some lonesome valley" (Hurston 1942, 144).

After ten days in Eatonville, Hurston moved on, taking careful precautions as she ventured into unfamiliar territory. She kept a pistol in her car and avoided "whites only" signs. She primarily stayed at rooming houses or private homes because most hotels and even restaurants were off-limits to a black woman. Though Hurston evinced no obvious frustration or resentment at the ways she had to operate in a segregated and often violently racialized world, her attitude toward such injustices is difficult to gauge from her writing. In "How It Feels to Be Colored Me," she declared, "Sometimes, I feel discriminated against but it does not make me angry. It merely astonishes me. How *can* any deny themselves the pleasure of my company! It's beyond me" (Hurston 1979, 155). Such bold self-confidence reads as a radical indictment of the sheer inanity of racism, but it ignores the slights, insults, inconveniences, and dangers Hurston must have encountered in her travels. Carla Kaplan warns against romanticizing Hurston's travels with her Model T and pistol: "The truth is that she worked hard under harsh conditions: traveling in blistering heat, sleeping in her car when 'colored' hotel rooms couldn't be had, defending herself against jealous women, putting up with bedbugs, lack of sanitation, and poor food in some of the turpentine camps, sawmills, and phosphate mines she visited" (Kaplan 2003, 52). Though Hurston figures as a radical trailblazer in our contemporary imagination, such pioneering work was often unglamorous and dispiriting.

Hurston's writing and private letters of the time affirm her decision to focus primarily on her work and ignore the hostility she perceived among the whites she encountered. She wrote to Annie Nathan Meyer back in New York that "the poor whites down here have the harshest and most unlovely faces on earth" (Kaplan 2003, 92, letter from Hurston to Meyer in 1927). Later she came to view whites almost as part of the landscape: "Flowers are gorgeous now, crackers not troubling me at all—hope they don't begin as I go farther down state" (Kaplan 2003, 94, letter from Hurston to Lawrence Jordan in 1927). As she proceeded in her fieldwork, she eventually learned to drop her "Barnardese" and collected colorful idioms among the black people she met. But she still found difficulties in meeting Boas's expectations. He noted that her findings largely repeated what others had collected and did not yield new insights. Despite returning to many beloved locations, Hurston missed her life and friends in Harlem. And although her work required her to socialize with people, she could not stay long enough to establish meaningful connections. Moreover, the queen of many a rent party now had to act primarily as a listener, to note the specific gestures of a certain dance or rhythm of a song rather than throw herself into the fun. Hurston believed in the purpose and desired the insights of anthropology, but its objective approach was an uneasy fit with her exuberant personality.

Hurston took the opportunity afforded by her travels to visit a few of her siblings in Memphis. Her oldest brother, Bob, had become an accomplished doctor, and upon their reunion, he apologized for not doing more to support her education when she lived with his family. Her younger brother Ben also lived in the city, working as a pharmacist. He had married and, more than many of their other siblings, shared his older sister's wit and humor. The brothers filled Hurston in on the details of the lives of other family members: Clifford Joel was a high school principal in Alabama, Dick worked as a chef, and Sarah, recently a new mother, was still married to her preacher husband. Hurston shared with them news from John Cornelius and updates on Everett, who was a postal worker in Brooklyn.

Hurston made one other side trip while in the South, to St. Augustine, Florida, where she met her longtime beau Herbert Sheen. After nearly five years of weathering a long-distance relationship and at least two breakups in between, the two married on May 19, 1927. Aware that it should have been "the happiest day of my life," Hurston was immediately consumed by doubts: "For the first time since I met him, I asked if I really were in love, or if this had been a habit" (Hurston 1942, 204). In a letter written to Sheen decades later, Hurston described a "vision-dream" she had the night before the wedding. Reminiscent of her childhood visions, the nightmare involved "a dark barrier" that "kept falling between us." She explained that the dream left her with an abiding sense of doom: "It made me forever fearful that you would escape out of my life. It all seemed unreal in a way, I mean our union. We appeared like shadowy figures seen through an opal. It was terrible" (Kaplan 2003, 725–726, letter from Hurston to Sheen in 1955). Sheen was then at Chicago's Rush Medical College, and though he remained a few days with his new wife in Florida, he had little interest in the work or substance of collecting folklore. It was clear that he wanted to return to his world, while Hurston was happy to remain in hers. This dynamic would not change throughout their short-lived marriage.

Perhaps because of her private reservations, Hurston did not tell her correspondents back in New York about her marriage. She may also have calculated that Boas, Meyer, and Woodson would have perceived her momentous news as a distraction from the work she was sent to do. Instead, Hurston continued her work by heading to Mobile, Alabama, where she spoke with Cudjo Lewis, a man many considered to be the last living survivor of the Middle Passage. This accomplishment was followed by a surprise meeting with Langston Hughes, who, following a reading at Fisk University, decided to travel through the South on his own. The friends had previously discussed the possibility of touring together, and their chance encounter was the perfect opportunity to make that old plan a reality. After a meal of fried fish and watermelon, they headed north in Sassy Susie together.

Despite Hughes's financial difficulties and his inability to drive, he proved to be an ideal road companion. They shared hours of spirited conversation and laughter. Perhaps because of Hughes's ambiguous sexuality and Hurston's own recent marriage, the two shared a bond that was familial and friendly, rather than romantic. Although their friendship ended in discord following a disagreement over their collaboration on the play *Mule Bone*, their bond remains one of the most famous in all of American literary history. They deeply supported one another's art and vision, even as they sometimes sparred on issues of representation and audience. Hurston at times found Hughes's poetry to cater to "what the 'white folks had exalted,'" ironically a charge that was later levied at her by Richard Wright and other black writers (Kaplan 2003, 84, letter from Hurston to Countee Cullen in 1926). Hughes for his part understood how adept Hurston was at pleasing whites in power. In his autobiography, he writes:

> In her youth she was always getting scholarships and things from wealthy white people, some of whom simply paid her to just sit around and represent the Negro race for them, she did it in such a racy fashion. . . . To many of her white friends, no doubt she was a perfect "darkie," in the nice meaning they give the term—that is a naïve, childlike, sweet humorous, and highly colored Negro. (Hughes 1986, 239)

Both writers understood their common struggle to publish fresh creative work in a world dominated by whites and the compromises this sometimes necessitated. Hughes also shared Hurston's passion for folk culture and took scrupulous notes of his own while she continued to gather material for Boas. They continued to discuss working on a folk opera together and shared developments in their personal lives. Hurston confessed to her marriage to Sheen as well as her doubts about the relationship, and Hughes told her about Charlotte Mason, an affluent widow in New York who financed many of his projects.

On their way north, the two writers spoke at the Tuskegee Institute and met with the former literary editor of *The Crisis*, Jessie Fauset. Together they visited the grave of Tuskegee founder and former presidential advisor Booker T. Washington. In Georgia, they also went to the Toomer plantation, which inspired Jean Toomer to pen his Harlem Renaissance masterpiece *Cane* (1923). After learning that Bessie Smith would be performing in Macon, Hurston and Hughes drove there and discovered that the

> ### Cane
>
> Published in 1923, Jean Toomer's groundbreaking novel *Cane* has become a classic of High Modernism. Although Toomer identified as mixed race, he wrote eloquently about the black community in a novel that helped ease his own racial disquiet. Organized into three sections, *Cane* is considered by many to be one of the greatest pieces of African American literature. The book begins by describing rural blacks in Georgia, then moves on to urban African Americans living in Chicago and Washington, D.C. It closes with a long piece entitled "Kabnis," which is based on Toomer's own experiences of encountering rural black life. Though it was not widely read at the time of its publication, *Cane* was called by Langston Hughes "the finest prose written by a Negro in America."[1] Nearly a century after its publication, *Cane* is now widely praised for its bold experimentation and impressionistic aesthetic. Eschewing stereotypes in his nuanced depiction of the diversity of black life, Toomer affirms the humanity and complexity of his characters. Perhaps drawing an affinity between Toomer and Hurston, Alice Walker engraved the phrase "A Genius of the South" on Hurston's gravestone. The line comes from Toomer's poem "Georgia Dusk," which appears in the novel.
>
> ---
>
> 1. Hughes, Langston, "The Negro Artist and the Racial Mountain," in *The Norton Anthology of African American Literature*, 3rd ed., vol. 1, ed. Henry Louis Gates Jr. and Valerie A. Smith (New York: W. W. Norton, 2014), 1320–1324.

famous blues singer was staying in their hotel. Smith's singing and lifestyle had particular resonance for Hurston; both women worked and traveled without a partner, committing themselves to their own desires rather than pleasing anyone else. The writers also visited a hoodoo doctor in Georgia, though Hurston was left unimpressed by the conjurer's elaborate performance. Before returning to New York, they lunched in Pennsylvania with one of Hughes's former professors.

Hurston settled back into her West Sixty-Sixth Street apartment, which Dorothy West and Helene Johnson had sublet while she was away. She began work on her final report for Boas and concluded a few tasks for Woodson, who refused to pay her two weeks of wages. Because Woodson supplied part of her fellowship money, he asked that she complete a few research assignments for him. One required her to track down some county court records and another involved transcribing documents concerning Fort Moosa, a black settlement that dates to the seventeenth century. The Fort Moosa account was later published in Woodson's *The Journal of Negro History*.

In the same issue of Woodson's journal, dated October 1927, Hurston's first scholarly article appeared: "Cudjo's Own Story of the Last African

Slaver." Although she drew from the interview she conducted with Lewis in Mobile, after her death it was discovered that much of the article was plagiarized. Hurston took whole pages from Emma Langdon Roche's *Historic Sketches of the Old South* (1914), which she'd found at the Mobile Historical Society. Some of the essay clearly derives from Hurston's own research, such as new quotations from Lewis and revised descriptions of where he lived. A footnote states that the author "made some use" of records at the Mobile Historical Society (Hurston 1927, 648). However, such a disclaimer does not excuse the flagrant use of Roche's verbatim words (Hemenway 1977, 98). Because Hurston was never confronted with the plagiarism during her lifetime and her mentors, including Boas and Woodson, never detected any wrongdoing, we can only speculate on Hurston's motivations. When she'd begun to compose her article, she'd written a friend, Thomas Jones, the president of Fisk University, to describe her frustration with the task: "Returned to New York and began to re-write and arrange the material for Scientific publications, and while doing so, began to see the pity of all the flaming glory of being buried in scientific journals" (Kaplan 2003, 315, letter from Hurston to Jones in 1934). Although Hurston's disdain for the rigors of academia is understandable, this seems like a slight justification for her extensive appropriation of Roche's material.

The essay was penned after Woodson withheld her wages, and she wrote to Hughes that she hated "that improperly born wretch" (Kaplan 2003, 99, letter from Hurston to Hughes in 1927). Hurston had little interest in the additional tasks Woodson demanded of her, and plagiarizing may have been the quickest way to finish an essay that was ultimately for him. Though it is tempting to read her misdeed as a form of resistance against a known taskmaster—Hughes left a job working for the overly strict Woodson to become a busboy—Hurston's theft of Roche's work represents a significant failure of integrity. Hemenway speculates that Hurston may have wanted to get caught in an "unconscious attempt at academic suicide"; discovery by Boas or Woodson would have allowed her to be free of the rigid and often impersonal approach of anthropological fieldwork (Hemenway 1977, 99). Valerie Boyd speculates that "Hurston believed the report was only for Woodson's files; she did not expect it to be published" (Boyd 2003, 154). More likely, Hurston simply did what was simplest and most expedient for her. As her career would eventually prove, she was less a brilliant anthropologist than a dazzling storyteller for whom the difference between fact and fiction was secondary to the sheer power of language.

As promised, Hughes encouraged Hurston to meet his patron Charlotte Mason shortly after their return to New York. Alain Locke was instrumental in setting up the momentous encounter. When Hurston entered Mason's penthouse at 399 Park Avenue in September 1927, she recognized the final image from her childhood visions: two women with "queer-shaped flowers such as I had never seen." The flowers were calla lilies, which Cornelia Chapin, Mason's young assistant, was arranging in a vase when Hurston walked into the apartment. She remembered the import of her earlier dream: "When I had come to these women, then I would be at the end of my pilgrimage, but not the end of my life. Then I would know peace and love and what goes with those things, and not before" (Hurston 1942, 42).

Hurston later wrote to Hughes that much of her initial conversation with Mason centered on her hope to write a black folk opera. Mason—or Godmother, as she insisted on being called by her protégés—was yet another Negrotarian who believed African Americans to be "utterly sincere in living." This interest in sincerity may explain Mason's interest in Hurston, who struck the older woman as refreshingly free of academic affectation. Unlike other black writers living in New York, Hurston spoke with Southern phrases and intonations at the ready. However, given Hurston's keen ability to size up new acquaintances, especially white patrons, it is difficult not to imagine that she neatly played into Mason's desires. Her description of Mason in *Dust Tracks on a Road* takes on a nearly mythical quality: "Godmother could be as tender as Mother love when she felt that you had been right spiritually. But anything, however clever, in you that felt like insincerity to her called forth her well known 'That is nothing! It has no soul in it'" (Hurston 1942, 145). Nonetheless, the two women had much in common. Mason had dabbled in anthropology, studying for a time the tribes of the Great Plains. Born into a wealthy family, she then inherited her husband's sizable estate after his death in 1903. Mason used her fortune to underwrite the research for Natalie Curtis's 1907 collection of songs and legends, *The Indians Book*, as well as to support the work of such artists as Aaron Douglas and Miguel Covarrubias.

Despite her dedication to the culture and artistry of African American and indigenous peoples, Mason subscribed to some troubling racial views. She advocated a kind of racial essentialism known as primitivism, which celebrated the savage wisdom and intuition of "primitive" people, especially Native Americans and African Americans. These populations were believed to have more organic relationships to the natural world and even to larger cosmic forces that opposed the sterility of white civilization. In Mason's worldview, people of color might redeem white culture through their rich artistry and creative energies. Much of Hurston's own experience aligned with aspects of Mason's understanding of black culture. After all, Hurston claimed to have first seen Mason in a vision she had as a child. Hurston called Mason "just as pagan as I" and claimed that there was "a psychic bond between us." Hurston swore that "she could read my mind, not only when I was in her presence, but thousands of miles away"

(Hurston 1942, 144). Such descriptions must have delighted Mason; by immersing herself among black artists, she could prove her own seemingly progressive beliefs and demonstrate that she had evolved beyond the rationality and conventionality of white culture.

Mason selected the artists she funded largely under the advice of Alain Locke, who introduced her to Hughes, Douglas, and Claude McKay, among many others. She insisted that all of her beneficiaries adhere to two rules: they must call her "Godmother" and they must never identify her as a patron. Hughes noted that Mason "possessed the power to control people's lives—pick them up and put them down when and where she wished" (Hughes 1986, 324). Though Hughes went on to laud Mason's charm, knowledge, and progressive ideas, it is difficult to disentangle the financial needs of the artists she supported from their loving portraits of her. Hughes acknowledged the tension between who Mason wanted him to be and who he actually was: "She wanted me to be primitive and know and feel the intuitions of the primitive. But, unfortunately, I did not feel the rhythms of the primitive surging through me, and so I could not live and write as though I did" (Hughes 1986, 325). Even as Mason idealized Hughes as a model icon of Africa, she kept Hughes outfitted in tailored suits and made sure he had tickets to the hottest performances in town; for her, he was a handsome talent to display. Boyd characterizes such fraught artist-patron relationships as "not so much volunteer slavery as luxurious servitude" (Boyd 2003, 158). The disparity in power between Godmother and her protégés—and the thousands of dollars that passed between them—muddles any clear understanding of how writers like Hurston and Hughes viewed her, as well as how they responded to her demands and expectations.

Unlike many of the other artists that Mason funded, Hurston signed an employment contract in December 1927 that specified that she was to conduct research specifically for Mason. She was not hired to pursue her own work but rather to undertake research that Mason specifically wanted on African Americans but was unable to collect herself. The contract states that Hurston was "to seek out, compile and collect all information possible, both written and oral, concerning the music, poetry, folk-lore, literature, hoodoo, conjure, manifestations of art and kindred subjects" among Southern blacks (Hurston 1927, contractual agreement with Mason). This information was to be given only to Mason and could not be used without her explicit consent. Along with a camera and a car, Hurston would receive two hundred dollars a month for the next two years.

Days after she signed her contract with Mason, Hurston headed South to Mobile. While arranging matters with Godmother in New York, she lived for a while with her husband in her West Sixty-Sixth apartment. Although they attended a few dinners and social events together, Hurston's relationship with Sheen was strained. Some of her friends did not even know that she had been married, since she continued to live her life as independently as before. Her trip South was an ideal escape from what was quickly becoming a burdensome relationship. By March 1929, she admitted to Hughes that she had cut the relationship off in January and had plans to end it formally: "I am going to divorce Herbert as soon as this is over. He tries to hold me back and be generally obstructive." Her letters to Hughes at this time express the kind of shared passion for black folk culture that Sheen never understood: "I am getting inside of Negro art and lore. I am beginning to see really and when you join me I shall point things out and see if you see them as I do" (Kaplan 2003, 114, letter from Hurston to Hughes in 1928). With little interest in Hurston's central ambitions, Sheen was soon to become a distant figure, though the two did maintain an intimate friendship well into the final decade of Hurston's life. Once the divorce was finalized, she told Mason, "Don't think I am upset, for your lil Zora is playing on her harp like David. He [Sheen] was one of the obstacles that worried me" (Kaplan 2003, 222, letter from Hurston to Mason in 1932).

Hurston began her second research expedition by first returning to interview Cudjo Lewis, who she referred to as Kossola, his African name.[1] Worried that he would soon die, Hurston made the most of her time with him. She brought him Georgia peaches, Virginia ham, and Bee Brand insect powder for the mosquitos. At Kossola's home in the town of Plateau, Alabama, Hurston learned about his capture by the Dahomey. He recalled his life among his own people, the Takkoi, as well as his trip across the Atlantic on the *Clotilda*, the last slave ship known to have crossed the Atlantic. At seventy-five, Kossola was beset by sorrows. He had survived his wife and six children by two decades but was especially distraught over the death of his favorite son, David, by a train. These tragedies compounded the loss of his family in Africa. Hurston described his yearning as a "sense of mutilation" that "gave me something to feel about" (Hurston 1942, 168). Hurston told Mason about Kossola; Godmother, along with Locke, felt strongly that his story should be protected from whites. Hurston thus advised Kossola to avoid talking with other anthropologists, though he eventually reached out to Mason directly. In a letter he dictated to Mason, he calls her "dear friend" and explains that he shared his story with others because he was struggling financially (Hurston 2018, xxi). Hurston followed up to make sure that Kossola received the money Mason sent to him.

---

1. Multiple spellings of "Kossola" are used by Hurston in different texts. In *Dust Tracks on a Road*, she spells his name "Kossola," though in *Barracoon* she uses "Kossula." Consistent with the spelling used by Deborah J. Plant in her introduction and other notes included in *Barracoon*, I use the spelling "Kossola."

In February, Hurston officially received her bachelor's degree in English from Barnard, but as if to prove how little she cared for such formalities, at the time of the conferral, she was on her own in Florida, collecting material for Mason. She had recently moved into a room at the Everglades Cypress Lumber Company in Loughman, Florida. The boardinghouse was run by a woman whose daughter, Babe Hill, had shot her husband to death. The family's matriarch was typical of the women at the work camp who fought hard and loved hard. Hurston studiously recorded their vivid threats toward one another and lent her guitar to others so there could be music along with the after-work conversations with visiting men. However, Hurston found a degree of resistance among the camp residents. Though friendly, they seemed evasive if she pressed too hard and tended to dodge her questions with pleasantries. At last, a young man told her that her fancy Chevrolet was part of the problem. It was suspicious and roused concern that she might be a detective or some other officer of the law. The camp included a good number of fugitives or former inmates who were wary of anyone asking too many questions. Hurston quickly improvised a story of her own to encourage the trust of others; she identified herself as a bootlegger who'd had some trouble in Jacksonville and Miami. Her shiny car suddenly became a prop in her story, rather than a liability.

However, this story proved to be troublesome in other ways. At the next payday party, which involved guitar playing and square dancing, Hurston was dismayed that no one asked her to dance. Once again, Hurston had to be told what the problem was; various men were interested in her, but her pricey clothes suggested that she was rich. In order "to prove that I was their kind" (Hurston 1942, 26), Hurston concocted another story about how she once had money, but it was all gone now. Perhaps convinced by her authentic accent, men soon filled her dance card, and she led a raucous rendition of "John Henry" while standing on a table. After the party, Hurston made her car available to others and eventually disclosed the true reason for her visit. At first, the workers were confused that anyone would want to collect "lies," but Hurston convinced them by holding a "lying contest" that ended with prizes and square dancing. Following the contest, workers began coming to her individually to share their own stories.

Although Hurston was not writing fiction during her research trip, she was clearly inspired creatively. Her work was certainly anthropological in nature, but where previously she was beholden to the mandates of Boas and Woodson, now she was free to collect material as she saw fit, although her contract prevented her from using her findings for anything beyond the purview of Mason. Nonetheless, she envisioned new possibilities opening up through the stories, idioms, and practices she documented. Perhaps thinking of her earlier "The Eatonville Anthology," she wrote to Hughes, "I can really write a Village Anthology now," but worried how Mason would understand her enthusiasm: "I am wary about mentioning it to Godmother for fear she will think I'm shirking," as she was all too aware that "I must not publish without her consent" (Kaplan 2003, 115, letter from Hurston to Hughes in 1928). During her travels, Hurston wrote most frequently to Hughes though diligently kept Mason apprised of her work. She stopped communicating with Meyer, Fannie Hurst, and Carl Van Vechten, perhaps skeptical that her white friends would understand the importance of her discoveries. Instead, Hughes received the most enthusiastic accounts of her encounters, as if only he could appreciate their significance and share her excitement. She read his poetry to the men and women at the work camps, mines, and turpentine stills she visited and found that they applauded his work far more than the critics who reviewed his books in the press. He in turn kept her up-to-date on developments in New York, including the gala wedding of Countee Cullen to the daughter of W. E. B. Du Bois, as well as the groom's escape to Paris with his best man. Cullen was a well-known homosexual, and apparently only his new wife, Yolande, was left in the dark about his sexuality. Finally, Hughes counseled Hurston to write to their benefactor more often, rather than rely too much on their "psychic" connection.

The other person who Hurston corresponded with during this time was Locke. Since the publication of *The New Negro*, Locke had ascended to an important place in African American letters, and with Mason's ear, he wielded significant influence over the future direction of black art. Sensitive to such a position, Hurston sent a triangle to Locke with a large *L* at the apex and "L. H." and "Z. H." at the bottom corners. The diagram represented her vision for the future of African American literature. Locke would lead the campaign supported by the artistry of Hurston and Hughes. Though Locke was a natural leader with his many connections, both artistic and financial, he could also be an irritant to Hurston. His letters are full of practical but often tiresome, advice about how best to conduct her research. He warned her to protect her most novel discoveries from other anthropologists who might publish her findings first or dilute their impact. He also urged her to draw connections between certain images, like those involving snakes or water, to larger African mythologies. Hurston was careful to maintain a good relationship with Locke, no doubt aware that any sign of trouble or misdirection would get back to Mason, but her letters to Hughes indicate a greater affinity and understanding between the younger writers.

In April, she wrote to Hughes explaining that she had come to identify "5 general laws" concerning the nature of African Americans. Wary of telling Mason and Locke about her findings (she guessed that Locke would want to "hustle out a volume right away"), she shared with Hughes a brief description, knowing that with him "a word is enough to make you grasp it all" (Kaplan 2003, 115–116, letter from Hurston to Hughes in 1928). Among these general laws, Hurston concluded that the "Negro's outstanding characteristic is drama" and further noted that angularity, repetition, ferocity, a lack of reverence as well as the use of dialect best define the people she studied. Hurston's emphasis on these qualities clarifies her growing interest in developing a robust African American theater. She appealed to Hughes to help her realize her dream, writing that she always assumed he would be a collaborator: "Of course, you know I didn't dream of that theatre as a one-man stunt. I had you helping 50-50 from the start. In fact, I am perfectly willing to be 40 to your 60 since you are always so much more practical than I. But I know it is going to be Glorious! A really new departure in the drama" (Kaplan 2003, 117, letter from Hurston to Hughes in 1928). Hurston's interest in drama also affirms a collaborative vision of black folk art that resonates with some of her early work. "The Eatonville Anthology," for example, captures an artistic sensibility that is deeply rooted in an entire community's language and narrative legacy.

By this time, Hurston had at last mastered the art of soliciting stories and opinions from the people she encountered as she traveled. She soon shifted attention from female to male workers, developing a strong camaraderie with men who would no doubt have reminded her of the storytellers from Joe Clarke's porch. However, this easy rapport, which led Hurston to join a group of men at the cypress swamp, caught the ire of at least one woman. Lucy, who worked at a sawmill in Polk County, became jealous of Hurston's relationship with a man named Slim, who had once been her boyfriend. With his talent for singing and guitar playing, he was an important source for Hurston. She often bought him drinks and let him ride in her car, fostering a dynamic that could easily be read as sexual in nature. Lucy soon started insulting and threatening Hurston. The fight culminated at a payday party in which Lucy approached Hurston with a knife. Fortunately, Hurston had previously befriended a powerful woman named Big Sweet, who wrestled Lucy to the floor. Big Sweet was known in the camp as a formidable fighter whom even men identified as "uh whole woman and half uh man" (Hurston 1935, 152). She had vowed to fight and protect Hurston, whose anthropological mission she honored even if she did not fully understand it. Big Sweet's attack on Lucy precipitated a massive brawl at the party. Suddenly surrounded by open blades, razors, and ice picks, Hurston ran, knowing that Big Sweet needed no help from her. Eager to flee the fracas, she jumped into her car and headed out of town.

After over four months of productive research in and around Loughman, Hurston headed to Magazine, Alabama, where she stayed for most of the summer. She had acquired what could constitute a whole volume of material and told Hughes that she was "learning better technique" to solicit stories and expressions and had even gathered a collection of love letters. She routinely held storytelling contests in the towns she visited, making her job of collecting tales a competitive affair that elicited multiple gems. Hurston was especially interested in idioms with double meaning or double words like "sitting-chair" or "cook-pot." Two hundred miles up the Tombigbee River, Hurston was delighted to meet another "of the original Africans," a woman who was older than Cudjo and "a better talker" (Kaplan 2003, 122–123, letter from Hurston to Hughes in 1928). Though she disclosed this discovery to Hughes, she vowed not to tell Mason about this exciting subject. Instead, she sent Mason the diploma she at last received from Barnard in May 1928.

Increasingly, Hurston struggled to maintain good relations with Mason. After the wealthy widow sent her a copy of the newly published *Negro Workaday Songs* (1926) by white scholars Howard Odum and Guy Johnson, Hurston replied with a brief critique of the book, stating that "white people could not be trusted to collect the lore of others" (Kaplan 2003, 121, letter from Hurston to Locke in 1928). Elaborating on this idea to Hughes, she admitted, "It makes me sick to see how these cheap white folks are grabbing up our stuff and ruining it. I am almost sick—my one consolation being that they never do it right and so there is still a chance for us" (Kaplan 2003, 126, letter from Hurston to Hughes in 1928). Though Hurston had tried to distinguish Mason from such usurpers, her patron became upset. Hurston may have relied too heavily on their psychic connection or misjudged how her written words would read to the septuagenarian. Soon after Mason excused Hurston for this mistake, she became newly upset after reading her protégé's essay "How It Feels to Be Colored Me," which was published in the May issue of *The World Tomorrow*. Mason was not upset by the content of the essay, which remains one of the most famous in all of Hurston's oeuvre. In it, Hurston delights in the contradictions of race—both reveling in a kind of essential power that comes on when she listens to jazz in a Harlem cabaret and transcending all categories as a cosmic being who creates her own way: "I am the eternal feminine with its string of beads" (Hurston 1979, 155). Mason instead took issue with its very publication, arguing that Hurston's contract prevented her from publishing any of her own creative work. Though the contract was explicit in only barring Hurston from publishing material based on the work she collected for Mason, Godmother was adamant in maintaining that her protégé must first receive approval before publishing anything.

Though Hurston could easily have cited the details of the contract to justify her actions, she wisely chose not to confront Mason with what she saw as her misunderstanding of their agreement. Such an approach could jeopardize their financial relationship and Hurston's future work. Instead, she concocted an elaborate explanation. She told Mason that the essay had been submitted to *The World Tomorrow*, a magazine that now employed

Wallace Thurman, in order to pay back the costs of printing *Fire!!* years earlier. Even Locke supported this story and told Mason that the essay had been submitted before the two women had even met, adding that Hurston had not made any money off its publication. Mason at last relented and forgave Hurston for the debacle.

Mason's domineering approach to Hurston paralleled her relationship to other artists she supported. Godmother insisted on closely supervising their work and at times intervened upon their creative choices. Hurston presented unique challenges to Mason because of their geographic distance as well as the young writer's obvious independent streak. No matter how gracious Hurston appeared in her letters, conflict between the two was inevitable. Though Mason understood herself as a force for the betterment of the Negro race, her often imperious behavior reflects the ingrained entitlements of a wealthy white woman. Like Hughes, Hurston was effectively ensnared by the golden opportunity Mason provided. Only with the widow's generous support could she travel and gather the material that would demonstrate the creative genius evident in black folklife. But without the ability to publish or use such material, Hurston was forced to keep all findings secret and obliged to keep her patron satisfied.

In August, Hurston rented a house in Algiers, a neighborhood in New Orleans, for ten dollars a month. Here Hurston began planning how she would at last use all of the material she had amassed. There was enough for multiple volumes on folk stories, children's games, black drama, work songs, religion, and love letters. And still there were new leads to follow. In New Orleans, she discovered the home of Marie Leveau, a Creole practitioner of voodoo who lived in the 1800s. Though a devoted Catholic, Leveau was known for her powerful spells and potions. Her legacy was continued by her daughter, who looked so similar to her mother that many believed her to be the original Leveau, blessed with exceptional beauty and longevity. Leveau's mixed ancestry reflects the syncretistic nature of voodoo. The illegitimate daughter of a free man of color and a Creole mother, Leveau combined her Catholicism with African practices nurtured often in secret through antebellum slavery. The very word *voodoo*, sometimes spelled as *hoodoo* or *vodou*, derives from the Fon language used in West Africa and signifies "spirit" or "deity." Ancient beliefs combined with influences from the Caribbean, in particular from Martinique and Haiti, to create a varied set of practices that thrived in the vibrant melting pot of New Orleans. Though Hurston recognized that voodoo adapts to specific geographic and cultural locales, she noted that it "is burning with a flame in America, with all the intensity of a suppressed religion. It has its thousands of secret adherents" (Hurston 1935, 183).

Eager to learn about spells that could cure everything from venereal diseases to unemployment, Hurston apprenticed herself to at least five different voodoo masters in the area. To prepare for her initiation, she often had to fast or remain celibate for a certain period of time. Such requirements were mild compared to the actual rituals, which involved elaborate baths with special ingredients and the reading of biblical texts for days at a time. Perhaps the most gruesome rite of passage was the "Black Cat Bone" ritual; Hurston had to boil a black cat in a large cauldron until its bones broke off. According to her mentor Father Joe Watson, the bone of a black cat would allow a conjurer to walk out of sight. Hurston mentions the ritual in *Mules and Men*, but it is not entirely clear how the specific cat bone was selected to become her talisman: "The bones of the cat must be passed through my mouth until one tasted bitter." Hurston then mentions that she may have slipped into a trance, though by the next morning she is home "with a small white bone for me to carry" (Hurston 1935, 221). Hurston writes of her voodoo experiences with not just interest and curiosity but genuine belief. Describing its origin, she notes, "The way we tell it, hoodoo started way back there before everything" (Hurston 1935, 183). With the collective pronoun "we," Hurston claims voodoo history and culture as her own. This came to be far more than an academic exploration but a celebration of her own powers and knowledge.

By October, Hurston had moved to a house on Amelia Street in New Orleans where she was closer to the action of the city. There she worked closely with Father Watson, who was known as "the Frizzy Rooster" because of his powerful ability to remove curses; like a frizzled chicken, he scratched everywhere to find buried hexes planted by enemies. Under his guidance, she was named the "Boss of Candles." Father Watson declared, "You have the power to light candles and put out candles, and to work with spirits anywhere on earth" (Hurston 1935, 216). With this new power, Hurston was able to work on her own with clients. She remedied a number of domestic disputes for a small fee and, with the assistance of Father Watson, helped curb the ambitions of a local preacher.

With the conjurer Kitty Brown, who specialized in uniting lovers, Hurston was instructed in the rarely performed death dance. The ritual was called forth by a woman whose lover had left her for another and squandered their savings. Involving male and female dancers who performed for three hours, often in obscene poses, the ritual promised to kill the unfaithful lover within nine days. Fortunately, this end did not come to pass; the man, after experiencing alarming chest pains, returned to his original lover, and she called off the death spell.

Hurston also apprenticed with Luke Turner, who claimed to be the nephew of Marie Leveau. He often worked wearing the skin of a rattlesnake that had been a part of Leveau's original altar. Though Hurston approached Turner after she had gained considerable experience working with other conjurers, he was skeptical of her motives and abilities. He at last consented to accept her as a pupil after they sat together before his altar. As they faced each other across candles and incense, Hurston "forgot my fears, forgot myself, and things began to happen. Things for which I can find no words, since I had experienced nothing before that would furnish a simile" (Hurston 1931, 358). Turner agreed to take Hurston on, dispensing with his usual fee because he was so taken with her innate power. As part of her initiation, he ordered her to sleep for nine days with one stocking on and the other leg bare. She then arrived at his home with new underwear and snakeskins to begin an additional stage of the process. Turner directed Hurston to lie naked, facedown upon the snakeskins for three days and nights accompanied only by a pitcher of water. By the second day, Hurston began having intense dreams that lasted until the end of the initiation. She awoke without hunger and filled with a profound sense of exaltation. Turner then bestowed the title "the Rain-Bringer" upon Hurston and painted a lightning symbol on her back along with two eyes on her cheeks to affirm "that I could see in more ways than one" (Hurston 1935, 200). Turner cut her finger to squeeze her blood into a chalice mixed with wine. After he and others added their own blood, they all drank from the brew. Turner was so impressed by Hurston that he asked her to become his conjuring partner. Though he also predicted his own death in just over a year and asked Hurston to stay with him until his final end, she moved on, having other commitments to honor.

Hurston had not begun her study of voodoo to become a master conjurer and take over the work of a renowned practitioner like Turner. She was still beholden to her contract with Mason and invested in exploring and ultimately sharing the wisdom of the folklore she gathered. However, this aim posed challenges to keeping the secrets she had learned through her various initiations. To write about her experiences candidly would betray the culture she had come to understand and admire. Though popular representations of voodoo remained laughable to her, the silence of the initiated demanded that she be circumspect in how she wrote or even spoke about her months in New Orleans. Hurston sought advice from her old mentor at Barnard, Franz Boas. She began by thanking him for providing her with the skills that allowed her to successfully penetrate the world of voodoo. Hurston was forthcoming with Boas about the strict terms of her agreement with Mason (though was careful not to disclose the identity of her patron) but expressed her interest in understanding the significance of the work she had gathered. Though she lacked an academic affiliation, Hurston was beginning to establish herself in the field of anthropology. She had become a member of the American Folklore Society and would eventually join the American Ethnological Society and the American Anthropological Society.

Many of Hurston's questions for Boas involved how to organize and understand the material she had gathered. She asked about making connections between baptism and water worship or clothing adornments and body painting. The range of stories and accounts of various religious and cultural practices was voluminous.

After returning to Jacksonville for a family visit in early April 1929, she headed to Eau Gallie, a hamlet on the Indian River. There she rented a cabin and tried to map out her plans for her research. She sent a collection of pieces to Mason and Hughes to review. She hoped to have separate volumes on religion, including a verbatim transcript of a Baptist church service. While enjoying the beauty of the coastal village, Hurston imagined establishing an African American art colony that might include Hughes, Thurman, Nugent, and Aaron Douglas. Overlooking "the most beautiful river in the world," the land offered "a lovely place to retire and write on occasion" (Kaplan 2003, 145–146, letter from Hurston to Hughes in 1929). She wondered if A'Lelia Walker, the only surviving daughter of self-made millionaire Madame C. J. Walker, might invest in the property. This dream was one of many grand projects Hurston envisioned but never developed.

Her musings were soon overtaken by her interest in Bahamian culture. In Liberty City, Hurston became enraptured by a "jumping dance" that convinced her that the "music of the Bahaman Negroes was more original, dynamic, and African, than American Negro songs." Insisting that she "just had to know more," she quickly sailed to Nassau, where she fell in love with the music of the island (Hurston 1942, 157). After learning that

---

AARON DOUGLAS

Often referred to as "the father of black American art," Aaron Douglas was a key figure in the Harlem Renaissance. After earning a bachelor of fine arts from the University of Nebraska, Lincoln, Douglas moved to New York City, where he soon became a vital part of Harlem's cultural life. His illustrations of African American life appeared in *Opportunity* and *The Crisis* and helped win him the commission to illustrate the cover of Alain Locke's influential *The New Negro* (1925). Douglas's signature style merges a modernist sensibility with African art. Much of his work uses silhouettes that create powerful urban and industrial images. Douglas traveled widely, studying in France before returning to New York to create one of his best-known works, a series of murals entitled *Aspects of Negro Life*. The four panels depict scenes of music, work, dance, and triumph. Douglas was also a dedicated educator. He founded the art department at Fisk University along with the school's impressive Carl Van Vechten Gallery. The recipient of many prestigious grants and fellowships, Douglas remained an active painter and lecturer until his death in 1979.

some Bahamians could trace their ancestry back to specific African tribes, Huston resolved to collect folklore from the natives to compare it to the stories and history of black Americans. In a few weeks, she learned the jumping dance, collected numerous songs, and recorded reels of folk dances. On one of her last nights there, a horrible hurricane hit the island. With the natives overwhelmed by the disaster, Hurston was not able to stay long enough to work with the voodoo or obeah practitioners there.

When Hurston returned to Miami, she learned of an exciting opportunity from Boas. The anthropology department at Columbia was beginning a new study on various ethnic groups, and her old mentor wanted her to join the research team in New Orleans, where they were especially interested in understanding the musical talents of African Americans. Because her contract with Mason was due to expire at the end of 1929, Hurston figured this might be the ideal moment to conclude their work together. However, Mason refused to release Hurston and demanded she remain in her service. Though she still could not mention Mason specifically, Hurston explained to Boas that she was bound by her current employer from pursuing any other research projects. However, she agreed to return to New Orleans under the guise of collecting more material to consult with one of Boas's collaborators and provide important contact information of residents she knew who could assist with their study. Boas was pleased with this arrangement and hoped that Hurston would help make inroads on his study of Creole culture. However, he warned his associate to keep a close eye on Hurston: "Please be sure to check Miss Hurston in regard to accuracy. I have no reason to doubt her, but temperamentally, she is so much more artistic rather than scientific that she has to be held down" (Boas 1929, letter to Otto Klineberg). While Hurston worked on Boas's investigation, she also pursued additional leads on stories about conjure and witchcraft.

Even as Hurston's research was going well, she encountered other problems that continued to tax her relationship with Mason. After miles on highways and backroads, Hurston's Chevy needed to be replaced. Hurston explained her request to Mason, who accused her protégé of taking advantage of her goodwill. When the car broke down again, Hurston bargained for a new one. Mason learned of the deal when she was called as a reference. In her anger she asked, "Why couldn't Negroes be trusted?" Hurston confided to Hughes that Mason's response "hurt me thru and thru" (Kaplan 2003, 156, letter from Hurston to Hughes in winter 1929/1930). Although Mason eventually sent $400 to pay for the car, it had to be traded in for another model, which left Hurston out $300. Hurston vented to Hughes about her many travails with Mason, and he counseled her to tell the truth about the new car and assured her that Godmother loved all of her children.

Hurston returned to the Bahamas for Carnival, then headed back to New York in the early spring of 1930. The city had transformed since she'd last lived there. The crash of 1929 devastated financial markets and left people sleeping in subways or on front stoops. However, the changes sweeping the country's working class and poor had almost no impact on Mason and her penthouse apartment. There, Mason demanded to see the footage Hurston had gathered. Hurston obliged by showing her images of Cudjo Lewis, the Loughman sawmill camp, and various children and women playing or talking among themselves. Impressed with what she saw, Mason arranged for Hurston to live and work in a room in Westfield, a few doors away from where Hughes was writing his first novel.

The old friends were delighted to be reunited. Hughes helped review and edit the material Hurston had gathered. They were often joined by Louise Thompson, whom Mason had hired the previous year as Hughes's secretary. Hurston knew Thompson's name because she had briefly been married to Wallace Thurman. Thompson had previously worked as a secretarial science teacher at Hampton Institute. She set to work typing up Hurston's vast trove of material. There was so much to collate that Thompson often worked well into the night preparing Hurston's many manuscripts. The three got along very well, and Thompson's Manhattan apartment became a welcome distraction from their work in Westfield.

Though Hurston had initially envisioned multiple volumes for her material, she settled on writing a single book that would include the best of her folktales and her work on conjure. Locke, as Mason's favorite advisor, offered overweening criticism to Hurston and urged her to finish the manuscript by May 18, Mason's birthday. Instead, Hurston gave her benefactor a lengthy letter that extolled her to the point of mockery. She began, "Darling my God-Flower" and then continued,

> May I, on your emergence day sing with my broken harp the small song of love that I am able to sing? It is a small song from a big heart. Oh, my lovely just-born flower, if back there when you fluttered pink into this drab world— if they had but known how much joy and love you would/should bring! How much of the white light of God you would diffuse into soft radiance for the eyes of the primitives, the wise ones would have stood awed before your cradle and brought great gifts from afar. (Kaplan 2003, 187–188, letter from Hurston to Mason in 1930)

It is impossible to read this letter without imagining a smirking Hurston, barely containing her laughter. Though she seems to have had genuine affection for Mason, there was no escaping her patron's condescending racial views. Mason may have wanted to uplift the Negro race, but she did so always aware of her own unimpeachable authority. Thompson believed that Mason was in fact racist, while many of her beneficiaries felt coerced into performing a version of black primitivism. Hurston, for her part, never mistook her relationship with Mason as friendship. Godmother was her benefactor, and their encounters are best understood as transactional. Hurston needed Mason's money and acted accordingly. Flattery, no matter how overweening, assured Mason of her power and kept Hurston sufficiently funded. Thompson recalled how Mason occasionally sent Hurston an exotic dress to wear. Hurston would immediately call Godmother to gush over how beautiful she looked in it, but after hanging up the phone, she would turn to her friend and note with a laugh that she would never wear such a thing. She did what she needed to keep her work funded, no small feat during the first years of the Great Depression.

Although Hurston knew how to charm Mason, there were limits to her ability to get what she wanted from her patron. Boas was so pleased with Hurston's work in New Orleans that he recommended her for a graduate fellowship. This was a rare opportunity for a black woman to pursue a doctorate at an Ivy League institution, and Hurston was eager to make the most of it. When the General Education Board denied Boas's request because it only assisted teachers at black colleges, he asked Hurston to see if she might secure funding from her mysterious benefactor. Hurston wrote back that such efforts proved futile. She explained cryptically, "The 'Angel' is cold towards the degrees, but will put up money for further research. I have broached the subject from several angles but it got chill blains no matter how I put it" (Kaplan 2003, 190, letter from Hurston to Boas in 1930). Mason had already expressed reservations about Boas's interventions, and her earlier concerns about ownership over the material Hurston had gathered would have made graduate work impossible. Hurston exhibited less disappointment than might be expected by Mason's refusal to let her pursue a doctorate. She may simply have been glad that Godmother continued to fund her work, which was ultimately more important than the acquisition of a fancy degree. And as her life would prove, there were still many other opportunities ahead.

5

Mule Bone

Hurston's interest in graduate school may also have dissipated because she had at last begun substantial work on the folk opera she envisioned writing with Hughes. With such brilliant creative minds working together, the collaboration could only be a success. However, this partnership and its subsequent fallout proved to be one of the greatest tragedies in Hurston's life. Marred by jealousy, insecurity, and rampant miscommunication, what once promised to be a union of two of the greatest living writers of their generation ended in bitter resentment and the destruction of one of her closest friendships.

As Hurston and Hughes's project developed, it took the name *Mule Bone* and transformed into a folk comedy. This shift from opera to comedy was in part a response to an observation made by Theresa Helburn, who worked at the Theatre Guild and bemoaned the many scripts that described a somber, if not tragic, picture of African American life. A comedy would stand out among other projects and offer a distinctive take on black culture. Although Hurston had already composed a few scenes based on the original idea hatched with Hughes, she was willing to change direction and offered her short story "The Bone of Contention" as the basis for the play. The Eatonville tale involves two hunters who both shoot at a wild turkey. Arguing over who actually made the kill, one of the men hits the other with a mule bone and runs off with the turkey. Dave, the man who was left unconscious by the blow, brings the other man, Jim, to trial at the Baptist church. The feud takes on a religious dimension, as Dave is Baptist and Jim is Methodist, and members of their respective churches each take sides. After much discussion focusing on whether a mule bone can be considered a deadly weapon, Jim is found guilty of assaulting Dave. After exiling Jim for two years, the mayor welcomes the townspeople to fight one another over the verdict, but they are not to use guns, razors, or, of course, mule bones.

The story was one that Hurston often recounted at parties, and she adorned it with descriptive images resonant of her Eatonville childhood. Hughes made some key revisions, making the object of contention a woman rather than a turkey and setting the final scene on a railroad track. It is impossible to know what other additions or specific phrases came from Hurston or Hughes, since both writers revised their account of its genesis after it led to a devastating rift between them. Hughes insisted in his autobiography that he "plotted out and typed the play based on her story" (Hughes 1986, 320). However, his biographer, Arnold Rampersad, concludes that "Hurston's contribution was almost certainly the greater" (Rampersad 1988, 184). Initially, such distinctions hardly mattered, as the friends worked on the play together with Louise Thompson acting as their typist. Hurston enjoyed acting out the parts with exaggerated voices for each character and testing the lines that would draw the biggest laughs. Progress on the play was swift; by May 1930, two of three acts were complete. However, as the trio discussed details of its finances, serious difficulties began to emerge.

Because the two writers did not have enough money to pay Thompson for her secretarial work, Hughes suggested that they split three ways any profits generated by the play. Hurston questioned this arrangement, since the real creative labor of the play came from the artists, not the play's typist. Thompson rejected Hurston's offer to receive five dollars a day and suggested instead that she be compensated in the future. Hurston was wary of such an arrangement and became suspicious that Hughes and Thompson had come to an agreement behind her back. They at last agreed to tell Charlotte Mason about the project, perhaps as a way to find a compromise. However, Mason ordered the play to be dropped until Hurston finished her folklore work. According to Hurston, she then stopped actively writing the play. Instead, she left Westfield to return to the South to complete some additional research for her book. Hughes, meanwhile, believed that Hurston would continue work on the last act of the play. He had bright hopes for *Mule Bone* and at the end of the summer went to Moylan, Pennsylvania, to attend a theatrical workshop run by Jasper Deeter, the head of the Hedgerow Players. Dedicated to producing innovative theater, Deeter hoped to organize an all-black season of plays for the fall. He named Hughes the playwright in residence and was delighted to read portions of *Mule Bone*, which he anticipated would be a great success.

Hughes then told Hurston about Deeter's enthusiasm and asked about the development of the final act. She refused to send him anything and claimed that the play belonged to her because he had not written any of the dialogue. This response was especially troubling to Hughes, because his relationship with Mason had started to deteriorate. While dining on caviar with Mason at her Park Avenue penthouse, Hughes began to feel guilty as he considered so many who were barely able to survive in the trying economic times. These feelings were exacerbated by Mason's orders to write when she demanded. He at last asked that they reconsider the terms of their financial arrangement. Rather than receive a monthly allowance, he preferred to receive gifts that would effectively come with no strings attached. Mason conceded, though she also called him ungrateful and disloyal. More significantly, it was unclear if and when her gifts would appear. Hughes suddenly found himself desperate for her previous largesse. In September, Mason suddenly dismissed Thompson from her secretarial position. Hughes worried that he too would be cut off entirely.

Aware of these developments, Hurston did her best to placate Mason and demonstrate her unwavering commitment to her benefactor's vision. Hurston was caught between two very important relationships; while she valued her friendship with Hughes, she would be lost without Mason's support. Moreover, she had begun to question Hughes's loyalty given her concerns about Thompson's role in *Mule Bone*. While Hughes became physically ill following his argument with Mason, Hurston focused on her work. She received approval to publish some of her research findings, including "Dance Songs and Tales from the Bahamas," which appeared in the July–September 1930 issue of the *Journal of American Folklore*. The article may have reflected Hurston's attempt to pursue her own way amid the feud between Mason and Hughes. Mason had little interest in Hurston's work in the Bahamas and expected that none of her material from the island would be included in her eventual volume on black folklore of the American South.

By the end of the year, both Hurston and Hughes were back in New York, but work on *Mule Bone* was contentious and difficult. This was just the beginning of what has been called "the most notorious literary quarrel in African-American cultural history" (Louis Gates Jr. 1991, 5). According to Hughes, Hurston skipped appointments with him or made excuses about why she needed to leave when he arrived. She deliberately misplaced copies of certain scenes or complained that she was not well enough to write. When they finally spoke about the play, she insisted on major changes, such as replacing the woman with the original turkey, a shift first suggested by Hughes. Although he found her behavior troubling, he assumed they were still good friends and that she was simply distracted by other tasks.

Hurston, however, nursed resentments left over from their quarrel over how Thompson would be paid. She also noted that the very people she believed to have conspired against her were now out of Mason's favor. Consorting with either of them might trouble the more focused attention she now received from her patron. She thus avoided Hughes as best she could and, as a result, prevented any meaningful reconciliation between the old friends. Though it is easy to judge Hurston's actions as petty and small-minded, the effects of the Great Depression must have also frightened her. She observed to a friend, "Some of my friends are all tired and worn out—looking like death eating crackers" (Kaplan 2003, 190, letter from Hurston to Lawrence Jordan in 1930). People in New York, and Harlem specifically, were struggling economically as never before. It would no doubt be difficult and disheartening for Hurston to return to waitressing or housecleaning, even though, as Jacqueline Jones notes, over 80 percent of black women had done domestic work by the end of the decade (Jones 1986). Because Harlem had prospered so significantly in the 1920s, the stock market crash was especially devastating to the area. Black ownership of real estate plummeted from 35 percent to hardly 5 percent, and black businesses suffered acutely. Even the empire of hair-care entrepreneur Madame C. J. Walker languished. Her daughter and heir, A'Lelia Walker, was forced to sell much of her private art and antique collection. Despite these difficulties, the 1930s proved to be one of Hurston's most fruitful

---

THE GREAT DEPRESSION AND THE GREAT MIGRATION

In the years before the Great Depression, African Americans labored primarily in positions that did not require formal education, such as domestic work, manual labor, and jobs in the service economy. With the stock market crash of 1929, many of these jobs disappeared or were given to whites in sudden need of employment. As the "last hired and first fired," African Americans suffered acutely in the 1930s. They had the highest unemployment rate of any group during this time; by 1932, almost half of all African Americans were out of work. The worst conditions were in the South, where Reconstruction had failed to bring opportunity to lands still devastated by slavery and the Civil War. This lack of opportunity, coupled with growing violence against African Americans, led to the Great Migration, the movement of hundreds of thousands of blacks from the rural South to the urban North. The Great Migration fueled the energy of the Harlem Renaissance and fostered the kind of political activism that anticipated the civil rights movement. In 1935, Mary McLeod Bethune founded the National Council of Negro Women, while the Southern Negro Youth Congress formed two years later. These and other organizations signaled a new political presence for African Americans.

decades, in part because she was no stranger to financial difficulty. With a mixture of canny courtships of mentors and a furious work ethic, Hurston discovered that she could make a living through writing and research.

Even as Hurston did her best to please Mason, Godmother was increasingly less interested in supporting her African American protégés. She discussed reducing Hurston's monthly allowance and asked her to sell her car. Hurston tried to keep her usual sum for the final month of the year so that she could purchase a blanket and an oil stove, which would make for a cheaper heat source for the coming winter. Mason agreed to give Hurston $150 per month until the publication of her book, which would hopefully provide her with a degree of financial independence. Since she had expected a bigger cut in her allowance, Hurston was delighted with this arrangement and wrote to Mason with effusive thanks and praise. However, Mason was insulted by what she perceived to be a complaint in Hurston's letter and in her rage took her protégé's seeming ingratitude as evidence of "the reason the whole white world says 'You can't do anything with Negroes. They are unreliable'" (Mason 1931).

Though Hurston had somewhat abandoned Hughes in part to strengthen her relationship with Mason, by the beginning of 1931, she was in conflict

---

C. J. Walker

Madam C. J. Walker was the first female self-made millionaire in the United States. Born Sarah Breedlove, the entrepreneur and social activist was the first of her five siblings to be born into freedom. After a series of failed marriages, Walker moved to St. Louis with her daughter, A'Lelia, where she worked as a laundress and then as an agent for Annie Turnbo Malone, an African American hair-care specialist and entrepreneur. Walker soon devised her own product lines, and with the help of her new husband, Charles Walker, she presented herself as Madam C. J. Walker, a hairdresser and retailer of cosmetic creams. The couple worked as business partners and traveled throughout the country, together expanding their customer base. In 1908, they moved to Pittsburgh, where they opened a beauty salon and founded Lelia College to train hair specialists. However, Indianapolis eventually became the headquarters of the Madame C. J. Walker Manufacturing Company, which included a factory, hair salon, beauty school, and laboratory to test new products. By the second decade of the twentieth century, Walker employed thousands of women as sales agents. In signature white shirts and black skirts, they went door-to-door touting the transformational results of Walker's beauty products. As Walker's fortune grew, so did her philanthropic activity. She supported numerous schools for African Americans, and as an executive committee member of the New York chapter of the NAACP, she spoke out on a wide range of political issues.

with both of them. In January, Hughes wrote to Van Vechten to report that while visiting his family in Cleveland, he learned that the Gilpin Players, an amateur group of black actors directed by Rowena and Russell Jelliffe, were preparing to present *Mule Bone* next month. Outraged at the seeming deception of his old friend, he asked, "Is there something about the very word theatre that turns people into thieves?" (Hughes 1931, letter to Van Vechten).

But Hurston was just as surprised to learn of the plans for *Mule Bone* and had no knowledge of the agent who had brought the play to the Gilpin Players. She wrote back to Hughes quickly and elaborated on her anger at his eagerness to include Thompson in their plans. Though Hurston claimed, "I don't care who you love nor whom you marry, nor whom you bestow your worldly goods upon," it is impossible not to read Hurston's reply as tinged with the jealousy of a lover (Boyd 2003, 208). Thompson clearly threatened her relationship with Hughes, and Hurston replied by spurning them both. She concluded by stating that she had at last decided to write her own version of the play, which eliminated any contributions Hughes had made. Before Hughes received Hurston's letter, he called her, and she explained that she did not know how the Gilpin Players had obtained a copy of the play. The mystery was only clarified when Hughes called Carl Van Vechten, who explained that he had been absolutely delighted with an early draft Hurston had shared with him. In his enthusiasm, he had passed the manuscript on to an agent, who later presented it to Rowena Jelliffe in Cleveland. Although the various strands of the play had yet to come together—act one included the turkey, but later scenes described a love triangle—the Gilpin Players went ahead with production.

Later in January, Hurston went to see Van Vechten in person, and he explained that he had not known about the planned performance until Hughes called him. He later wrote to Hughes that Hurston cried about the misunderstanding and the fallout it had caused. Both Hurston and Van Vechten were concerned that a premature staging of the play would destroy its chance to become a major success in New York. Perhaps more important was the abiding issue of its authorship. Hurston wrote to Hughes that the play was ultimately hers: "It was my story from the beginning to end. It is my dialogue; my situations" (Kaplan 2003, 202, letter from Hurston to Hughes in 1931). In a postscript, she even adds, "I don't think you can point out any situations or dialogue that are yours. You made some suggestions, but they are not incorporated in the play" (Kaplan 2003, 202, letter from Hurston to Hughes in 1931).

Hughes was enraged by Hurston's letter and immediately contacted his lawyer, Arthur Spingarn. Acknowledging that Hurston had been a significant collaborator on the play, Hughes offered to grant her two-thirds of all royalties while he pocketed the final third. Meanwhile, Hurston consulted with Mason, telling her that the story on which *Mule Bone* is based was derived from her research and much of the language reflects her Eatonville upbringing. It appears that Hurston was most concerned that Louise Thompson would receive creative credit for the play and in some way upstage the relationship she had long enjoyed with Hughes. Because he was out of favor with Mason, Hughes was desperate to have the play performed. It would be an easy source of income and confidence for him. He thus wrote to Hurston reminding her that the Gilpin Players were well respected and that *Mule Bone* would open with significant local publicity. Although it was not Broadway, it would not, he suggested, "be a bad beginning for our first play, and for the first Negro folk-comedy ever written" (Hughes 1931, letter to Hurston). Hurston was persuaded by Hughes's letter and decided that much of his poor behavior could be ascribed to the negative influence of Thompson. Writing to Mason about the issue, she presented herself as a generous advisor, almost as if she had now taken on the role of Godmother: "Personally, I think that he has so much in him that it is worth my swallowing and forgetting if by extending a friendly hand I can bring him back into the fold." She noted that "Langston is weak. Weak as water," and without Mason's "noble influence," he was susceptible to the machinations of others: "When he has a vile wretch to push him he gets vile" (Kaplan 2003, 208, letter from Hurston to Mason in 1931). Hurston then sent a telegram authorizing the production of *Mule Bone*, though insisting that alterations could only be made by her. The Jelliffes were delighted with this news and invited Hurston to attend rehearsals, which would begin February 1. With matters seemingly at last settled, Hurston wrote again to Hughes, acknowledging that they had both "got worked up unnecessarily." She continued, "I am busy smoothing out my lovely brow at present and returning to normal. I am in fault in the end and you were in fault in the beginning. I shall freely acknowledge my share at anytime and place" (Kaplan 2003, 204, letter from Hurston to Hughes in 1931).

Soon after sending this promise of reconciliation, Hurston received a brief letter from Hughes written shortly after he read her claim to sole authorship. Dismissing her jealousy over Thompson, Hughes suggested that a lawsuit may be forthcoming. Hurston then received a call from the lawyer, Spingarn, and they met on January 24. Spingarn came around to Hurston's point of view on the matter of authorship and scolded Hughes for threatening to take her to court. Additional letters from Hughes indicate varying approaches to the matter. In one dated January 22, he again reiterates his willingness to accept a third of the royalties in deference to Hurston's greater contribution to the play. Aware that the manuscript still needed key revisions, he apologized to Hurston and welcomed the possibility of finding in Cleveland any kind of typist she might want. At last the two met face-to-face on February 2 in Cleveland. In part because Hurston had not arrived as promised on the first of the month to take part in the start of rehearsals, the Gilpin Players voted not to continue with the play's production. Nonetheless, Hurston and Hughes reached an agreement after airing out their many differences. Hughes admitted that the play was mostly Hurston's creation but noted that it was impossible to precisely identify his contribution. The two finally agreed to go forward with the production pending a positive reconsideration from the Gilpin Players.

But before the actors could reevaluate their decision about the play, Hurston reversed her position. She discovered that Thompson had come to Cleveland to testify against her to the Jelliffes earlier that year. In reality, Thompson had been in Cleveland for another matter but did speak to her friends the Jelliffes and supported Hughes's claim of dual authorship. Hurston was outraged to learn that Thompson even knew the Jelliffes and felt that the whole group had been orchestrating matters behind her back. She immediately called Rowena Jelliffe, who then proposed that they meet as a group to discuss the matter. Because Hughes was staying at his mother's home, where he was recovering from tonsillitis, they decided to meet there the same day, February 3. In a letter to Van Vechten recounting the scene, Hughes describes Hurston as upset and emotional. She verbally attacked Rowena, again accused Hughes of theft, and insulted Thompson. She refused to allow the play to go forward. Hughes could do little more than watch Hurston wave manuscripts in his face, though he reports getting out of bed to restrain his mother, who was unnerved by the tumult. That evening Hurston wrote to Mason announcing that the play had been stopped and she "SMASHED THEM ALL" (Kaplan 2003, 209, letter from Hurston to Mason in 1931).

Despite claiming victory, Hurston lost much through this angry outburst. The play would not be performed by the Gilpin Players and, in fact, would never be staged in her lifetime. But more importantly, by not letting Hughes or Jelliffe explain Thompson's visit to Cleveland, she lost one of the most important friendships of her life. Rather than seek understanding, Hurston doubled down on her anger and that week attended a party given by Hughes's college fraternity. Knowing Hughes would be too sick to make it, Hurston spent the evening telling others that Hughes had tried to steal her work. She also shared her ire with Mason, who wrote a letter to Hughes full of "ungodly things" (Hughes 1931, letter to Louise Thompson). The former friends exchanged a few more letters to tie up loose ends, but their friendship was irrevocably broken.

Mule Bone was never performed while either Hughes or Hurston was alive. They both came to regret their feud, and, in 1932, Hughes officially gave up all claim to the play. Years later, Hughes wondered if Hurston was still angry at him, while almost a decade later, Hurston admitted that she still cried over her breakup with Hughes; it was for her "the cross of my life" (Bontemps 1939, 44, letter to Hughes). But the two never conveyed their regrets to one another. Hemenway concludes that the fight over *Mule Bone* derived from "an honest misunderstanding" exacerbated by "bad behavior, shrill voices, and feigned innocence" (Hemenway 1977, 146, 136). Whatever the root cause of the feud—insecurity, jealousy, vanity, or desire for more celebrity—the end transformed two close friends into strangers who would never again correspond, much less collaborate.

6

Independence and *Jonah's Gourd Vine*

The end of Hurston's friendship with Langston Hughes coincided with the disintegration of the Harlem Renaissance. While the stock market crash of 1929 initiated the collapse of the movement, by 1931, key figures like Alain Locke, Charles S. Johnson, and James Weldon Johnson had left Harlem for more stable teaching positions at Howard and Fisk University. With Hughes in Havana after receiving the prestigious Harmon Foundation literature prize, Hurston found herself working alone on various projects. Unable to organize her folklore material into a single volume, she began writing a book focused entirely on Cudjo Lewis titled *Barracoon*. Two presses passed on the project, while another praised her material but noted that nothing yet amounted to a publishable manuscript. Still another suggested she translate it out of dialect. Hurston refused.

In 2018, over ninety years after Hurston first traveled to Plateau, Alabama to visit with Lewis, *Barracoon: The Story of the Last "Black Cargo"* was edited by Deborah G. Plant and published to enthusiastic reviews. Hurston's book gives voice to the man she called Kossola and visited repeatedly during the summer of 1929. Written largely from his point of view and seemingly in his unique language, *Barracoon* tells the story of how he was first captured by Dahomey warriors and held at the barracoons, or slave holding pens, at Ouidah and then survived the Middle Passage. For five and a half years, Kossola labored as a slave in Plateau-Magazine Point, Alabama, until Union soldiers informed him that he was free. However, liberation proved more bewildering than comforting as he made his way in what always remained a foreign world. Kossola lived to see World War I and the Great Depression but never returned to his homeland. Hurston approached him with many questions: "I want to know who you are and how you came to be a slave; and to what part of Africa do you belong, and how you fared as a slave, and how you have managed as a free man" (Hurston 2018, 19). Kossola shared his story with her, though his purpose was quite distinct from hers. While she observed of the slave trade, "All these words from the seller, but not one word from the sold" to affirm the importance of Kossola's story to supplement an inadequate historical record, Kossola rejoiced at the start of their conversations: "Thankee Jesus! Somebody come ast about Cudjo! I want tellee somebody who I is, so maybe dey go in de Afficky soil some day and callee my name and somebody say, 'Yeah, I know Kossula'" (Hurston 2018, 6, 19). After a lifetime of hardship and heartache, he was grateful to tell his story, but still longed to return home.

Kossola was born around 1841 in Banté, a town that was home to the Isha people of West Africa. Though not of royal heritage, Kossola's father had a large family, and his grandfather held land and livestock as an officer of the local king. As an adolescent, Kossola trained as a soldier and was preparing for induction into the secret male society known as *oro*, which enforced justice and provided security for the town. At nineteen, he was also anticipating marital rites, but in 1860, his town was awakened by a violent predawn raid. Dahomey warriors sliced off the heads of the Isha and hung them on their belts. Kossola and others were tied to a chain and marched to the barracoons, or slave barracks, at Ouidah. He and his companions had never seen the ocean. Once aboard the *Clotilda*, Kossola was kept below deck for thirteen days before being released to behold the fearsome sight of water all around him. He and the other slaves struggled to regain control of their muscles and calm their terror of the ocean's often wild noises. The *Clotilda* reached the Mississippi coast in July 1860. Kossola and his shipmates were held in bondage through the end of the Civil War.

Once emancipated, Kossola joined a group of other Africans who survived the *Clotilda* to establish Africa Town. They initially asked their former owner, James Meaher, to give them a piece of land, but after he refused, they raised enough money to buy two acres in Magazine Point. Sylviane A. Diouf writes that Africa Town was unique not only because it was composed of blacks, but because it honored those born in another country: "Black towns were safe havens from racism, but Africa Town was a refuge from Americans. . . . The very creation of Africa Town was an assertion that the Africans did not want to be part of any American community," African American or not (Diouf 2007, 157). Although many residents were practicing Christians, they tended to use their own language among

> ### AFRICATOWN
>
> Africatown, or AfricaTown USA, was founded by thirty-two West Africans who are recognized as the last known slaves to arrive in the United States. Although the Atlantic slave trade was banned in 1808, illegal smugglers continued to operate through the middle of the nineteenth century. In 1860, the schooner *Clotilda* arrived in Mobile Bay but was soon after burned in an attempt to hide its illicit cargo. Survivors of the *Clotilda* were ethnically Yoruba and Fon, and they eventually established Africatown three miles north of Mobile, Alabama. The African founders derived from present-day Nigeria and were taken captive by soldiers led by the King of Dahomey. Following their arrival in the United States, the enslaved Africans initially worked on a plantation owned by one of the men who owned the *Clotilda*. Even after they were emancipated following the end of the Civil War, they continued to farm this area. Cudjo Lewis was among the first settlers of Africatown and was frequently identified as one of the leaders of the group.
>
> In 2009, the historical district of Africatown, which now lies within the city limits of Mobile, was designated as a site on Mobile's African American Heritage Trail. It is now recognized by the National Park Service and is listed on the National Register of Historic Places.

themselves. In the mid-1860s, Kossola partnered with Abile, another survivor of the *Clotilda*, and the two married in 1880. They bestowed both an African and an American name to all six of their children. Having outlived all his children and his wife, Kossola at the time that Hurston met him was living with his daughter-in-law and grandchildren.

Hurston's narrative approach in *Barracoon* is unusual. Rather than order Kossola's experiences chronologically, she begins by presenting her initial encounter with him and describes at various points his reticence and even refusal to continue talking. As she transcribes his story, she maintains his vernacular as well as his linguistic rhythms. His repeated phrases describe a man at the end of his life, struggling to find meaning in his sorrows. The result honors his orality and unique perspective. Lynda Hall describes Hurston's narrative strategy as a kind of authorial erasure: "Through a deliberate act of suppression, she resists presenting her own point of view in a natural, or naturalistic, way and allows Kossula 'to tell his story in his own way'" (Hall 1996, 64). Plant likens Hurston's role to that of "a priest" who disappears in order to make his story the sole focus of the book (Hurston 2018, xxv). Hurston deliberately omits any commentary on Kossola's suffering, and as Hill observes, she "does not romanticize or in any way imply that ideals such as self-fulfillment or fully realized self-expression could emerge from such suffering as Kossula has known" (Hall

1996, 67). There is no simple redemption to his tale, no easy moral to take away.

An additional aspect of the book that many readers may have found troubling is Kossola's description of the Africans who were complicit in the slave trade. Even Hurston had difficulty accepting this fact of history, as she explains in *Dust Tracks on a Road*:

> But the inescapable fact that stuck in my craw, was: my people had sold me and the white people had bought me. That did away with the folklore I had been brought up on—that the white people had gone to Africa, waved a red handkerchief at the Africans and lured them aboard ship and sailed away. I know that civilized money stirred up African greed. . . . But, if the African princes had been as pure and innocent as I would like to think, it could not have happened. No, my own people had butchered and killed, exterminated whole nations and tore families apart, for a profit before the strangers got their chance at a cut. (Hurston 1942, 165)

Kossola's account of African brutality is far more bracing than his description of slave life in the antebellum South. The worst violence in the text occurs between blacks, not by white masters upon black slaves. Although this does nothing to mitigate the atrocities committed by Southern whites and often abetted by Northerners, Kossola's story profoundly reorients our understanding of slavery's origins. With her usual insight and bold self-reflection, Hurston wonders what she might have done in place of the African slave traders. She questions, "If I were King, let us say, over the Western Hemisphere tomorrow, instead of who I am, what would I consider right and just? Would I put the clock of Justice on my ambition and send her out a-whoring after conquests? It is something to ponder over with fear" (Hurston 1942, 166). After penning *Barracoon* and learning all of the intimate details of Kossola's suffering, Hurston could not resolutely declare that she would not also be corrupted by power. She would not exempt herself from what she understood as "the universal nature of greed and glory" (Hurston 1942, 165). Hurston's suggestion that she too might have been complicit in the worst of history's horrors speaks to the profound difficulties of a text like *Barracoon*. Kossola's story dispenses with any easy mythology attached to slavery. There is no clear dividing line separating the races between good and bad but instead a vast legacy of suffering that seems almost sadistic in its relentless attack upon Kossola.

It is not surprising then that Hurston could not find a publisher for *Barracoon*. With the country gripped by the Great Depression, Kossola's story would find no ready readership. It is even understandable that Hurston never returned to *Barracoon* once she achieved greater literary fame. Boyd wonders if Hurston had resolved to save her most compelling material from Cudjo Lewis "for her own work" (Boyd 2003, 154). However, none of her fiction approaches anything like Kossola's story. With her imprimatur, the book as it now appears in published form might have intrigued readers of her time eager for more from the author of *Mules and Men* and *Tell My Horse*. However, Hurston chose not to pursue its publication even in the often financially desperate final years of her life. Kossola's story may simply have been too disturbing for Hurston to revisit, much less release to the public. Instead, *Barracoon* languished in the Howard archive for decades before readers could appreciate this stunning tragedy.

Hurston accepted the rejection of *Barracoon* by Viking and Boni publishing houses with little complaint. She soon turned her attention elsewhere. In June, Hurston escaped the city and her frustrations by joining Fannie Hurst on a trip to Maine. The two women made for an unusual sight on the road and drew a good deal of unwanted attention. Unaccustomed to the realities of racial discrimination, Hurst was quick to protest hotels and restaurants that refused to serve them together. In one instance, she told a frowning waiter that Hurston was an African princess. Awed by such a royal guest, the waiter delivered impeccable service. Hurston was more annoyed than amused by Hurst's response to prejudice and later remarked, "Who would think that a good meal could be so bitter?" (Hurst 1960, 20). Rather than share the white woman's righteous anger, Hurston found Hurst's grandstanding and deception tiresome. It did little more than pose another obstacle to the continuation of their journey. Hurston was at times wary of Hurst's celebrity friends, confiding to a black pen pal that "they are OFTEN insincere. Their show of friendship mere patronage" (Kaplan 2003, 80, letter from Hurston to Constance Sheen in 1926). After a stop in Saratoga Springs, Hurst suggested they visit Niagara Falls rather than drive to Maine. Eager to see the famous tourist site, Hurston agreed, and they then explored a number of towns on the Canadian border. At some point, they were joined by the Arctic explorer Vilhjalmur Stefansson, Hurst's lover and the actual reason behind the trip. They never made it to Maine but instead returned to New York through Rochester.

Hurston's trip with Hurst offered a brief respite from her pressing financial concerns. She now only received half of her previous salary from Charlotte Mason, and thus it was imperative for her to find other outlets of support. In addition to covering her usual bills, Hurston also needed enough money to buy agar-agar, a medicine required for a digestive condition she developed after her trip to the Bahamas. Concerned about Hurston's health, Mason put her in touch with the writer Paul Chapin, another of her "godchildren," who in turn referred her to a specialist in Brooklyn. This episode became the basis for Hurston's 1944 essay, "My Most Humiliating Jim Crow Experience." When Hurston arrived, she was directed to what was called "a private examination room" but which clearly was used for other purposes: "Under any other circumstances, I would have sworn it was a closet where the soiled towels and uniforms were tossed until called for by the laundry." When the doctor arrived, it was clear that "he meant to get me off the premises as quickly as possible" (Hurston 1979, 163). Hurston decided to stay and endure his basic exam "to torture him more," eventually leaving with a prescription and a twenty-dollar bill she never paid. She concluded, "I went away feeling the pathos of the Anglo-Saxon civilization. And I still mean pathos, for I know that anything with such a false foundation cannot last. Whom the gods would destroy, they first made mad" (Hurston 1979, 164). In her usual sly and understated manner, Hurston ends the essay by aligning herself with the gods. She is clearly incensed by the end of the visit with the doctor, but it is an anger that takes on divine power. Moreover, even as Hurston leaves without confronting the doctor for his bad behavior, she suggests that destruction is coming. Below the surface of her hat, set "at a reckless angle" as she exits the office, is a promise of impending doom (Hurston 1979, 164).

Though she would suffer from periodic digestive problems until the end of her life, Hurston recovered from the immediate symptoms of her illness and soon found a new job writing for *Fast and Furious*, an African American revue, as well as for another show called *Jungle Scandals*. With the failure of *Mule Bone* still in mind, Hurston sought to at last make her mark in the theater. Although she admitted that neither of the revues were accomplished pieces, she began composing a play version of her short story "Spunk," which she hoped would demonstrate her development as a dramatist.

That summer, Hurston learned that her husband, Herbert Sheen, working as a physician in St. Louis, had met another woman and wished to marry again. In July, Hurston agreed to the long-awaited divorce. Looking back at their separation, Sheen noted that his first wife "was a little too accommodating. I often wished that she had refused to get a divorce. I would have been a lot better off" (Sheen, interview by Robert E. Hemenway). Though Hurston abandoned a degree of financial stability by divorcing Sheen, she aspired toward a marriage of passion, partnership, and love. While she professed to still love Sheen deeply, their strong individual interests made sustained intimacy all but impossible.

As usual, Hurston did not dwell upon personal wounds but instead focused on the projects at hand. Mason urged her to continue her work with *Fast and Furious* and *Jungle Scandals* and reminded her that African American theater was in need of strong creative voices. However, when *Fast and Furious* debuted at the New Yorker Theater in September, it was met with harsh reviews. Hurston could have predicted the negative response to the revue after she clashed with the producer over artistic concerns. She resigned herself to using the performance for a quick payout, though after *Fast and Furious* closed within a week, she was left with only $75 of the $525 she had expected. Her plans to move to a less expensive area in New Jersey were definitively foiled when *Jungle Scandals* was canceled soon after.

Desperate for a new source of revenue even as she remained committed to her writing, Hurston briefly considered opening what she termed "New York's Chicken Specialist," where she would serve all kinds of chicken dishes—chicken soup, chicken salad, fried chicken, and chicken a la king (Kaplan 2003, 229, letter from Hurston to Mason in 1931). She imagined that the mouthwatering business wouldn't even need advertisement and could survive alone on her kitchen skill and word of mouth. Though Hurston was a good cook, it's also possible that she presented this idea to Mason simply as evidence of her dedication to keep working hard. After deciding not to pursue the chicken shop, she resolved to use her experiences working on *Fast and Furious* to further her interest in presenting black folklife onstage. Rather than compose a drama or comedy, Hurston decided this time to focus on music. She sent some of the songs she had gathered during her travels to Hall Johnson, a prominent black choral director. Johnson had helped create the blockbuster show *The Green Pastures*, a retelling of biblical stories through the experiences of African Americans. The success of *The Green Pastures* and of shows like *Shuffle Along* and *Porgy and Bess* affirmed white interest in black-themed productions, though Hurston privately questioned the authenticity of such hits. Johnson, for his part, was skeptical that Hurston's songs could reach a wide audience without significant rearrangement. Hurston understood Johnson's response as "a determined effort to squeeze all of the rich black juice out of the songs and present a sort of musical octoroon to the public" (Hurston 1942, 280).

Rejecting Hall's assimilationist posture, Hurston demanded a more authentic performance, or what she called a "concert in the raw" that would celebrate the powerful dancing she saw in the Bahamas and the authentic black voices of the South (Kaplan 2003, 231, letter from Hurston to Mason in 1931). Although she returned to Hall suggesting that they draw from her dancers and his singers, she soon ended their partnership after she overheard some members of his choir maligning the West Indian performers she had brought to rehearsal. She titled her new solo production *In the Beginning: A Concert of Negro Secular Music* and insisted on casting dark-skinned singers and dancers. She promised, "No mulattoes at all" (Kaplan 2003, 233, letter from Hurston to Mason in 1931). Mason supported Hurston's decision and agreed to provide her with the footage she shot of the Fire Dance in the Bahamas. These films allowed Hurston to reconstruct the dances for her production, set for January 10, 1932, at the John Golden Theatre.

> ### Porgy and Bess
>
> The English-language opera *Porgy and Bess* was written by American composer George Gershwin. Though first performed in Boston in September 1935, it soon moved to Broadway in New York City. The opera is based on the 1925 Dubose Heyward novel *Porgy*. After reading the book, Gershwin traveled to Charleston, South Carolina, Heyward's home, to research the local culture and geography. Gershwin understood *Porgy and Bess* to be a folk opera, but rather than using original folk material, he composed his own. The libretto describes Porgy, a disabled black man who lives on the streets of Charleston. He struggles to rescue Bess from Crown, her violent boyfriend, and Sportin' Life, her drug dealer. Since its inception, *Porgy and Bess* has garnered controversy for its depiction of African American life. Many argue that it promotes base stereotypes and mocks, rather than celebrates, black forms of cultural expression. However, other critics suggest that it has been an important vehicle for black talent. In 2011, the Pulitzer Prize–winning playwright Suzan Lori-Parks returned to Broadway with her reimagined musical *The Gershwins' Porgy and Bess*, starring four-time Tony-winner Audra McDonald. In her version of the story, the characters are portrayed with more complex backstories, deepening the depictions offered in the original musical.

Eventually retitled *The Great Day*, this production consumed all of Hurston's energies. She declined another car trip with Hurst to the Midwest and instead began selling off personal items to pay for advertising and publicity photos for the production. Desperate for money, Hurston appealed to Mason for a loan, noting that she had never worked harder in her life except while gathering the original material for the show: "But I have nothing more to sell. I am on the brink [of] putting the thing over and it will break my heart to fall down now. . . . I am willing to make any sacrifice, meet any terms to give it a chance of success" (Kaplan 2003, 237–238, letter from Hurston to Mason in 1931). Hoping that the production would be picked up by an agent, Mason agreed to fund one night of the performance. Advertisements for *The Great Day* emphasized its authentic artistry and music that had not been rearranged or influenced by Harlem or Broadway styles. Instead, it would offer real African American work songs, lullabies, games, and a sermon. Though Hurston also hoped to include a conjure ritual, Mason objected, afraid that performing such a ceremony would undermine its spiritual power and offend its practitioners.

With Mason and Alain Locke in the audience along with many of Mason's godchildren, Hurston was nervous as the performance began. However, she recalled that from the very first scene, the audience was enraptured with the actors and dancers onstage. The musical chronicled a day at a Florida work camp, where the men sang "John Henry" and "Can't You Line It?" The men then headed home, where children played classic African American games like Chick-mah-chick and Mistah Frog and an itinerant preacher delivered a powerful sermon. The second act opened in a jook joint and included many popular secular songs. The performance concluded with the Fire Dance and a blues song. Following a tremendous burst of applause, Hurston was thrust on stage and "explained why I had done it. That music without motion was unnatural with Negroes, and what I had tried to do was to present Negro singing in a natural way—with action. I don't know what else I said, but the audience was kind and I walked off to an applauding house" (Hurston 1942, 283). Although *The Great Day* received glowing reviews, no one picked up the play, and Hurston was frustrated by its weak performance at the box office. She ended up owing over eighty dollars to cover expenses and once again had to turn to Mason for help.

Hurston now owed over six hundred dollars to Mason and believed the only way she could at last pay her debt was by putting on another show. Although Hurston was responsible for writing and organizing *The Great Day*, the play's material remained the possession of Mason, and Hurston was obliged to ask for permission to do anything further with it. Perhaps venting her own frustration with the performance's failure to make good on her investment, Mason scolded Hurston for not consulting her throughout its development. Her independent approach to the production had assumed Mason's goodwill and financial backing. To prevent such behavior in the future, Mason insisted on a legally binding agreement that outlined what sections of the concert program Hurston could use in the future. The document also asked that any royalties be used to pay back the money still owed to Mason and closed with a reminder that Hurston's most lasting contribution would be the books she had still yet to write.

In part because publishers, hit hard by the Depression, generally avoided African American subject matter at this time, Hurston continued to focus on presenting theatrical work. Now blessed with Mason's permission, she began work on a revised version of her concert titled *From Sun to Sun*. The production opened at The New School for Social Research on March 29. The performance was similar to *The Great Day* but included Hurston's one-act play, *The Fiery Chariot*, about a slave who prays to die as a way to escape his bondage. One night his master appears before him pretending to be God. Dressed in a white sheet, the master asks his slave to join him in heaven. The slave changes his mind and tries to escape his master, leading to a farcical end. Once again, Hurston ended her concert with the Fire Dance, which always brought the audience to their feet.

As with *The Great Day, From Sun to Sun* garnered positive reviews but no profit. Exasperated with yet another failure at the box office, Mason consulted with Locke and discussed her belief that Hurston was too prone to exploitation by others and did not have the vision necessary to succeed. Locke, who had often been skeptical of Hurston's talents, questioned why Mason continued to offer such generous financial support. Less than a week after the performance, Locke visited Hurston and made clear his and Mason's misgivings. He noted that her apartment was too expensive and directed her to seek a teaching position at a black college. He also took this opportunity to critique her writing, which had failed to progress from its last draft. Hurston tried to defend the changes she had made in her work and explained that part of the problem was that her health had never fully recovered. Unable to pay for the medicine she needed for intestinal difficulties, she had little energy to focus on her writing.

After this dispiriting meeting, Hurston wrote to Mason and proposed a solution to some of the concerns Locke had raised. She requested money to go back to Eatonville, where living expenses would be far cheaper and she could focus on her work while regaining her strength among friends and family. Mason finally agreed to fund Hurston's return, though she griped about having to pay her outstanding phone and heating bills. Hurston was so destitute that she had only one pair of shoes, which were bursting along the toe line. Mason gave her six dollars for a new pair along with a one-way ticket to Eatonville. With her return imminent, Hurston felt that "somehow a great weight seems lifted from me. I have been trying to analyze myself and see why I feel so happy. But I do" (Kaplan 2003, 253, letter from Hurston to Mason in 1932).

Within a week of her arrival in Eatonville, Hurston described herself as "happier than I have been for years" and "renewed like the eagle" (Kaplan 2003, 254, letter from Hurston to Mason in 1932). Away from the noise and bustle of New York, Hurston began tending a garden of watermelon, beans, okra, and tomatoes. Far removed from her late Harlem nights, Hurston went to bed early and woke with the sun. She now only received fifty dollars per month from Mason and looked for new ways to make money. Within a month, she proposed staging *From Sun to Sun* locally to Edwin Osgood Grover, a creative arts professor at Rollins College, located in Winter Park, an affluent town close to Eatonville. Grover and others were impressed by Hurston, and with Mason's approval, they began preparing for the concert.

Hurston delighted in returning to her childhood home. She never put on airs or gloated about her New York connections. Instead, she basked in the creative language of the townspeople, learned the chicken dance from a child, and contemplated new ventures like starting a vocational adult school or buying a lakefront property. Though she was not able to find teaching work, she anticipated a steadier income in the fall, when her concert would begin its performances. Hurston asked that Mason continue to support her through October, promising that she would then "be off of your financial hands forever" and Mason would at last be able to see her as before, as "the Zora of the Eatonville gatepost, again" (Kaplan 2003, 273, letters from Hurston to Mason on September 16 and 28, 1932). Although it would be impossible not to miss Mason's monthly checks, Hurston surely looked forward to her financial independence. She would no longer have to account for every expense, from cough syrup to sanitary pads, nor worry how her actions might offend the ever-temperamental Mason.

By the end of the year, Hurston was finally freed from Mason's watchful eye and her artistic demands. With this independence, she found new energy and focus for her work. She returned to fiction, writing short stories and working on what would become her first novel, *Jonah's Gourd Vine* (1934). Far from the expectations of New York publishers, Hurston at last completed her volume on folklore, which she entitled *Mules and Men*. However, she put the manuscript aside to dedicate herself to the Rollins concert. With Bob Wunsch, the college's theater director, she trained performers for the opening of *From Sun to Sun*, set for January 20, 1933. She persuaded her uncle, the Rev. Isaiah Hurston, to serve as the play's itinerant preacher, and she found a number of skilled vocalists from local church choirs. Wunsch hosted Hurston in one of his fall classes, where she regaled his students with work songs and stories. Although Hurston found these pursuits satisfying, she continued to struggle financially. She managed to collect small sums speaking at local clubs but was also beholden to friendly neighbors who shared their garden harvests with her. Hurston was too proud to ask for loans or favors from her new friends and associates. However, she heaped thanks on Mason when she sent her a generous check for Christmas, writing, "Godmother Darling, your Christmas present was the finest thing that could have happened to me" (Kaplan 2003, 276, letter from Hurston to Mason in 1932). Despite her new independence and surroundings, some dynamics were hard to change.

Hurston refused to find a steady job because she so firmly believed in the importance of establishing a strong African American theater. She would rather wash her face with laundry soap than give up her dream of harnessing and showcasing black talent: "If we can give real creative urge a push forward here, the world will see a New Negro and justify our efforts. That is pay" (Kaplan 2003, 277, letter from Hurston to Mason in 1932). Hurston pursued her passion even as she continued to struggle with intestinal difficulties. She often had to lead rehearsals sitting on a car cushion, which helped ease her discomfort. However, Hurston faced more than just health challenges in putting on the Florida debut of *From Sun to Sun*. Although the president of Rollins agreed to stage the concert at an on-campus theater, he insisted that African Americans not be allowed in the audience. Hurston was unable to contest the president's decision, but she did arrange for a performance in Eatonville at the Hungerford School as well as an invitation-only premiere at a small theater called The Museum. The January 27 event at the Rollins's Recreation Hall for a whites-only audience would at least be a repeat performance and not the show's debut. *From Sun to Sun* proved to be a real hit, with even the president lauding the performance. In addition to providing program notes for the secular songs, Hurston acted in "The Fiery Chariot" and led one of the concert dances. Soon the performers went on the road with *From Sun to Sun*, appearing in many Florida cities.

The success of the concert was tempered by unfortunate developments in Hurston's personal life. Around this time, she learned that her older sister had died of pneumonia and that Mason was in the hospital after breaking her hip. Though Hurston did not want to share her sadness with others, she grieved these tragedies deeply: "It's as if the sun had lain down in the cradle of eternity" (Kaplan 2003, 282, letter from Hurston to Locke in 1933). Previously when Mason had fallen ill, Hurston had used her conjure skills to send her positive energy, but this time, Mason did not even reply to Hurston's letters, and she had to seek further information about Godmother's health from Locke.

Hurston responded to these tragedies by focusing more intently on her work and specifically on honing her skills as a creative writer. Though it had been many years since she'd last published a short story, she remained committed to applying her knowledge of black folklore and life to her fiction. During this time, she penned one of her most acclaimed short stories, "The Gilded Six-Bits." Uncertain of its value, she shared it with Wunsch, who asked to read it to his creative writing students. More importantly, he gave it to the editors of *Story* magazine, who published it in the August 1933 issue. Although Hurston only received twenty dollars for the story, it proved to be foundational to her future career as a literary writer.

"The Gilded Six-Bits" both maintains and departs from Hurston's previous stories. As in "Sweat" and "John Redding Goes to Sea," Eatonville provides the backdrop, this time for the loving but conflicted marriage of Missie May and Joe Banks. However, while "Sweat" describes the destructive relationship of Delia and Sykes, "The Gilded Six-Bits" offers a more hopeful perspective on marriage. Although Missie May and Joe Banks have a playful dynamic, Missie May has an affair with Slemmons, the seemingly affluent owner of a new ice cream parlor. Joe is heartbroken by this infidelity, but the couple remain committed to one another. They reunite and eventually make a family together. Much of the beauty and innovation of the story derives from Hurston's careful portrayal of Missie May, who is at once sexually vibrant and emotionally complex. She makes a mistake in sleeping with Slemmons, but this act does not define her. Rather, she chooses the hard work of repairing her relationship with Joe, moving past common stereotypes of sexual licentiousness associated with black women. The story rejects an easy idealization of marriage to show that romance is sustained by forgiveness and acceptance of another's faults and strengths.

Perhaps because *Story* magazine had a wider readership than the black magazines Hurston had previously published in, she soon received inquiries from publishers interested in her work. Four presses asked if she had a book-length fiction manuscript to send them. Hurston was most impressed by Bertram Lippincott's "gentle-like letter," which gave her a sense of security: as she explained, "Exposing my efforts did not seem so rash to me after reading his letter" (Hurston 1942, 173). She responded that she was in fact writing a novel. Although she later admitted that she had not written a single word of what would become *Jonah's Gourd Vine*, that week she moved to Sanford to begin writing. Away from close friends and family, Hurston devoted herself to an idea conceived a decade ago, when she was first collecting folklore in the South. She would write the story of her parents, focusing in particular on the enormous strengths and flaws of her father. When she'd first thought of such a book, the task of writing a novel had seemed too daunting, and she'd worried that it would never find a publisher. She knew that publishers preferred black authors to write about racial issues. While Hurston's primary characters would of course be black, she had no interest in focusing on the problem of race.

With the confidence and vision of her forty-some years, as well as the encouragement of Lippincott's letter, Hurston at last decided to begin writing in earnest. Paying $1.50 a week in rent, she holed herself up in a small house to write in pencil a fictionalized version of her parents' marriage. Though she ran out of money in two weeks, she kept writing, managing on the fifty cents a week her cousin provided for groceries. Hurston kept her parents' names in *Jonah's Gourd Vine*, a novel that is primarily an homage to her father. It showcases in equal measure his talents and his weaknesses, offering a kind of belated reconciliation between daughter and father. The manuscript took Hurston a mere nine weeks to complete.

By September, Hurston found a stenographer to type up her handwritten manuscript. She was so broke that she had to borrow the two dollars required to send it to Lippincott's office in Philadelphia. With the text off her hands, Hurston found work with the Seminole County Chamber of Commerce to offer a mobile version of her concert. She organized a sound truck to drive through the city's streets followed by her band of performers. Although the job offered twenty-five dollars a day, her landlady was tired of enduring weeks of unpaid rent and evicted Hurston. The very same day she had to find storage for her meager belongings, she received a telegram from Lippincott. In the tumult of the day's performance, Hurston stuck the message in her purse and did not read it until she was buying a much-needed new pair of shoes. The telegram stated that Lippincott had accepted *Jonah's Gourd Vine* and would offer her a $200 advance for its publication. Hurston remembered the moment as one of the highlights of her life: "I tore out of that place with one old shoe and one new one on and ran to the Western Union office. Lippincott had asked for an answer by wire and they got it! Terms accepted. I never expect to have a greater thrill than that wire gave me" (Hurston 1942, 175).

Lippincott scheduled the release of *Jonah's Gourd Vine* for May 1934. From a new rental home in Sanford, Hurston wrote to her former friends and mentors to ask for their support for her first novel. She requested an introduction from Fannie Hurst and an endorsement from Carl Van Vechten. She also instructed her editor to send advance copies to such influential black scholars as James Weldon Johnson and W. E. B. Du Bois. Although the $200 advance more than covered her immediate necessities and even allowed her to put the down payment on a car, Hurston was paid far less than her white contemporaries and soon had to find other ways to pay her bills. She continued to partner with the Rollins College Dramatic Art Department, putting on *All de Live Long Day* in January 1934. The performance included some earlier material but also debuted a new one-act dramatization of a folktale by Hurston, *De Possum's Tail Hairs*. Rollins College proved to be a good fit for Hurston. Under the direction of Hamilton Holt, the school had converted its curriculum away from a lecture format to focus on small seminars and individual engagement with faculty. Holt also instituted a somewhat tongue-in-cheek program of faculty chairs, which included a Professor of Evil and another each for Leisure, Books, and Things in General. Despite her Barnard education, Hurston was wary of academic pretention and found in Holt a fellow champion of "undistinguished Americans" (Holt 2000).

Hurston also dedicated herself to writing an application for a prestigious Guggenheim fellowship to study the roots of black American cultural practices in West Africa. Although Hurston's proposal was strong and her earlier fieldwork attested to her ability to gather important material, she chose a list of recommenders who failed to make a persuasive case for her. Rather than select black scholars like Alain Locke, Carter G. Woodson, or Charles S. Johnson, who knew her work well, she opted for a group of distinguished white intellectuals she presumed would impress the selection committee. Unfortunately, none of these individuals offered an unequivocally positive assessment of Hurston's talents and vision. While Carl Van Vechten had only praise for Hurston, his two-sentence recommendation was hardly a ringing endorsement. Hurst complimented Hurston but also took care to note that she had an uneven work ethic. Franz Boas's verdict was more surprising, as the once-supportive mentor identified her as lacking the talents necessary for such a distinguished award. Not surprisingly, Hurston did not receive the fellowship.

She did, however, at last land a teaching position at a black school, Bethune-Cookman College. Hurston was asked by the school's founder, the educator and civil rights activist Mary McLeod Bethune, to organize a school of dramatic arts at Bethune-Cookman. Although Hurston was delighted with the opportunity, she soon encountered a number of difficulties. The student body was too small to create the performances she had produced in the past, and Bethune constantly intervened in Hurston's directorial work. Carla Kaplan observes that Hurston was better suited to schools like Rollins that treated her like an "exotic," rather than all-black institutions that had less obvious expectations: "It was one thing to perform black folklore to white audiences who found it new and exciting. It was altogether another thing to stage black folklore in a black context with audiences experiencing various scenarios as overly familiar, embarrassing, or belittling" (Kaplan 2003, 179). Hurston described herself as "plugging away in the dark," unable to fulfill her vision for the school. By the spring, she decided to abandon the position (Kaplan 2003, 294, letter from Hurston to Locke).

With Lippincott due to publish *Mules and Men*, her volume of folktales, soon after *Jonah's Gourd Vine*, Hurston headed to St. Louis in May to attend the National Folk Festival. The event began with a thousand-person choir singing Negro spirituals and included dance and song performances by lumberjacks, Indians, Mormons, Appalachian fiddlers, Vermont balladeers, and many others. The festival highlighted the mixing of academic and nonacademic scholars and practitioners of American folklore that constituted the still-emerging discipline. Hurston's own prominence as an expert in black folklore had grown with the publication of *Negro* (1934), an anthology edited by Nancy Cunard that included six of Hurston's essays. Of these short works, "Characteristics of Negro Expression" remains the most influential, even as its descriptions tend toward troubling stereotypes. For example, Hurston writes: "It is said that Negroes keep nothing secret, that they have no reserve" (Hurston 2014, 1057). While such statements play on ideas of African American simplicity, she also offers a more cogent analysis of black dialect and styles of speaking earlier in the essay. "Characteristics of Negro Expression" is strongest in revealing the linguistic sophistication of black grammatical constructions and the poetry of its vernacular.

These important insights were soon dwarfed by the publication of *Jonah's Gourd Vine*, which embodied many of the theoretical premises Hurston outlined in her essays. In this novel, Hurston transformed her parents into legendary figures. Like her father, the novel's John Pearson evolves from a manual laborer to an eloquent preacher whose oratorical skills prove to be both his glory and his folly. With his smooth tongue, he talks women into his bed, much to the pain and dismay of his hardworking wife. Even as he remains unfaithful, John recognizes his utter dependence on Lucy, who cares for their children. Hurston explained in a letter to James Weldon Johnson her aim in writing the novel: "I have tried to present a Negro, preacher who is neither funny nor an imitation Puritan ramrod in pants. Just the human being and poet that he must be to succeed in a Negro pulpit.... I see a preacher as a man outside of the pulpit and so far as I am concerned he should be free to follow his bent as other men" (Kaplan 2003, 298, letter from Hurston to Johnson). Even as Hurston sought to describe the complex humanity of her characters, she also imbued them with biblical significance. The title refers to a biblical story involving a vine that grows overnight to protect Jonah from the hot sun. However, God then plants a worm that kills the vine, demonstrating how quickly life can be destroyed. John's progress reflects the sudden growth of the vine, and just as Hurston's father ended a broken man, her novel's protagonist is brought low by his adultery and abusive behavior.

Before its publication, Hurston was terrified of the reviews her debut book would receive. However, the advance praise for *Jonah's Gourd Vine* helped create genuine excitement and interest. Hurst penned a laudatory introduction and suggested that not even Langston Hughes had written such an accomplished piece of writing. Van Vechten was also smitten by the novel, while Bertram Lippincott envisioned a movie version starring Paul Robeson. Hurston's publisher gushed to others about the book's originality, remarking, "I have never read anything like JONAH'S GOURD VINE. It has a style and rhythm that a white writer simply could not do and I do not see how it can fail to make a big impression" (Lippincott 1934, letter to Grover). Although many of the reviews that appeared in mainstream publications were laced with racialized language, they were remarkably positive in their assessment of the novel. Writing in the *New York Times Book Review*, Margaret Wallace called it "the most vital and original novel about the American Negro that has yet been written by a member of the Negro race" (Wallace 1934). Race was also operative in reviews that appeared in black publications, which tended to judge the book based on its representative value. One of the harshest responses to the novel was published in *The Crisis*; calling the book "quite disappointing and a failure as a novel," it attacked Hurston's desire "to write a novel about a backward Negro people, using their peculiar speech and manners to express their lives" (Burris 1934). Most reviewers praised the rich, metaphorical language of the text, even as some found it difficult to understand or questioned whether such eloquence could actually come from black mouths. No one, however, could deny the sheer force of *Jonah's Gourd Vine* and the emergence of a major literary talent.

7

Jamaica, Haiti, and *Their Eyes Were Watching God*

Hurston returned to New York to promote *Jonah's Gourd Vine* but was eager to get back to Florida, where she could attend to the final draft of *Mules and Men*. Bertram Lippincott instructed her to revise her manuscript so that a nonacademic audience could appreciate its contributions and insights. To this end, Hurston included parts of her own narrative in the book, describing her experiences collecting the material she presents. Though she worried the new version would not be sufficiently scientific for Franz Boas, she sent it to her former professor to ask him to write an introduction. He agreed, and Lippincott set the publication date for 1935. Hurston continued to write, publishing "The Fire and the Cloud" in *Challenge*, a new journal started by Dorothy West. The short story imagines a dialogue between a lizard and Moses as he prepares to lead his people across the River Jordan.

That fall, Hurston headed north to Chicago, where she was invited to produce a version of her folk concert. Along the way, she stopped in Nashville to visit some old friends at Fisk University, including Charles S. Johnson and Lorenzo Dow Turner. In Chicago, she spoke at a series of women's clubs and gave a few public addresses. While staying at the South Parkway branch of the YWCA, Hurston organized her Chicago concert, which she renamed *Singing Steel*. The November shows garnered positive reviews and the attention of representatives of the Julius Rosenwald Fund. They suggested that Hurston apply for a fellowship from their foundation, which aimed to promote "Negro welfare" and "black-white relations." At the time, it was the only funding source primarily dedicated to supporting African American artists. Over thirty years, it raised more than $20 million and provided grants to such luminaries as W. E. B. Du Bois and James Baldwin. It is especially significant that the Rosenwald trustees sought Hurston out, rather than the other way around. She was clearly a rising talent, and they were eager to provide her with the resources she needed. In her application, she explained that "the major problem in my field" lay in the nature of its researchers. Collecting, she declared, "must be done by individuals feeling the material as well as seeing it objectively. In order to feel and appreciate the nuances one must be of the group" (Hurston, "Fellowship application," 1934). Her budget came to $4,407.50, and she hoped that after two and a half years, her work would lead to her PhD. Five days after she mailed her application, she received a two-year fellowship of $3,000 to pursue a doctorate in anthropology at Columbia University. This award exceeded the usual amount given and reflected the great confidence the fund president, Edwin Embree, had in her ability to contribute significantly to a broader understanding of black cultural life.

In December, Hurston published a short essay, "Race Cannot Become Great Until It Recognizes Its Talent" in the *Washington Tribune*. Affirming the value of black folk culture, Hurston warned her fellow African Americans to cease emulating Western art. The result of such imitation, she warned, would only be an "intellectual lynching" that destroyed the most vital source of African American expression and creativity: "Fawn as you will. Spend an eternity standing awe-struck. Roll your eyes in ecstasy and ape his every move, but until we have placed something upon his street corner that is our own, we are right back where we were when they filed our iron collars off" (Hurston, "Race Cannot," 1934). Hurston expanded on this subject in an essay submitted to *The American Mercury* that same year. The never published "You Don't Know Us Negroes" indicts depictions of black life of the last decade, which constitute in her view "the oleomargarine era in Negro writing." Simplistic characterizations of African American life fortified damaging stereotypes that led whites to believe that "First thing on waking we laugh or skeer ourselves into another buck and wing, and so life goes." She demanded that writers, both black and white, "treat the public to some butter" for "Negro reality is a hundred times more imaginative than anything that has ever been hatched up over a typewriter" (Hurston, "You Don't Know," 1934).

After using a moving allowance from the Rosenwald Fund to relocate to New York, Hurston began her studies under Boas. Perhaps anticipating doubts about her ability to complete such scholarly work, she wrote to him: "Now I realize that this is going to call for rigorous routine and discipline, which every body seems to feel that I need. So be it. I want to do it.

I have always wanted to do it and nobody will have any trouble about my applying myself" (Kaplan 2003, 326, letter from Hurston to Boas in 1934). Hurston returned to a Harlem transformed by the Great Depression and bereft of its former artistic leaders such as Langston Hughes, who was in Mexico, and Wallace Thurman, who had died at the end of 1934. While Hurston had previously straddled two social worlds—Harlem and Columbia—now she was firmly committed to her studies. Due to her extensive fieldwork and the lack of classes on black culture at Columbia, she and Boas outlined a specialized course of study for her. She would first take classes to give her a foundation in ethnology and then travel to Haiti to research the development of hoodoo.

Unfortunately, Embree objected to this plan. Although the fellowship only asked for the approval of Hurston's mentors at Columbia, Embree cut her funding from $3,000 to $700, effectively guaranteeing only one semester of sponsorship. Embree later wrote to Charles S. Johnson expressing concern that Hurston lacked the personal and intellectual discipline to be successful. At the end of this period, Hurston could apply to other fellowship programs, but the Rosenwald Fund was no longer obligated to contribute to her education. Valerie Boyd speculates that the real reason Embree pulled Hurston's funding is due to an article that ran in *The New York World-Telegram* in early February. In "Author Plans to Upbraid Own Race: Zora Hurston Denies There Is 'Tragedy' in Being Negro," she is quoted as saying that she had considered passing on a Rosenwald fellowship to study at Columbia in order to write "a book that would give her own people 'an awful going over,' particularly the ones who talk about the tragedy of being Negroes" (McDougal 1935). Shortly after Embree slashed Hurston's fellowship, he wrote to Boas explaining that he and others at the Rosenwald Fund were concerned by her excessive initiative in expressing her opinions, which would no doubt be a distraction to producing serious scholarship. Boas intervened and promised that he and others at Columbia would direct Hurston's studies and provide her with the guidance necessary to complete her research but Embree was not persuaded. Although Hurston considered pursuing her research with famed anthropologist Melville Herskovits at Northwestern, which was developing a graduate program in African and African American studies, she ultimately resolved to continue her work at Columbia.

Hurston took the stipend provided for her first semester but stopped attending her classes. Instead, she used the money to support her creative writing. With little interest in teaching, she directed her attention to writing a new novel. An April profile of her in New York's *Amsterdam News* described her habit of writing in bed at night and her belief that creative writing could not be taught but was instead the product of natural talent. Many of Hurston's usual correspondents noted that she was less responsive than usual during this period. However, this time around she was not just consumed by a new project of her own. Instead, as she described it, she "met the man who was really to lay me by the heels." Percival McGuire Punter was a twenty-three-year-old graduate student at Columbia who Hurston had met three years earlier, when he'd performed in the first production of *The Great Day*. Although Hurston had taken note of the handsome singer, their relationship did not initially extend beyond work. Now, however, both took significant notice of one another, and Hurston recalled, "I did not just fall in love. I made a parachute jump" (Hurston 1942, 205). Punter was initially uncertain of his ability to woo such a talented and confident woman. The son of West Indian parents, he had, as Hurston noted, "nothing to offer but what it takes—a bright soul, a fine mind in a fine body, and courage" (Hurston 1942, 207). Although Hurston identified Punter as the love of her life and the two enjoyed discussing art and literature, the relationship soon encountered difficulties. Hurston enjoyed a modest celebrity in New York, and Punter struggled to reconcile her independence and success with their relationship. He became possessive and insecure about how to best act like a man before such an accomplished woman. His solution was to propose to Hurston and ask her to renounce her career. While Hurston was content to marry him, she could not give up her writing:

> I really wanted to do anything he wanted me to do, but that one thing I could not do. It was not just my contract with my publishers, it was that I had things clawing inside of me that must be said. I could not see that my work should make any difference in marriage. He was all and everything else to me but that. One did not conflict with the other in my mind. But it was different with him. (Hurston 1942, 208)

Despite this fundamental difference, Hurston and Punter could not part ways. One night, their jealousies and resentments escalated, and Hurston slapped him. Punter hit back, and soon they were trading attacks, though Hurston noted, "No broken bones, you understand, and no black eyes." They quickly made up, consoling one another on the floor. Punter then went out to buy a pie, and Hurston brewed hot chocolate.

Despite their reconciliation, Hurston concluded that she "was too deeply in love to be my old self" and worried that she would soon be a drag on his career prospects (Hurston 1942, 209). She decided to leave town without even telling him, hoping that he would soon get over his heartache and she could continue with her work. In June, Hurston headed South with New York University Professor Mary Elizabeth Barnicle to collect African American folk songs. Joined by college student Alan Lomax, they worked out of a small house on St. Simons island off the Georgia coast. Lomax was wowed by Hurston's easy rapport with the folk singers who happily presented their songs. They then headed to Eatonville and Belle Glade, where

> **WPA**
>
> President Franklin Roosevelt established the Works Progress Administration (WPA) in 1935 as part of his ambitious New Deal to reinvigorate the American economy. The employment and infrastructure program was a direct response to the Great Depression. Over eight years, the WPA employed more than eight million Americans. The WPA (which was renamed the Work Projects Administration in 1939) primarily employed unskilled male workers on public infrastructure projects. Under the WPA, more than 4,000 new schools were built, 130 new hospitals established, 9,000 miles of storm drains and sewer lines laid, 29,000 new bridges constructed, 150 new airfields created, and over twenty million trees planted; additionally, 280,000 miles of roads were either paved or repaired. The WPA administered the Federal Project Number One, which included five parts: the Federal Art Project, the Federal Music Project, the Federal Theater Project, the Federal Writers' Project, and the Historical Records Survey. Tens of thousands of artists and scholars were employed through the WPA. They presented countless performances, exhibits, and artistic events for communities across the nation. The Federal Writers' Project also created the American Guide Series, guidebooks for every state in the union, and worked to promote reading among children. The WPA was closed in June 1943. Unemployment levels had shrunk to less than 2 percent, and as weapon production increased due to World War II, many workers found well-paying jobs in the armed services and defense industries. The WPA simply was not needed as before.

they focused on collecting work songs and spirituals. While Lomax and Barnicle continued on to the Bahamas, Hurston returned to New York, where she could not resist returning to Punter.

Although she had made good use of the Rosenwald fellowship, noting in a letter to Embree that she'd written two plays and drafted her next novel under its sponsorship, she once again had to look for work. Fortunately, Hurston found a job working for the "Negro Unit" of the Work Projects Administration's Federal Theater Project in New York. For $23.66 a week, she was a "dramatic coach," working on *Walk Together Chillun!*, the first production of the Harlem unit, and helping organize an April staging of an all-black *Macbeth* set in Haiti. Hurston remained in her WPA job for six months, through the publication of *Mules and Men* in October 1935.

Hurston's second book garnered immediate critical acclaim. Though long in the making, *Mules and Men* was a testament to Hurston's dedicated fieldwork and deft narrative skills. The book documents folklore and hoodoo practices while also including details of Hurston's own experiences and failures collecting this material. Boas, who wrote the preface for the book's first edition, comments on Hurston's ability to insert herself among the communities she studies. He identifies "the charm of a loveable personality" as what allows her to "penetrate through that affected demeanor by which the Negro excludes the White observer effectively from participating in his true inner life" (Hurston 1935, reprinted 1990, xiii). Although this somewhat condescending comment makes her success a result of charisma rather than intelligence and insight, it highlights what for white readers was the most novel aspect of the book: Hurston's rapport with her subjects. Reviewers applauded Hurston's ability to establish an intimate connection with both the storytellers she encounters and readers who are far removed from the practices she chronicles. For many whites, the book was a revelation, providing an inside view on black life apart from the dictates and expectations of dominant society. Though Hurston received unanimous praise for her rendering of black dialect, Sterling Brown, writing in *New Masses*, criticized the book for ignoring the anger and violence roiling black communities in the South. For Hurston, such issues were better addressed in other ways; literature need not be the mouthpiece for racial injustice. Moreover, the text's long road to publication was impacted by considerations of its white publishers, who were less inclined to print controversial material. Throughout her life, Hurston sought to turn away from the "sobbing school of Negrohood" to celebrate the vitality of black life (Hurston, "How It Feels," 1979, 153). She was less interested in the tragedies of injustice than in the resilience of story, laughter, and song. *Mules and Men* does not offer a simplistic caricature of the happy darky but instead mines the complexities of black folklife.

One of the greatest insights of the book also elucidates part of Hurston's own life. In her struggle to collect material from her subjects, she describes encountering what she terms "feather-bed resistance":

> The Negro, in spite of his open-faced laughter, his seeming acquiescence, is particularly evasive. You see we are a polite people and we do not say to our questioner, "Get out of here!" We smile and tell him or her something that satisfies the white person because, knowing so little about us, he doesn't know what he is missing. The Indian resists curiosity by a stony silence. The Negro offers a feather-bed resistance. That is, we let the probe enter, but it never comes out. It gets smothered under a lot of laughter and pleasantries.
>
> The theory behind our tactics: "The white man is always trying to know into somebody else's business. All right, I'll set something outside the door of my mind for him to play with and handle. He can read my writing but he sho' can't read my mind. I'll put this play toy in his hand, and he will seize it and go away. Then I'll say my say and sing my song." (Hurston 1942, 2–3)

Boas praised Hurston for being able to move past the "feather-bed resistance" of the black communities she studied, but many of her relationships, particularly with white people in positions of power, demonstrate her own deft use of this strategy. Hurston was a master at satisfying whites by at times fulfilling and at other moments upending their desires and expectations. She knew how to appease a patron like Charlotte Mason and make the most of a friend like Fannie Hurst. There is both sincerity and deception at play in "feather-bed resistance," a genuine response to connection but also a reluctance to engage too intimately with a stranger. Kaplan observes that this is a strategy "necessitated by social inequality" (Kaplan 2003, 21). It is a tool of the disempowered to both protect the self and get ahead in a white-dominated world. Hurston's own use of "feather-bed resistance" is marked by a somewhat more aggressive approach. Boyd writes that "by all accounts, Zora Neale Hurston possessed a quality that enabled her to walk into a roomful of strangers and, a few minutes and a few stories later, leave them so completely charmed and so utterly impressed that they sometimes found themselves offering to help her in any way they could" (Boyd 2003, 107–108). Hurston transformed "feather-bed resistance" into a performative posture that enticed patrons, impressed fans, and left much of her inner self safely hidden.

Mules and Men elevated Hurston into a nationally recognized expert on African American culture. Her old friend Fannie Hurst asked her for a signed photograph and penned a recommendation for Hurston's second Guggenheim application. This time, she landed the fellowship. She proposed to study obeah practices in the Caribbean, the very project she had hoped to complete with Rosenwald funding but without the constraints of coursework. Her successful Guggenheim application reveals what may have been her fundamental ambition in pursuing graduate work to begin with: to search for the Moses legend in Caribbean folklore. She planned on writing a novel centered on a black folk hero based upon the biblical prophet. Hurston sought to use her intimate knowledge of black folk culture to inform her fictional work, sharply departing from the scientific approach of Boas and other anthropologists. She had at last found a way to marry her two primary passions and elevate her own unique artistic vision. This focus departed from her previous enthusiasm to develop a robust black theater, which she understood as central to the black experience. As she explained in "Characteristics of Negro Expression," there is one thing "that permeates [the Negro's] entire self. And that thing is drama" (Hurston 2014, 1050). While Hurston remained committed to the joys of the theater, publishing two well-received books demonstrated the power and influence of the written word. No longer beholden to the often-divergent opinions of a cast production, Hurston was at last free to craft her art as she saw fit.

In March 1936, Hurston was notified that she had been awarded a one-year $2,000 grant to study magic practices in the West Indies. She immediately quit her job at the Federal Theater Project and prepared for her departure. After receiving a clean bill of health, Hurston at last ended her relationship with Punter. She knew that "this was my chance to release him, and fight myself free from my obsession" (Hurston 1942, 210). She refused to write to him, knowing that if he answered, her conviction would waver. Though Hurston agonized over the end of their relationship, Punter later reported that he could not compete with her dedication to her work. He never saw her doubt her decision.

Hurston arrived in Port-au-Prince in April and soon sent a postcard to Carl Van Vechten, affirming that she was eager to move on from Punter: "Weather fine, men plentiful" (Kaplan 2003, 371, letter from Hurston to Van Vechten in 1936). She soon moved on to Jamaica, where she confirmed that the Guggenheim Foundation had indeed sent her funding through the Barclays Bank in Kingston. Her arrival caught the attention of a local newspaper, the *Daily Gleaner*, which featured an article on her entitled "U.S. Woman on Hoodoo Hunt in Jamaica." She appeared in a photograph wearing jodhpurs and riding boots, ready to explore the back country.

From Kingston, Hurston headed to St. Andrew's and St. Mary's parishes. The people in Jamaica proved to be highly class and color conscious. Hurston noted that "the upper class, these 'coloured people' who have white blood in them . . . feel like suing you if you call them Negroes" (Kaplan 2003, 376–377, letter from Hurston to Henry Allen Moe in 1936). Hurston was dismayed by such blatant colorism and what she perceived as "a frantic stampede white-ward to escape from Jamaica's black mass" (Hurston 1938, 6). Such inclinations were anathema to the daughter of Eatonville. She was also disappointed by the rampant misogyny she encountered in Jamaica. In *Tell My Horse* (1938), her account of voodoo and other cultural practices in Haiti and Jamaica, Hurston describes a man who bemoaned the waste of American women who "were destroyed by their brains." He concluded, "Being a woman is the only thing that you can do with any real genius and you refuse to do that" (Hurston 1938, 16). Adopting a detached, scientific stance, Hurston argued with the man but was unable to sway him. The man was useful, however, in directing her to an unusual practice on the island. He described female specialists who instructed new brides or the future mistresses of wealthy men in the arts of sexual pleasure. Hurston was able to shadow one of these practitioners for two weeks, learning how "to bring complete innocence and complete competence together in the same girl" (Hurston 1938, 18). Before the young women are given to their husbands or patrons, they are told "You are made for love and comfort. Think of yourself in that way and no other" (Hurston 1938, 20).

Hurston was glad to be an outsider to this world. She recognized that to be a woman in the United States was a thing apart from being a woman in the Caribbean, where men assumed that female bodies were made for their pleasure. She further noted the complications caused by class and color.

While wealth could improve a woman's prospects, to be "poor and black" was to be "in a bad way indeed in that man's world. She had better pray to the Lord to turn her into a donkey and be done with the thing" (Hurston 1938, 58). As a visiting American, however, Hurston escaped such designations. She was honored with a curry goat feast prepared by moonlight, a tribute usually reserved for a man. She also participated in a variety of sacred rituals, including "Nine Night" ceremonies, which celebrate the dead while also casting them away from the world of the living.

A highlight of her time in Jamaica was her stay with a self-governing Maroon group in Accompong. The Maroons were descended from fierce fighters who'd escaped the shackles of slavery and set up communities in the remote mountain regions. Hurston had to climb most of the way to the highest peaks of St. Catherine herself because the mule that had been sent to carry her refused to cooperate. Although initially disappointed to discover that a student of noted anthropologist Melville Herskovits was already stationed with the Accompong Maroons, Hurston soon found a way to gather especially distinctive material. She began working with Medicine Man, the Maroons' conjure doctor. He awed her by commanding countless chirping frogs to silence and then instructing her in the value of various plants. Hurston also participated in a three-day-long hunt for a wild boar that produced the delicious jerk pork she had come to love.

Maroon Groups

Maroon groups were formed by fugitive slaves who escaped their masters along with other individuals who were born free. These communities varied significantly in their general stability and social practices. Some were largely composed of wandering men who were able to survive by raiding. Others included men and women and were stable enough to plant their own crops and develop trading partnerships with other groups. Maroon communities thrived more in the colonial period than in the nineteenth century. As the United States developed as a nation, laws became more restrictive, plantations more strict, and the vast uninhabited space of the country was soon claimed by white settlers. This made escape more perilous for enslaved people. Maroon communities often mixed with Native American tribes, creating creole cultural practices. In Cuba and Puerto Rico, the strongest Maroon groups were located in mountainous regions that offered protection from outsiders. The Jamaican Maroons were so fierce in their opposition to British rule that they signed treaties in the mid-eighteenth century that secured their freedom almost a century before the 1833 Slavery Abolition Act. The Black Seminoles of Florida are among the most successful Maroon groups in the United States.

Hurston left Jamaica in late September, noting that the Maroons were themselves worth an entire year of study. She concluded that "Jamaica is a seething Africa under its British exterior" (Kaplan 2003, 379, letter from Hurston to Moe in 1936). From Kingston, Hurston returned to Haiti for an additional six months of study. Less than a month after her arrival in Port-au-Prince, Hurston wrote to Henry Allen Moe of the Guggenheim Foundation to ask if she could apply for a second fellowship to continue her work there. Overwhelmed by the history and culture of the island, she guessed that she already had material for two books: "There is so much to write about in these waters," she explained, adding, "I have grown in every direction in these six months" (Kaplan 2003, 387, letter from Hurston to Moe in 1936).

While most of Hurston's time in Jamaica had been spent traveling through all of the country's parishes, in Haiti, Hurston rented a house in the suburbs of the capital. She hired an attentive maid named Lucille, worked on her Creole, and focused on educating herself in local hoodoo practices. She was especially interested in zombies and claimed that she had evidence of "eight authentic cases" (Kaplan 2003, 389, letter from Hurston to Moe in 1937). By January, she wrote to Moe with details on two books, one to be entitled *Bush*, which would explore life in both Haiti and Jamaica. She included a detailed outline of *Tell My Horse*, which would address the "Nine Night" ceremony and the pre-wedding preparations for young women and include a discussion of Haitian gods and zombies. In addition to these ambitious plans that she described to Moe, Hurston also found inspiration for a new novel. Now settled in a comfortable house in Haiti, she at last confronted her lingering feelings for Punter. However, rather than reach out to him, she channeled her emotions into her writing. She later explained that "the plot was far from the circumstances, but I tried to embalm all the tenderness of my passion for him in *Their Eyes Were Watching God*" (Hurston 1942, 211). She completed the book in seven weeks.

Hurston sent her new manuscript to her publisher on December 19, 1936. As if to distract herself from this startling accomplishment, she quickly headed to La Gonave, a satellite island off the coast of Port-au-Prince. The beautiful island was said to have the shape of a goddess riding a whale. There, Hurston enjoyed the holidays in the company of the island's chief of police and learned various folk games. As the new year dawned, Hurston came to recognize that voodoo encompassed far more than she'd anticipated. She would need more time to understand and write about this network of beliefs, gods, and practices, noting, "It is like explaining the planetary theory on a postage stamp" (Kaplan 2003, 391, letter from Hurston to Moe in 1937). She realized, "It is more than the sympathetic magic that is practiced by the hoodoo doctors in the United States. It is as formal as the Catholic church anywhere" (Kaplan 2003, 390, letter from Hurston to Moe in 1937). In a letter to Moe, she acknowledged that her exploration of voodoo practices had affected her own beliefs, though she had not become a convert. What was most clear to Hurston was the need to spend more time understanding the range and depth of voodoo.

After her time in La Gonave, Hurston traveled to Archahaie, a central site of Haitian voodoo practice and home to Dieu Donnez St. Leger, an especially well-respected voodoo priest. Hurston studied with Donnez for the remainder of her time in Haiti. Under his tutelage, she learned the songs and dances of various ceremonies. She also observed him leading sacred rituals, including one in which he raised the dead. Following a sacrifice of pigeons and chickens, Hurston witnessed a dead man sit up and open his eyes. The deceased was another priest, and Donnez successfully transferred his power to another. Because of the fascinating spectacles she witnessed there, when Hurston's funding ran out in March, she lamented not spending all of her year abroad in Haiti, though she hardly regretted her travels through Jamaica.

Hurston returned to New York and the news that Lippincott was preparing *Their Eyes Were Watching God* for publication in the fall. He was so pleased with the manuscript that there was no need to revise it significantly. Though delighted with this news, Hurston was most concerned with finding a way to continue her research in Haiti. In March, she learned that the Guggenheim Foundation had renewed her fellowship. Despite her eagerness to return, she had to wait until May to begin her travels due to a delay with her passport. On the twenty-third, she boarded a Panama steamer to Port-au-Prince, enjoying a spacious cabin and delicious food along the way. Initially met with seasonal monsoons, Hurston soon continued her earlier studies of voodoo practices. She underwent the first ceremony to become consecrated for the priesthood and was preparing for the next stage of initiation when she began receiving warnings to temper her curiosity. At one point, Lucille, her maid, warned her about consulting with priests she did not know well. There were some who practiced harmful magic that led to the creation of zombies. Fascinated by the prospect of reanimating the dead, Hurston even went so far as to photograph a woman at a hospital who had been given a drug to simulate the effects of death; the woman was rendered a kind of zombie, unable to speak or act independently but able to work in the fields. A Haitian doctor explained that if Hurston discovered the secret to the undead, she would indeed make a significant contribution to science, but questioned at what price: "Perhaps it will cost you more than you are willing to pay, perhaps things will be required of you that you cannot stand. Suppose you were forced to—could you endure to see a human being killed?" (Hurston 1938, 205).

Moved by the doctor's considerations, Hurston ceased her investigations into zombies, though she continued with her research in other ways.

However, her work was put on hold in June, when she suddenly became sick. She wrote to Moe in dramatic capitalization, "I HAVE HAD A VIOLENT GASTRIC DISTURBANCE" (Kaplan 2003, 403, letter from Hurston to Moe in 1937). For two weeks she lay in bed before finally managing to travel to Port-au-Prince, where she withdrew enough money to return to the United States. She intended to drop the money off at the consul, but he was so struck by her weak condition that he took her into his own home. By the time she wrote to Moe, she was already on the road to recovery and planning to finish her writing back in the United States. However, Hurston extended her stay in Haiti through September so that she could stay for "something big" on the eighteenth (Kaplan 2003, 403, letter from Hurston to Moe in 1937). Though she never clarified what had induced her to miss the launch of *Their Eyes Were Watching God* on the sixteenth, it must have been spectacular.

By the time Hurston returned to New York, her new book was the talk of the critics. *The New York Times* and the *New York Herald Tribune* printed glowing reviews. Writing for the *Times*, Lucille Tomkins called it a "well nigh perfect story," concluding, "It is about Negroes, and a good deal of it is written in dialect, but really it is about everyone, at least every one who isn't so civilized that he has lost the capacity for glory" (Tomkins 1937). The most obvious innovation of *Their Eyes Were Watching God* is Hurston's integration of various forms of English. On Joe Starks's front porch, Eatonville townspeople debate one another in black vernacular, staging philosophical discussions in richly metaphorical language. The third-person narrator presents Janie's story in tones that draw from the King James Bible and romantic poetry. The result is a stunning amalgamation of prose that affirms the diversity of American English.

Their Eyes Were Watching God is Hurston's masterpiece, a searching rumination on one woman's path to fulfillment and joy. Though raised by her grandmother Nanny, an ex-slave who warns against wanting and dreaming too much, Janie Crawford escapes such curtailed expectations to find happiness and pleasure. Because Nanny works for a white family, Janie grows up surrounded by white children. She only realizes she is black when she sees a photograph of herself among the others. This recognition of her racial identity is met with neither sadness nor joy; instead, it signals Janie's limited self-conception and understanding of the wider world. It is simply a point of departure for a much broader perspective on herself and others.

Because of Janie's youth and inexperience, Nanny seeks to control her granddaughter's life and secure a stable future for her. By contrast, Janie is hungry for love, beauty, and pleasure. One of the most potent images of the text involves a blossoming pear tree. Janie often sits beneath the tree, marveling at nature's fertile images: "It had called her to come and gaze on a mystery. From barren brown stems to glistening leaf-buds; from the leaf-buds to snowy virginity of bloom. It stirred her tremendously.... The rose of the world was breathing out smell. It followed her through all her waking moments and caressed her in her sleep" (Hurston 1937, 10). Beneath the pear tree, she comes to recognize her budding sexuality and kisses a local boy. Nanny spies her granddaughter in the act and warns her that in this world, white men have all the power while "de nigger woman is de mule uh de world so fur as Ah can see" (Hurston 1937, 14). More in sadness than in anger, she marries Janie off to Logan Killicks, a middle-aged farmer. After a few months, Janie realizes that she will never love her strict, hardworking husband: "She knew now that marriage did not make love. Janie's first dream was dead, so she became a woman" (Hurston 1937, 24). Such comments are typical of the novel's rich, insightful language, which charts how Janie not only becomes a woman but loves and thrives on her own.

Hurston's exploration of the different ways men and women navigate the world is one of the hallmarks of the text. Janie's journey to self-discovery is largely premised upon her growing confidence to shape life according to her dreams. Hurston begins the novel with a now-canonical meditation on how men and women approach the world:

> Ships at a distance have every man's wish on board. For some they come in with the tide. For others they sail forever on the horizon, never out of sight, never landing until the Watcher turns his eyes away in resignation, his dreams mocked to death by Time. That is the life of men.
>
> Now, women forget all those things they don't want to remember, and remember everything they don't want to forget. The dream is the truth. Then they act and do things accordingly. (Hurston 1937, 1)

Although Janie is not a simplistic stand-in for her creator, much of Hurston's own life vision permeates the text. She was a woman who lived true to her dreams, forgetting what she did not want to remember and remembering what she did not want to forget. In that selective vision of her own life, we find the truth of Hurston.

Janie soon abandons Logan after she meets Joe Starks, a wandering dreamer with big plans. He steals Janie away to Eatonville, which is ripe for Joe's grand ambitions. He soon buys two hundred acres of land, builds a store and post office, and assembles a town meeting. Before long, he is named mayor of the town and awes the townspeople with a ceremony to commemorate the lighting of Eatonville's first streetlamp. Although Janie is impressed by his gumption, Joe does not provide the love and passion she seeks. He insists that she refrains from participating in the often-raucous talk on the store's front porch, and as he ages, he begins demeaning her in front of others. When she finally responds to his derision with a sharp retort, Janie demonstrates to the townspeople how quick and eloquent she can be. Soon after this exchange, Joe dies and Janie becomes a wealthy widow.

Still attractive and eager to explore life's possibilities, Janie meets Tea Cake, a charming young laborer who woos her with sweet talk and humor. They quickly marry and enjoy a partnership in which they laugh and play together. He encourages her to be free and to savor all of life's pleasures with him. With the townspeople scandalized by their union, the two lovers leave Eatonville. They join seasonal workers picking beans together in the field or "the muck" and delight in the games, dance, and storytelling of the community. Where Janie was silenced by Joe in his store, in the home she shares with Tea Cake, she becomes a vital and vocal partner. Although their relationship is not perfect and they struggle through Tea Cake's desire to assert his masculine power, they remain united by a deep passion. As June Jordan declared, Janie and Tea Cake's relationship makes *Their Eyes Were Watching God* "the most successful, convincing, and exemplary novel of Blacklove that we have. Period" (Jordan 1974, 6).

Ultimately, only Mother Nature poses a challenge to their love. A devastating hurricane sweeps through the camp, scattering their friends and destroying their community. They flee to escape the rising waters. While fighting off a rabid dog that was threatening Janie, Tea Cake is bitten by the animal. He soon falls into a paranoid madness, turning upon his wife in his deluded state with accusations of infidelity. He attempts to kill Janie, and in self-defense, she shoots him dead. She is put on trial by a jury of white men and is acquitted. After these travails, Janie returns to Eatonville, where her neighbors assume that Tea Cake has run off with all her money. Her friend Pheoby Watson visits Janie to discover the truth, and the book concludes with Janie passing on her story. Though she has lost Tea Cake, she returns triumphant, having experienced a life of passion and joy. She encourages Pheoby to embrace her own life: "It's uh known fact, Pheoby, you got tuh go there to know there. Yo' papa and yo' mama and nobody else can't tell yuh and show yuh. Two things everybody's got tuh do fuh theyselves. They got tuh go tuh God, and they gut tuh find out about livin' fuh theyselves" (Hurston 1937, 192).

While Hurston drew from her affair with Punter to describe Janie's relationship to Tea Cake, the book is clearly fiction. This use of real life to create art mimics Hurston's reliance on her deep understanding of folklore to portray the town of Eatonville and the work camp where Janie and Tea Cake live. *Their Eyes Were Watching God* combines all of Hurston's talents and knowledge while reflecting the wisdom of a lifetime. At the time of its publication, there was no book comparable to its depiction of black life or its bold affirmation of female experience. While it is easy to label the text feminist, just as Hurston was wary of racial markers, she likely would have pushed back against any simplistic categorization. The book explores how a woman claims her own voice, even as it takes seriously its male characters in all their ambitions and failures. Hurston did not shy away from depicting sexism, and it is worth noting that though Tea Cake adores Janie, he also operates under troubling assumptions about how men and women should act. In one passage, he physically abuses her to show everyone at the work camp that he is in control. While the novel hardly condones this behavior, Janie does not challenge Tea Cake's actions. Hurston allows readers to think through the insecurity that underlies this beating as well as the troubling love that causes Janie to endure such violence. It is also fruitful to read this scene against Janie's eventual murder of Tea Cake. She concludes by asserting ultimate physical authority over him. Hurston presents us with complex characters who are not defined by single acts but evolve throughout the novel.

Although there is much to admire in this bold, innovative book, Richard Wright, three years from publishing his monumental *Native Son* (1940), worried in the pages of *New Masses* that *Their Eyes Were Watching God* confirmed base stereotypes of African Americans and failed to address the discrimination and injustice faced by blacks in the South. Although *Their Eyes Were Watching God* does depict examples of black workers subject to ruthless white authorities—after the hurricane, Tea Cake and others are forced at gunpoint to bury the dead—Wright bemoaned the absence of an explicit critique of America's rampant racism and classism. He had already outlined in "Blueprint for Negro Writing" his belief that black writing must be an agent for political change. Moreover, although he recognized that Hurston could write well, he found her writing too beholden to stereotype to stake out a new frontier of African American literary expression: "Her prose is cloaked in that facile sensuality that has dogged Negro expression since the days of Phillis Wheatley." He concluded, "The sensory sweet of her novel carries no theme, no message, no thought" (Wright 1937). Wright's perspective has not withstood the passage of time. Though *Their Eyes Were Watching God* is not in line with the kind of protest fiction he advocated, it demonstrates a deep awareness of black subjugation. Hurston chose not to make oppression the focus of her novel. Instead, she depicts black people primarily confronting one another—in love and competition, in frustration and hope. The result is a book that does not cater to white readers and their expectations, but instead places black agency and self-sufficiency at the center of its artistic vision.

Their Eyes Were Watching God opened numerous doors for Hurston. Soon after its publication, she was invited to write a profile on Fannie Hurst for the *Saturday Review of Literature*. Hurston appeared in the new edition of *Who's Who in America* and was interviewed for a piece in *The New York World-Telegram*. She also received congratulations on her novel from award-winning poet Edna St. Vincent Millay. With the rest of her Guggenheim funds, Hurston found an apartment in Jamaica, Queens, where she promoted *Their Eyes Were Watching God* and began work on her book documenting her Caribbean travels. She resisted the temptation to call Punter, focusing instead on events like the Boston and New York book fairs. Though she hoped to stage a folk concert using material she'd gathered in Jamaica and Haiti, she conceded to the pressures of her publishers, who urged her to finish the manuscript that would become *Tell My Horse*.

In January 1938, the overwhelming critical praise she received for *Their Eyes Were Watching God* was sharply curtailed by an essay in *Opportunity*. Alain Locke customarily assessed the previous year's output of black literature, and in his survey of 1937, he paid special attention to Hurston's novel. Though he commended her "gift for poetic phrase, for rare dialect, and folk humor," he found the book wanting. Her descriptions remained on "the surface of her community and her characters," failing to dive "deep either to the inner psychology of characterization or to sharp analysis of the social background." He asked when "the Negro novelist of maturity," implying that Hurston was not such a writer, would "come to grips with motive fiction and social document fiction" (Locke 2014). Although Wright's review of *Their Eyes Were Watching God* was certainly harsher, Locke had been Hurston's former professor and longtime mentor, if not exactly friend. Moreover, while Wright had yet to break through into mainstream literary circles, Locke remained a trusted voice of the African American intelligentsia.

Hurston responded by sending an angry screed to *Opportunity* entitled "The Chick with One Hen." The magazine editors declined to publish the one-and-a-half-page essay, no doubt because its caustic tone would have scandalized its readers. Hurston calls Locke's review "an example of rank dishonesty" and a "conscious fraud." She claims he knows "nothing about Negroes" and "nothing about either criticism or editing." After stating that he "has not produced one single idea, or suggestion of an idea that he can call his own," she explains that his critique of *Their Eyes Were Watching God* is based in her refusal to write like Sterling Brown, the only "chick" left to this mother "hen." Hurston closes the essay with the promise: "I will send my toe-nails to debate him on what he knows about Negroes and Negro life, and I will come personally to debate him on what he knows about literature on the subject. This one who lives by quotations trying to criticize people who live by life!!" (Hurston 1938).

Hurston shared her opinion of Locke with friends and colleagues including James Weldon Johnson. She wrote to him, "And if you will admit the truth you know that Alain Leroy Locke is a malicious, spiteful little snot that thinks he ought to be the leading Negro because of his degrees. Foiled in that, he spends his time trying to cut the ground from under everybody else" (Kaplan 2003, 413, letter from Hurston to Johnson in 1938). Hurston wrote to Johnson from Eatonville, where she had returned to complete her manuscript on Haiti and Jamaica. In leaving New York, Hurston also left the debates on black literature that were so pressing to people like Locke. The "social document fiction" he asked of African American writers was soon to be exemplified by the work of Richard Wright. Challenging Wright's conviction that black writers "must have in their consciousness the foreshortened picture of the whole, nourishing culture from which they were torn in Africa, and of the long, complex (and for the most part, unconscious) struggle to regain in some form and under alien conditions of life a *whole* culture again," Hurston penned the 1938 essay "Art and Such" for the Florida Federal Writers' Project (Wright 1937, 131). She begins by chronicling the history of race leaders after slavery and into Reconstruction, noting that white educated elites present themselves as authorities on the black population, often without having any meaningful connection to them. These race leaders, she explains, focus on "race problems," lamenting various social ills rather than embracing the freedom to write about whatever they like. Rather than sing of sorrows, she argues, black writers should "sing a song to the morning." She refuses the precondition that "the one subject for a Negro is the Race and its sufferings and so the song of the morning must be choked back" and wryly adds, "I will write of a lynching instead." Hurston was adamant in defying the race leaders who insisted on returning to the "same old theme" and "same old phrases," championing instead her choice to celebrate the originality, resilience, and beauty of black folklife (Hurston 1999, 142).

In Eatonville, Hurston lived in a rented former jook joint and tried to capture her experiences in Jamaica and Haiti on the page. This was especially challenging because she believed that she had material for as many as three books, but her publisher insisted that she turn in only one. At last, on March 26, she sent a manuscript to Lippincott, and the book was slated for an October publication date. Soon after, the *Saturday Review* invited her to review Richard Wright's collection of short stories, *Uncle Tom's Children* (1938), which had won an award sponsored by *Story* magazine. Much like Wright had done in his review of *Their Eyes Were Watching God*, Hurston had to admit that Wright was a skilled writer, though she found his grasp of dialect notably wanting. However, she most bemoaned that his talents were not directed on something beyond "the spectacular." In this "book about hatreds," Hurston observed, "all the characters . . . are elemental and brutish" (Hurston 1938). Violence, rather than understanding and sympathy, pervades the book and signals a hopelessness in Wright's vision of the South. Despite Hurston's forceful opinion, Wright would soon become the most famous and influential African American writer of his generation. The same year *Uncle Tom's Children* was published, *Time* magazine identified him as the most promising black novelist to ever write. Decades later, however, both Wright and Hurston are considered pillars of the African American literary canon.

8

Wanderings and Fame

In April, Hurston's Guggenheim fellowship was nearly at its end and with it her primary source of income. To support herself, she accepted a job with the Federal Writers' Project gathering information for *The Florida Negro*, an account of local black life. Working for $63 a month, Hurston was to collect material on black cultural practices. Some scholars claim that Hurston was embarrassed by her work at the FWP because it was a form of government relief. Her letters are unusually reticent on the subject, as if she did not want to disclose the full nature of her position to her family and friends. However, her reluctance to discuss her position at the FWP may also have derived from the mistreatment she suffered there. The office was segregated, and black staff were not allowed to attend editorial conferences. They also had to turn their time sheets in to an office located in a black section of Jacksonville. Carita Dogget Corse, the FWP director, however, made allowances for Hurston due to her literary success and celebrity. She invited Hurston to the Jacksonville office, where she impressed the staff with her glamour and New York stories. However, one junior interviewer noted the incongruity of a published novelist working for such a meager salary. Hurston was certainly qualified to be the editor for the entire project, but instead, she made less money that the typist.

Corse was impressed by Hurston, who took her to a church service in the black community. Soon, Hurston had the entire congregation on their feet and clapping. People even began rolling on the floor. Corse worried that things were getting out of control and she asked to leave. Due in part to that encounter, Corse found Hurston to be vibrant but at times difficult to manage. Hurston sometimes disappeared without telling her supervisor where she was going or when she would return. In one case, she went to Washington, D.C., to coordinate a group of performers called the "Chanters" for the National Folk Festival. They began by performing at the Winter Park Women's Club, raising enough money to pay for their three-day trip. In Washington, Hurston also met the Federal Writers' Project national director, Henry Alsberg. Charmed by the charismatic writer, Alsberg asked Corse to give Hurston a raise and put her in charge of Florida's Negro Unit. Pamela Bordelon writes that "Alsberg's liberal recommendation that Hurston be made an editor sent shock waves through Florida's WPA organization, which controlled the state FWP's employment and finances. In the Southern scheme of things, blacks were not given supervisory positions, even if they were more capable or better suited" (Bordelon 1999, 16). Corse was reluctant to pay Hurston a higher wage than some of her white coworkers. Instead, she offered Hurston a travel allowance of $75 and the paltry title of "Negro editor," which came with no benefits. Hurston fully recognized the insult of this treatment and referred to herself as Corse's "pet darkey" (Kaplan 2003, 418, letter from Hurston to Carita Corse in 1938). Though she was often mentioned to the national office, she did not even have a desk in any of the FWP offices. Despite this racist treatment, Hurston collected her monthly salary and used her free time to write. She preferred writing in her backyard and sometimes moved a card table outside to spend the day working on a novel about Moses.

Stetson Kennedy, Hurston's supervisor at the Florida FWP, recalls how Hurston's strengths as a writer made for an uneasy fit with the mandate of the program's mission: "There we editors were doing our very best to see to it that everything that went into the *Guide* was couched not only in staid Federalese but also in the specific guidebook jargon set forth in the FWP *Style Manual*; and there was Zora, turning in these veritable prose poems of African eloquence and imagery!" (Kennedy 1991, 65). Although all of Hurston's contributions were cut from the final edition of *The Florida Negro*, in 1999, Pamela Bordelon collected and edited Hurston's writings for the FWP in *Go Gator and Muddy the Water: Writings by Zora Neale Hurston from the Federal Writers' Project*. Hurston's influence over the entire project was also felt when she traveled to Washington, D.C., to discuss the work with Sterling Brown, who was then acting as a national director for Negro affairs for the FWP, and W. E. B. Du Bois, who was a consultant on the project. They fought over Hurston's description of the 1920 white mob attack that left as many as sixty African Americans dead and transformed Ocoee, Florida, into an all-white town. In defending her muted description of the event, Hurston reportedly claimed to have been an eyewitness to the massacre (Kennedy 1991).

In June of 1938, Hurston traveled to New York to attend the funeral of James Weldon Johnson, one of her longtime correspondents and friends. The year before, she'd written an essay about him called "My People, My People!," which lightly teased that he was so solemn and beneficent as to be a kind of royalty: "If some day I looked out of my window on Seventh Avenue and saw him in an ermine robe and a great procession going to the Cathedral of St. John the Divine to be crowned I wouldn't be a bit surprised. Maybe he'd make a mighty fine king at that" (Hurston 1942, 238). Over 2,500 people gathered to pay their respects to Johnson at Salem Methodist Episcopal Church, including Langston Hughes and Carl Van Vechten.

When Hurston returned to Eatonville, Winifred, the daughter of her brother Bob, came to live with her. Winifred's older sister, Wilhelmina, had moved to Eatonville earlier and had lived with Hurston before getting married to an orange picker and moving into her own place. Wilhelmina often wrote to Winifred describing the happy times she'd spent with her aunt. When Winifred came to live with Hurston, she found a job at a nursing home and regularly enjoyed her aunt's cooking. She remembered that her aunt frequently wore overalls, especially when she was working at home, but could also dress quite fashionably to go out.

JAMES WELDON JOHNSON

James Weldon Johnson was one of the most influential African American figures of the early twentieth century. An author, lawyer, educator, and civil rights activist, he was an early leader of the NAACP. In 1920, he became the first African American executive secretary of the organization, staying in that position for a whole decade. A poet, novelist, and editor of black spirituals, Johnson was also gifted musically and wrote the song "Lift Every Voice and Sing," which became known as the "Negro National Anthem." His anonymously published novel, *The Autobiography of an Ex-Colored Man* (1912), remains a classic among passing narratives—that is, books that explore the experience of people with African ancestry presenting themselves as white in social life. Johnson also edited *The Book of American Negro Poetry* (1922), which helped organize and define the nature of African American poetic expression. Like Hurston, Johnson was deeply invested in the study of black folklife. His book of poetry, *God's Trombones* (1927), reflects a trip he took to rural Georgia while he was a freshman at Atlanta University. Johnson was deeply shaped by this experience as well as by three months he spent as a young man teaching the descendants of former slaves. Johnson's diverse artistic and social contributions were united by a fierce commitment to African American education at all levels.

Hurston continued working for the FWP, though her communication with the state office was often erratic. But her absences were often followed by the delivery of wonderful songs, stories, and legends that wowed her coworkers. As one interviewer recalled, "We did not care, how, where, or when Zora had come by them—each and every one was priceless, and we hastened to sprinkle them through the *Florida Guide* manuscript for flavoring" (Boyd 2003, 318). Hurston wrote a number of essays specifically for *The Florida Negro*. "The Sanctified Church" describes forms of black worship and notes their effect on American music. Though Hurston hoped that "Art and Such" would be included in *The Florida Negro*, her opinionated stance on the state of black letters proved too controversial for the editors. "Go Gator and Muddy the Water" summarized her basic understanding of folklore and its importance, calling it "the boiled-down juice of human living" (Hurston 1999, 69). Other essays described games played by African American children as well as an account of "Negro Mythical Places," which include "Diddy-Wah-Diddy," a heaven of no work and abundant good food, and "Beluthahatchee," where "all unpleasant doings and sayings are forgotten" (Hurston 1999, 108). The extensive cutting that Hurston's work received by the volume's white editors may be explained by her refusal to pander to racist stereotypes, something that other staff writers indulged.

In October, Hurston returned to New York for the publication of *Tell My Horse*. The title comes from the phrase used by the god Guede when he first spoke. Because Guede was invisible, he spoke through the person that he had mounted as a person mounts a horse. The god would then act through his person or horse. The phrase was also adopted by poor Haitians as a preface to expressing frustrations or resentments toward the upper class. "Tell my horse" was a way of speaking with courage what could not be said without the support or excuse of a god. By choosing this phrase as the title of her book, Hurston affirmed her desire to speak without fear about what she had learned in Haiti and Jamaica. Despite this call to brave revelation, Hurston does not always clarify the details of certain voodoo practices and her chapter on zombies is constrained by her hesitation to learn too much about their origin.

Tell My Horse lacks the narrative coherency of *Mules and Men*. Where the earlier book on American black folklife presents Hurston as a character—initially stumbling in her attempt to connect with the people she meets and at last finding ways to gain their trust—this book is more episodic. It unites essays on various topics based on her experiences in Haiti and Jamaica but lacks an overarching organizational structure. *Mules and Men* took years to write. By contrast, *Tell My Horse* was rushed to press, though it contains far more material. Hurston conceded that the book was not and could not be comprehensive of voodoo, but it never clearly states what it specifically contributes to a broader understanding of the religion or its spiritual beliefs. Reviewers praised its fascinating subject matter and Hurston's obvious passion for the material but repeatedly noted that it was not well structured. Sales for the book were weak, though it sold very well in England under the title *Voodoo Gods: An Inquiry into Native Myths and Magic in Jamaica and Haiti*.

By December, Hurston was back in Florida, again working for the FWP. Corse found a task that was an ideal fit with Hurston's previous work for the stage: producing a theatrical rendition of Florida folklore. Hurston taught a group of black teenagers to perform the Fire Dance and other hits from her earlier folk concerts. She wrote the script for the production, which was shown twice at the WPA's National Exhibition of Skills in Orlando in the early months of 1939. Corse was delighted with the results, as was the predominantly white audience.

This success was followed by an invitation from the FWP to take part in a recording expedition throughout the state. Staff members were to use an audio recording machine to gather songs and stories from a broad range of populations, including Bahamians, Haitians, Latinos, and Greeks. Hurston was pleased to take part in this project, especially since her salary increased to just under eighty dollars per month. One of the first turpentine camps she visited was in White Springs. Operated by the Bullard family, it housed around eighty black families who lived in clapboard cottages with no windows or electricity. The family matriarch, Mary Bullard, settled Hurston into a large farmhouse nearby while she retired to a massive nineteenth-century home that included eight working fireplaces. Bullard was so amused by Hurston's intelligence and quick laughter that upon her departure, she gave the writer a deep red velvet toque that included a stylish ostrich plume.

Hurston also traveled to Cross City, a small town in northwestern Florida that was home to the Aycock and Lindsay Company, which was run by the gun-wielding Catherine Lindsay, best known as "Miss Catherine." The over-three hundred turpentine workers toiled under conditions that approximated chattel slavery. Hurston found subjects to be interviewed for the WPA's life-history program. The workers trusted her with more than just their folk stories and songs. They also told her about the physical and sexual abuse they suffered by the camp bosses. Anyone who dared to put up a fight was sunk with cement in the Gulf of Mexico. Hurston was troubled by these stories but was uncertain how to help the workers. She was reluctant to detail these abuses in full in her notes to the FWP home office but did include a number of disturbing descriptions of overworked individuals. Soon, white interviewers also heard of the problems, though addressing such issues was far beyond the scope of their official mission.

Hurston eventually left without affecting the situation in any meaningful way. However, her experiences left a deep impression, and she wrote an essay for the FWP called "Turpentine," which describes the experiences of John McFarlin, a turpentine woods rider.

Upon her return to Jacksonville in June, Hurston helped gather a group of railroad workers, musicians, and churchgoers at the Clara White Mission on Ashley Street to record their songs, stories, and conversations. However, the most notable voice on the recording is that of Hurston, who instructs and encourages the musicians and then sings a variety of songs herself. She also added introductions and comments between selections and answered questions from the white folklorists in attendance. At one point she describes how she came to learn the songs, a technique that speaks to her general approach to understanding and entering new cultural practices:

> I just get in a crowd with the people if they are singing and I listen as best I can. And then I start to joining in with a phrase or two and then finally I get so I can sing a verse, and then I keep on till I learn all the sounds and all the verses. And then I sing them back to the people until they tell me that I can sing 'em just like them. And then I take part and try it out on different people who already know the song, until they are quite satisfied that I know it. Then I carry it in my memory. (Boyd 2003, 324)

That same month Hurston married Albert Price III, who also worked at the WPA but in the education department. He was the twenty-three-year-old son of a distinguished Jacksonville family. His grandfather had cofounded the Afro-American Life Insurance Company, the first black insurance company established in the state of Florida. Hurston wrote her birth year as 1910 on her marriage license to Price, presenting herself as twenty-nine rather than forty-eight. It is not clear where or when Hurston met Price, though he was a member of the Jacksonville church that she had attended with her brother whenever she was in town. As with her previous marriage to Herbert Sheen, Hurston soon felt constrained by her relationship with Price. Her niece Winifred reported that "Aunt Zora doesn't have any business with a husband. She doesn't have time for that. 'Cause she likes to go when she gets ready. She didn't want anyone to tell her 'don't go, don't do,' or something like that. She was a career woman" (Bordelon 1997, 15). Although Price was good-looking, he was still in college and assumed that Hurston would provide for him until he finished his studies. Hurston soon grew impatient with his demands. He wanted her to live at his mother's house. He used her car, often leaving for long periods of time, and he verbally attacked her. Although Price stayed at either his mother's house or Hurston's small home in Jacksonville, he refused to contribute to any household expenses. Valerie Boyd speculates that this hasty marriage may have resulted from Hurston's longing for Percy Punter. Price resembled Punter in superficial ways; both were young and attractive with promising careers ahead. Although Price was more amenable to having Hurston follow her career, if only to support him, he was hardly an ideal mate. Within six weeks, Hurston abandoned her husband, her job, and her home state.

Hurston soon landed in Durham, North Carolina, where in the fall of 1939, she became a faculty member at the North Carolina College for Negroes. She arrived at the invitation of school president Dr. James E. Shepard, who had overseen the college from a small religious school to one of the most sought-after destinations for black students in the nation. Shepard was eager to establish a drama department and looked to Hurston for guidance. She envisioned making black plays about black life in a black style, warning students that cultural elites might frown upon their endeavors. Soon after moving to Durham, Hurston was invited to speak at the University of North Carolina, Chapel Hill, by the Carolina Playmakers, a university drama group. She impressed her all-white audience with her wit and stories, beginning with an encounter she'd had while driving onto campus. A university student yelled "Hi, nigger!" to which Hurston responded, "Hi, freshman!" from her convertible. The Pulitzer Prize–winning playwright and UNC professor Paul Green was so charmed by Hurston that he invited her to join his playwriting seminar. Though UNC did not have black students, the attendees at Green's groups espoused progressive views on race. Only one woman from Alabama argued against having Hurston participate, and rather than have the new star of his seminar undermined, Green asked the resentful student to leave. Hurston presented the group with selections from a comic folk opera she was working on.

In November, her next novel, *Moses, Man of the Mountain* (1939), was slated for publication. She had completed the manuscript while still working for the FWP. Carl Van Vechten enthused that it was the greatest work she had yet produced, and Bertram Lippincott anticipated excellent reviews. Hurston, however, had her doubts, writing to Van Vechten that she "fell far short of my ideal in the writing" (Kaplan 2003, 423, letter from Hurston to Van Vechten in 1939). *Moses, Man of the Mountain* is easily Hurston's most ambitious novel. It retells the story of Moses guiding the Hebrews out of Egypt but transposes it into an African American context. This overlaying of historical narratives imbues the novel with multiple meanings. Hurston draws from a long tradition of incorporating the Moses legend into black experience. The well-known spiritual "Go Down, Moses" as well as the description of Harriet Tubman as the "Moses of her people" attest to the ways in which African Americans have identified with the escape from Pharaoh's servitude.

Hurston had mulled over *Moses, Man of the Mountain* for years. Her interest in the Moses legend had helped guide some of her early work in the Caribbean. She'd discovered that in some regions, Moses is treated as a god and a supreme conjurer. In each iteration of the legend, Moses came to reflect the culture and values of his storytellers. Hurston endows her Moses with the wisdom and vision of the black folk world she adored. Although Moses speaks in the language of Eatonville, Hurston leaves his specific racial origin ambiguous. It is not clear if the Moses of her story is descended from the Hebrew couple Amram and Jochebed or is a descendent of an Egyptian princess and an Assyrian prince, the ruling elite who are presented as white Americans. Through his royal education, Moses comes to a deep appreciation of nature and develops into a skilled military leader. He laments the suffering of the Hebrews and kills an overseer who harshly beats a slave. When his possible Hebrew sister asks to speak with him, Moses is overcome with doubts about his origin. His uncle questions his birthright, and his wife accuses him of rape. Rather than face an attack by his power-hungry relatives, Moses leaves, crossing the Red Sea at a secret point. With this crossing, he leaves his past identity—he is no longer Egyptian, no longer highborn, and no longer beholden to past friends or enemies.

Awed by the disconcerting freedom to make himself anew, Moses decides to dedicate himself to nature. He follows the priest Jethro and marries his daughter Zipporah. For twenty years, he enjoys this peaceful life, mastering the vernacular of the people and surpassing Jethro in his hoodoo skills. He returns to Egypt to read the mysterious *Book of Thoth*, which contains secrets that transform him into a being with divine powers. Jethro then asks him to consider the plight of the Hebrews and apply his new powers to their struggle. Although Moses is initially reluctant to intervene, preferring to meditate and reflect on God on his own, he is persuaded after witnessing the burning bush and hearing the Voice. Moses travels to Egypt and confronts his uncle, the Pharaoh, commanding him to free the Hebrews. Pharaoh initially scoffs at this demand and assumes his priests can vanquish his nephew, but Moses unleashes multiple plagues upon the Egyptians. Pharaoh at last concedes, but as the slaves begin to leave, he directs his soldiers to capture them again. His army is drowned in the Red Sea, while the Hebrews flee to safety. Despite their escape, the Hebrews wander in the wilderness for forty years, haggling over Moses's leadership and eventually losing faith. They ultimately regain God's favor, receive the Ten Commandments, and at last enter the Promised Land.

While Hurston hewed closely to the biblical story of Moses, her novel is filled with sharp commentary on the nature of freedom and the consequences of race. She satirizes self-involved "race leaders" who are more interested in their own status than in the life of the people, and she critiques colorism in the black community. The seriousness of her subject matter is also mitigated by her characteristic humor and vibrant use of dialect. Moses speaks with unadorned insight when he instructs a follower, "When you find a man who has lost his way, you don't make fun of him and scorn him and leave him there. You show him the way. If you don't do that you just prove that you're sort of lost yourself" (Hurston 1939, 162). Although Moses is known as the great liberator, Hurston complicates this formulation by demonstrating all that he has sacrificed to play this role. He is a reluctant leader who would have preferred to lead a quiet life in nature rather than challenge Pharaoh and then contend with his often-querulous people. Hurston concludes less with the triumph of freedom than the ambiguity of Moses's attempt to make a better life for the Hebrews: "He had meant to make a perfect people, free and just, noble and strong, that should be a light for all the world and for time and eternity. And he wasn't sure he had succeeded. . . . He had found out that no man may make another free. Freedom was something internal" (Hurston 1939, 282). Despite his best efforts, Moses's victory is only as strong as his followers' embrace of their own lives. They must take responsibility for their freedom and embody the values they take to be meaningful. He cannot alone lead them to the Promised Land. Instead, they must become the agents of their own lives.

With its allegorical strength and rich complexities, *Moses, Man of the Mountain* received positive if somewhat reserved reviews. Critics from the *Saturday Review of Literature* and *The New York Times* were impressed by its force and vision but seemed somewhat bewildered by its unconventional approach. The most damning responses came from the leading black male writers of the time. Alain Locke called it "caricature instead of portraiture," noting that "black Moses is neither reverent nor epic, two things that I think that any Moses, Hebrew, Negroid or Nordic ought to be," while Ralph Ellison concluded that "for Negro fiction . . . it did nothing" (Locke 1940; Ellison 1941). Hurston's ambivalent Moses clashed with their strident opinions of how black literature should offer models of leadership and resistance. Although Hurston clearly addressed concerns relevant to a contemporary African American audience, she did so within a history and setting far removed from current discussions of the "race problem." *Moses, Man of the Mountain* remains a neglected book in Hurston's oeuvre, one whose ambition and scope reach far beyond a facile description of its subject. With *Their Eyes Were Watching God*, Hurston had leaped to counter critics, but in this case, she remained quiescent, perhaps aware of the novel's limitations. Though she likely disagreed with the specific critiques of Locke and Ellison, she admitted that the novel did not achieve what she had hoped: "I thought that in this book I would achieve my ideal, but it seems that I have not reached it yet but I shall keep trying" (Kaplan 2003, 422, letter from Hurston to Edwin Osgood Grover in 1939).

Far from the gossip of New York's literary circles, Hurston continued to devote herself to her work. North Carolina College President James Shepard hoped that Hurston would live on campus like most unmarried female faculty, but she insisted on finding her own place off campus, in a nearby log cabin. Shepard agreed to this arrangement in part because Hurston promised that some of her New York celebrity friends like Hurst and Van Vechten would soon visit the small college. While visiting in November, Arna Bontemps surmised that Hurston quite simply "had the president hypnotized" by her charm and vision. He recalled, "I remember she took me and introduced me to him. When she came in he started laughing and just settled back, you know, and dropped his cares to listen to Zora as usual" (Bontemps November 1970, interview by Robert E. Hemenway).

While all appeared well in Hurston's professional life, she had to weather the difficulties brought on by filing for divorce from Price. He refuted her accusations of drunkenness and cruelty, arguing that she had seduced him with no regard for his youth. He further claimed that she had a volatile temper and had given him a venereal disease and that he feared the voodoo powers she had mastered in Haiti. In a scathing letter, she returned his ring and expressed her ire over his false allegations:

> Here is my ring. By putting it into your hands, I hope this makes it unnecessary for you to come to see me for any reason what so ever. In fact, it is my earnest prayer that I never see you again, unless you are dead. If you will only be decent enough to die, I will buy me a red dress, send myself some flowers of congratulations, and come to your funeral. (Hurston 1942, letter to Albert Price)

In her divorce suit, Hurston described herself as "meek and humble," a woman who was "easy to be imposed upon" and never used "obscene language" (Kaplan 2003, 431). Such a self-portrait is laughable to anyone even remotely acquainted with Hurston, but Price's claim that he was vulnerable due to his youth is equally absurd. Despite the angry exchange documented in court records, Hurston was at last granted her petition to divorce.

In Durham, Hurston soon found another love interest. She wrote somewhat coyly to a friend, "Well, to tell you the truth, I am a little 'tetched' with love myself, though it has not gone beyond the palpitating stage. No commitments as yet. He has a magnificent bass voice. I am trying to find out if that is what I am stuck on or if it is the man himself. I do like strong, big wrassly men and he seems to fit the bill in many ways" (Kaplan 2003, 454, letter from Hurston to Jane Belo in 1940). Hurston might have added that a key trait she found appealing in men was youth. This unnamed interest of hers was reportedly a former student. Hurston's interest in men in their twenties may have been a reflection of her own desire for youth and a way to deny the deceptions about her own age. Younger men may also have been easier to control and delude, though—as Hurston had learned with Price—only for a time.

Hurston's rumored relationship with a former student, as well as her unconventional ways, ultimately eroded the goodwill Shepard harbored for her. Although the college prohibited social interaction between faculty and students, Hurston often invited students to her cabin in the woods. She defied the school's rules on limiting social interactions between male and female students, and she had a tendency to dress immodestly. Shepherd was aghast when he learned that Hurston was dating a student and quickly decided that she must be removed from the college's faculty. From Hurston's perspective, the school had also been a disappointment. She had not received the resources necessary to establish a credible drama program and she was frustrated by her teaching assignment. She insisted on postponing a play on campus and, to the likely ire of Shepard, suggested that it be presented at UNC rather than at NCCN. Hurston had continued her collaboration with Paul Green in Chapel Hill and hoped that he would help her finalize and produce her still-in-progress play, *John de Conqueror*. By March, however, the conflicts between Hurston and Shepard escalated, and she submitted her resignation. Her six-month employment there had not resulted in a single staged play, though she'd certainly brought a good deal of drama to the college.

With her furniture put in storage, Hurston drove to South Carolina to work with anthropologist Jane Belo to study the Gullah people of Beaufort. Belo had become a close friend of Hurston largely through their exchange of letters over many years. Belo also studied at Barnard and had traveled to Haiti in addition to the Dutch East Indies. Carla Kaplan, who collected Hurston's letters in a landmark 2003 volume, notes that Hurston's letters to Belo "are unlike any of the more than six hundred" published in her book. Hurston repeatedly refers to Belo as "Darling Jane" and peppers her letters with excessive "dears" and "loves." One letter concludes, "My love, my love, my love, my love, my love, my love!," while another signs off, "Darling, darling, darling, darling, darling, darling. Dear, dear, dear, dear, dear, dear, dear, dear. Love, love, love, love, love, love, love" (Kaplan 2003, 457, letter from Hurston to Belo in 1938). Once Belo married the anthropologist Frank Tennenbaum, this language vanished. Kaplan further notes that in *Dust Tracks on a Road*, Hurston affirms that she "fell in love with Jane Belo," begging the question of whether their relationship had ever been sexual (Hurston 1942, 228). While we can only speculate on the precise nature of their relationship, Hurston's affection for Belo as displayed by her numerous letters to her friend continued for years.

For $150 a month, Hurston joined Belo to live among and document the social and cultural life of the Gullah. The black communities in this region

> **GULLAH**
>
> The Gullah are a distinct group of African Americans with roots in South Carolina and Georgia. They live largely isolated from other communities in farming and fishing villages along the Atlantic coastal plain and on a series of Sea Islands close to the mainland. Their geographic distance from others has fostered the preservation of cultural practices that derive from Africa. The Gullah speak a creole language that is similar to Sierra Leone Krio and engage in many creative activities, from basket weaving to wood carving, that reflect African practices. Another aspect of their life that links them to the people of Sierra Leone is their rice-based cuisine. Slaves from the rice-growing region of West Africa were especially prized in the eighteenth century by white plantation owners who discovered that Atlantic coastal areas were ideal for rice cultivation. Africans from the "Rice Coast" were valued more highly because of their expertise with the crop. The Gullah people trace their roots to these slaves, and the similarities between their language and various African languages are quite striking. Songs and story fragments from Africa are evident in their cultural lore, uniting them to groups across the Atlantic.

trace their origins to West Africa. The slaves had developed their own language drawing from English and various African tongues to communicate with one another. Due to the geographic isolation of the area, the Gullah people developed an especially distinctive culture reflected in their foods, crafts, stories, and songs. Hurston and Belo attended church at Rev. George Washington's Commandment Keeper Seventh Day Church of God, which fiercely rejected white forms of worship. They marveled at the church music produced by guitars, cymbals, tambourines, rattle goers, and washboards and witnessed worshipers entering religious trances. This was of special interest to Belo, who was working on a study of ecstasy behavior in the church. Hurston continued the work after Belo returned to New York. She gathered her observations of the Seventh Day Church in the essay "Ritualistic Expression from the Lips of the Communicants of the Seventh Day Church of God," focusing in particular on vision and conversion experiences. Hurston became especially interested in the music of the area where local singers were producing spirituals that referred to current events. Although Belo had already gathered the material she wanted, she sent Hurston equipment to make a sound film and record the new church songs. Hurston was dismayed that this generous offer was accompanied by "two very enthusiastic Jews who want to take the spirituals for commercial purposes!" Horrified by this prospect, she wrote to Paul Green, insisting that he "DO SOMETHING," adding, "We cant let all that swell music get away from us like that" (Kaplan 2003, 458, letter from Hurston to Paul

Green in 1940). She asked him to immediately send recording equipment from the University of North Carolina so that she could make certain recordings for their planned collaboration and then direct the New Yorkers to less interesting works.

When Green agreed to this arrangement and promised both an audio recording machine and a technician to operate it, Hurston replied to Belo with a veneer of pert cooperation. She introduced the New York filmmakers to the Seventh Day Church and took part in much of the material they recorded. In the footage, she plays various instruments including the maracas and the drums, appearing not at all like an anthropologist but rather like another member of the congregation. The filmmakers developed some of their recordings for radio broadcasts on the WNYC *Adventures in Music* program. While this partnership proved more fruitful than expected, her collaboration with Green ended in disappointment. He invited Richard Wright to Chapel Hill on the heels of his enormously successful debut novel, *Native Son* (1940). Together they began working on a stage adaptation of the book. This new project explains Green's waning interest in Hurston's play. Frustrated with his failure to commit to her work, she at last wrote to him directly on the topic:

> I have the uncomfortable feeling that I have pestered you too much about this HIGH JOHN DE CONQUER. You have tried to feel it and you cant. So I will take High John out of your lap and go off an[d] sit up with him awhile. As I said, I will write through the thing and let you see what I have done. If you then feel like bothering with the thing again I will be very happy. If not, well then, you just don't feel that way. (Kaplan 2003, 455, letter from Hurston to Green in 1940)

As with so many of Hurston's possible creative partners from Hughes to Hurst, Green proved not to share her vision or energy. She resolved to finish the play on her own and returned to New York.

Back in Manhattan, Hurston at last indulged the temptation to call Percy Punter. She "cursed myself for the delay" because here again "was the shy, warm man I had left." As they spoke, their former feelings reappeared: "We both were stunned by the revelation that all along we had both thought and acted desperately in exile, and all to no purpose. We were still in the toils and after all my agony, I found out that he was a sucker for me, and he found out that I was in his bag" (Hurston 1942, 211). He admitted that without her to push him, he had settled into a tiresome desk job and also gained a few pounds. With her return, he began to envision new possibilities for himself. Hurston happily returned to "the real love affair of my life" (Hurston 1942, 207). She remained in New York through the start of 1941, trying to decide on her next project. The success of Langston Hughes's recently published autobiography, *The Big Sea* (1940), prompted Lippincott to encourage Hurston to pen her own story. Initially she

> ### NATIVE SON
>
> Richard Wright's *Native Son* remains one of the most important American novels of the twentieth century. Published in 1940, this groundbreaking tour de force tells the story of Bigger Thomas, a poor African American youth living in Chicago's South Side who inadvertently kills Mary Dalton, the daughter of a rich white couple who employ Bigger as a chauffeur. Wright portrays Bigger's murder of Mary as a consequence of the fear generated by his poverty and dim life opportunities. Bigger is eventually apprehended by the police and sentenced to death. *Native Son* helped define the genre of the American protest novel, texts that elucidate the social ills that plague the nation. The book was an immediate best seller and propelled Wright into the national spotlight, where he called upon black writers to use their craft to bring about massive social change. Despite *Native Son*'s commercial success and popularity, especially among white critics, some black writers, notably James Baldwin, argued that the novel indulged black stereotypes. Pointing to the limitations of protest fiction, Baldwin claimed that artistic merit and human complexity were compromised by a too obviously political agenda. This tension between the reformist impact of a book and its aesthetic value continues to be at the center of critical discussions concerning African American literature.

demurred, arguing that such a retrospective was inappropriate for her stage of life. Lippincott responded by suggesting that she conceive of it merely as the first volume.

Later that spring, Hurston ceded to Lippincott's request and moved to California to work on her autobiography. Her friend, the anthropologist and former modern dancer Katharine Edson Mershon, invited her to finish the book at her home in Altadena. Mershon supplied Hurston with everything she needed, from new clothes to a doctor to clear up the malaria she had contracted in Haiti, so that by July she had a first draft of *Dust Tracks on a Road*. During this time, she also published the short story "Cock Robin Beale Street" in the *Southern Literary Messenger*. The animal tale serves as a commentary on racial purity and miscegenation after questions about the color of Mrs. Sparrow's eggs lead to the death of Cock Robin. In California, Hurston met up with some familiar New York faces, including Ethel Waters and Etta Moten. Mershon proved to be an excellent hostess, driving Hurston up and down the state. Hurston was impressed by the state's natural beauty and diverse landscapes. However, she couldn't help but find California wanting in comparison to her beloved Florida:

> Of course, coming from Florida, I feel like the man when he saw a hunch back for the first time—it seems that California does wear its hips a bit high.

I mean all those mountains. Too much of the state is standing up on edge. To my notion, land is supposed to lie down and be walked on—not rearing up, staring you in the face. It is so big and imposing. But on the whole, California will do for a lovely state until God can make up something better. (Hurston 1942, 276)

Among the places that Mershon took Hurston was Hollywood. In October, Paramount Studios hired her as a writer and technical advisor. Although she vowed that the impressive $100-a-week position would be a means, not an end, Hurston could not persuade the studio to adapt any of her works for the big screen. However, a number of different studios seriously considered her work over the course of her career. Warner Brothers had reviewed *Their Eyes Were Watching God* even before it was published. *Dust Tracks on a Road* was also entertained as a possibility, but *Seraph on the Suwanee* (1948) generated the most interest. Both MGM and Warner Brothers lauded its relatable story and fresh approach before eventually passing on the manuscript. Hurston's dream of a movie version of one of her novels only came true in 2005, when Oprah Winfrey produced the film *Their Eyes Were Watching God*. Starring Halle Berry, the movie includes a script by acclaimed African American playwright Suzan Lori-Parks.

Hurston was living in California on December 7, 1941, the day that Pearl Harbor was attacked by Japanese planes and the effective start to U.S. involvement in World War II. Although Lippincott had received her manuscript months earlier, the war shifted his reading of *Dust Tracks on a Road*. He insisted that all criticisms of the U.S. government and its international relations be removed and that Hurston's discussion of how America failed to live up to its core values would have to be tempered. Hurston revised her manuscript in California and spent the holidays with Ethel Waters in her Los Angeles home. Waters was both a friend and a model for Hurston. They exchanged meaningful confidences while also pursuing highly successful careers. Just as Hurston was a pioneering black female novelist, Waters was the first African American actress to star in her own television show, *The Ethel Waters Show*. Both women succeeded in part by refusing the resentments of race. Like Hurston, Waters did not embrace *Native Son* as a prescription for the lives of all African Americans and instead focused on making the most of the opportunities before her.

Perhaps with such an attitude in mind, Hurston resigned from her position at Paramount on New Year's Eve. Hollywood was not ready for her work, and she could realize her creative vision more effectively in other places. Hurston began her long drive back east, stopping at various black colleges to lecture and meet with students. Her spring stay in St. Augustine was prolonged due to a variety of illnesses she'd contracted, including pneumonia, tonsillitis, and difficulties with her sinuses. For the summer, Hurston found a teaching position at Florida Normal and Industrial

College. Marjorie Kinnan Rawlings, who had recently won the Pulitzer Prize for her novel *The Yearling* (1938), lectured there in July. Hurston invited her to speak at the all-black Florida Normal College in St. Augustine. Rawlings was immediately charmed by Hurston. She invited her for tea the following day but later realized that problems would ensue because her apartment was located in the segregated Castle Warden Hotel. Though Rawlings sent an African American servant to wait for her guest and escort her upstairs, Hurston took care of matters herself. As soon as she realized the kind of establishment Rawlings lived in, she went through the kitchen and up to the top floor apartment without a problem. Both Rawlings and her husband, Norton Baskin, were dazzled by Hurston's humor, intelligence, and brilliance. Such effortless qualities posed fundamental challenges to Rawlings's antiquated notions of race. While she acknowledged Hurston's talents, however, she was afraid to renounce the social conventions that relegated African Americans to a secondary status.

Hurston and Rawlings went on to become friends and corresponded for many years. Hurston called her "my sister," someone who was deeply attuned to the past. Hurston especially admired Rawlings's novel *Cross Creek* (1942). She declared, "You have written the best thing on Negroes of any white writer who has ever lived." For Hurston, this nuanced portrayal was based on Rawlings's close observation of African American life and speech: "You looked at them and saw them as they are, instead of slobbering over them as other authors do. They talk real too, and act as I know them. You have done a remarkably able thing with the Negro idiom. It is so accurate" (Kaplan 2003, 486, letter from Hurston to Rawlings in 1943). Despite Hurston's admiration for *Cross Creek*, Rawlings expressed significant misgivings about African Americans generally. She used the word "nigger" both in her writings and her personal speech. However, Hurston challenged Rawlings's understanding of race, and the white woman seems to have become more progressive in her racial views as a result of their friendship. This shift occurred only after Hurston offered to become Rawlings's maid: "Even though I am busy, if it gets too awful, give a whoop and a holler and I will do what I can for you. I really mean that" (Kaplan 2003, 494–495, letter from Hurston to Rawlings in 1943). It is impossible to determine if Hurston meant this sincerely or was only offering exuberant sympathy for Rawlings's recent loss of her maid. In either case, it gave Rawlings new respect for African Americans.

As she readied her autobiography for publication, Hurston continued to write shorter pieces for various magazines. That summer she published "Story in Harlem Slang" in *The American Mercury*. Focused on two unemployed men, the tale is a departure from Hurston's usual emphasis on African American life in the rural South. Jelly and Sweet Back are Harlem hipsters looking for women to seduce in order to get a free meal and a place to stay. They set their sights on a young woman who can sling insults and sexual innuendo as deftly as the two men. She triumphs with her slick tongue and leaves them alone and hungry. The story was followed by "Glossary of Harlem Slang," which Hurston originally titled "Harlem Slanguage." The editors cut some of the more sexual references but saw fit to include definitions like "scooter-pooker" ("a professional at sex") and "jelly bean" ("a man who lives by sex, a pimp") (Hurston 1995, 227). The editors also eliminated some allusions to racial violence, transforming the story into a description of shiftless men rather than a commentary on the forces that brought them to poverty. In September, Hurston also published a profile of Lawrence Silas, a pioneering black cattleman, in *The Saturday Evening Post*.

Dust Tracks on a Road was published in November of 1942. The dust jacket on the first edition of the book reflects an outmoded approach to race and achievement: "She has lived in primitive simplicity in remote communities where folklore is a part of daily life. She has lived in the inner circles of literary New York, has known the glamour of Hollywood. All this comes to life in her story." This description assumes that real achievement happens in the big city while Hurston's childhood home is reduced to "primitive simplicity," a place better escaped than enjoyed. Such a trajectory speaks to mainstream assumptions about what success means, especially for an African American woman. Hurston's book hardly presents Eatonville as primitive or simple, just as it does not hold up life in the city as a signal achievement. Recognizing the tension between the substance of the book and its marketing is essential to understanding the text as a whole. Hurston did not want to write her autobiography, which created a degree of dissonance between who she actually was and what she disclosed in the book.

The dust jacket also ignores the complexity of Hurston's actual narrative and the challenges she faced in organizing her life into a coherent whole. Because she had been lying about her age for decades, Hurston was necessarily evasive about many of the key details of her life. In the book, she rarely provides specific reference to dates or periods of time in her life, instead presenting her story as largely episodic. She devotes much of the book to her early life and a description of the people who most influenced her, such as her parents and various teachers. At many points, she fails to provide key details about how or even where she lived. She emphasizes the significance of her early visions, adding a mythical quality to her narrative that glosses over her many omissions. Many of the most crucial episodes in her life are completely missing, including her friendship and fallout with Langston Hughes, her uneven relationship with Charlotte Mason, and her second marriage. These painful periods of her life would have been difficult to describe to a general audience. Their absence points to Hurston's skill at crafting a certain persona for herself. Just as she knew how to charm Mason to ensure another check for the month, Hurston presents a version of her life suitable for a broad readership. Hemenway surmises that it was "written self-consciously with a white audience in mind," leading to a text that is "at war with itself" (Hemenway 1977, 277–278). Many have been troubled by the book, including Alice Walker, who identifies it as "the most unfortunate thing Zora ever wrote" (Hemenway 1977, xvii).

Much of the debate over the book derives from its vexed origin. As she confided to friends, Hurston had little interest in writing her autobiography: "I did not want to write it at all, because it is too hard to reveal one's inner self, and still there is no use in writing that kind of book unless you do" (Kaplan 2003, 478, letter from Hurston to Hamilton Holt in 1943). However, once committed to the task, she placed self-invention over honesty; although readers would not receive her inner self, they would receive an idealized external self. This approach is consistent with many contemporary memoirists who take liberties with the truth in greater service to the story and to their own self-conception. Thus, even the selective or embellished truths that Hurston presents in the book provide insight into the woman that she was. Although we will never know how true her childhood visions were or the range of emotions she felt when encountering blatant acts of racism, the faith she invested in dreams and her seemingly indifferent attitude to the slights she endured at Barnard and other places tell us plenty about who she wanted to be.

Dust Tracks on a Road was also subject to Lippincott's editorial judgment. He excised two important chapters, "The Inside Light—Being a Salute to Friendship" and "Seeing the World as It Is." The first piece expressed deep gratitude to all of the people who had helped Hurston throughout her life and career. As she told Van Vechten, "In it, I tried to show my inside feelings for certain people, because I am not sure that I have ever made it clear how I feel, and as you have noted, I am such a poor letter-answerer. But I feel deeply, just the same. I regretted the loss of that chapter" (Kaplan 2003, 467–468, letter from Hurston to Van Vechten in 1942). She made the point more colorfully to another friend, "Now, I look like a hog under an acorn tree guzzling without ever looking up to see where the acorns came from" (Kaplan 2003, 478, letter from Hurston to Holt in 1943). Ironically, when Hurston was willing to expose her "inside feelings," Lippincott prevented her from doing so. *Dust Tracks on a Road* was an unusual if not radical book to publish. Few autobiographies of black female writers had been published since the handful of slave narratives penned by women in the nineteenth century. Just as those texts conformed to the expectations of a quintessential American story in which a self-reliant individual achieves success and freedom, Hurston's autobiography was shaped to focus on her personal gumption rather than the group of people who helped her along the way. Contemporary editions of the book include "The Inside Light—Being a Salute to Friendship," which ends with a Hurstonian flourish: "Make the attempt if you want to, but you will find that trying to go through life without friendship, is like milking a bear to get cream for your morning coffee. It is a whole lot of trouble, and then not worth much after you get it" (Hurston 1942, 277).

"Seeing the World as It Is" presents Hurston at her most political, and for obvious reasons, Lippincott refused to publish it. In the far-ranging essay, she excoriates Christian hypocrisy, noting the obvious disjuncture between sermons of peace and the call for war in Jesus's name. She similarly attacks the U.S. government for misguided foreign interventions that reek of paternalism and racism. In her rendering, the United States is a bullying older brother whose "little Latin brother" cannot be trusted because "he is so gay and fiesta-minded that he is liable to make arrangements that benefit nobody but himself." Thus it is "our big brotherly duty to teach him right from wrong" and "share with big brother before big brother comes down and kicks his teeth in" (Hurston 1942, 259). Few entities escape Hurston's sharp critique. The Communist Party may have some good ideas, but she refuses to "be connected with the flock" unless she can "shepherd my ownself" (Hurston 1942, 263). However, Hurston saves her greatest ire for those who champion "Race Pride" or "Race Consciousness." She claims that "Race Pride" is no virtue but "a sapping vice" that "has caused more suffering in the world than religious opinion, and that is saying a lot" (Hurston 1942, 249). She refutes the myth that there is a singular "Negro" representative of the race, claiming, "There is no single Negro nor single organization which can carry the thirteen million in any direction" (Hurston 1942, 251). Amid such diversity and inevitable discord, there could be no such thing as "Race Solidarity," and anyone who presents himself as a "Race Man" is a fraud, unable to recognize the greater unity of the nation. By contrast, she embraces an identity rooted apart from race: "Being an American, I am just like the rest of the Yankees, the Westerners, the Southerners, the Negroes, the Irish, the Indians, and the Jews" (Hurston 1942, 252). Although Hurston recognizes the reality of racism and the virulence of white supremacy, she understands such prejudice as emanating "out of a sense of incapability to which they refuse to give a voice." She challenges racist readers to prove their value: "If you are better than I, you can tell me about it if you want to, but then again, show me so I can know" (Hurston 1942, 253).

Shorn of its most controversial chapters, *Dust Tracks on a Road* was predictably derided by some black critics for ignoring the most serious issues confronting African Americans. Although the book in its original form does not substantially address Hurston's personal encounters with racial discrimination, it does not draw simplistic equivalences between black and white. As in her previous work, Hurston delights in black folk culture and distinguishes herself more as a child of Eatonville than as a child of the entire United States. She concludes the book writing that she has "no race prejudice of any kind," adding, "My kinfolks, and my 'skinfolks' are dearly loved" (Hurston 1942, 231). While prejudice is usually conceived as negative bias, Hurston seems to concede here a special disposition toward black people. This is not a matter of superiority but simply a passion for the culture and community that produced her.

White reviewers praised the book for its unique voice and uplifting story, spurring its strong initial sales of five thousand copies at first publication. The book cemented Hurston's status as a literary celebrity and ironically positioned her as a racial spokesperson, the very kind of figure she long derided. She became the most famous female African American writer in the country. Soon after the publication of *Dust Tracks on a Road*, Hurston was profiled in *Twentieth Century American Authors* and *Current Biography*. The book led to invitations to write for a number of popular magazines. While moving from St. Augustine to Daytona Beach, she finalized pieces for *The Saturday Evening Post* and *The American Mercury*. *Dust Tracks on a Road* also inspired much enthusiasm from friends and colleagues. Rollins College Professor Edwin Osgood Grover was so delighted with the book that he suggested various ways that she might expand her readership, even advising her to send a copy to first lady Eleanor Roosevelt. The president of Rollins College read the book in a single night and sent off a gushing fan letter the next day. Even Alain Locke wrote to send his congratulations and that of Charlotte Mason, who remained in a prolonged-care unit at New York Hospital. Hurston replied with frank gratitude, "You will never know how happy your letter made me. Really, I want your approval." Her conciliatory letter to Locke is far removed from the caustic response she penned to his review of *Moses, Man of the Mountain*. She suggests that in their old age they might renew their friendship: "Do let us see each other and run around town a bit, gas permitting. . . . Really, Alain, I am through being a smart-aleck. You must forget that I ever was one and let us have some fun while I am there" (Kaplan 2003, 473, letter from Hurston to Locke in 1943). With her literary reputation well-established, Hurston could more than afford to let go of feuds of the past.

In New York, Hurston reconnected with Van Vechten at his Park West apartment while sitting for various radio and newspaper interviews. Though she mostly recounted stories from her autobiography, she sparked some conflict with remarks she made in February to *The New York World-Telegram*: "The lot of the Negro is much better in the South than in the North. . . . There is, of course, segregation, no social intermingling. I can't go into certain white nightclubs or dine in first-class white hotels. But for everything put up in the South for white people there is the equivalent for the Negro. In other words, the Jim Crow system works" (Gilbert 1943). Hurston received immediate pushback from black leaders and politicians for comments that undermined a broad consensus in the African American community for increased integration across all areas of life. Two years earlier, President Franklin D. Roosevelt had outlawed racial discrimination in the national defense industry, and while segregation persisted in most areas of social life, including many parts of the U.S. military, the hope was that victory in World War II would force America to remedy its racial injustices. Roy Wilkins, who would later serve as the executive director of the National Association for the Advancement of Colored People, suggested in the *Amsterdam News* that Hurston's controversial remarks would increase her public profile but were simply nonsense because Jim Crow only served white supremacy. Wilkins wrote, "Miss Hurston is a bright person with a flair for actions and sayings that yield rich publicity dividends" and called for her to stop voicing such "arrant and even vicious nonsense" (Wilkins 1943).

Wilkins's essay appeared at the end of February, and on March 2, following a ceremony at Howard University where she received a distinguished alumna award, Hurston addressed his criticism. Hurston rejected her earlier statements and suggested that the reporter who interviewed her for the article in the *World-Telegram* had "left out the essentials or perhaps permitted his own views to gain ascendancy." She denied that she "ever said that Negroes are better off in the South," adding, "neither did I approve of segregation in the South or anywhere else" ("Zora Neale Hurston" 1943). Instead, she clarified that although racism existed in all parts of the country, she did notice a difference in the South, where people tended to be more open about their prejudices than in the North. Privately, Hurston agonized over the public misunderstanding, confessing to a friend, "I am positively ill over it. I know how impossible it is to get a retraction for a newspaper. I merely feel like dying, since I can get no chance to kill him. At any rate, the iron has entered my soul. I am now a bitter person where once I had tolerance" (Kaplan 2003, 475, letter from Hurston to Claude Barnett in 1943).

This experience led Hurston to become suspicious of "editors and the powers that be" that insist African American writers comment on the race problem in established ways. She explained, "The nation is too sentimental about us to know us. It has a cut-and-dried formula for us which must not be violated. Either there is no interest in knowing us, or a determination not to destroy the pattern made and provided. We are even supposed to use certain sentences at all times" (Kaplan 2003, 477, letter from Hurston to Douglas Gilbert in 1943). Hurston naturally railed against any expectation to conform to established beliefs, and her experiences as a Southerner led her to call out the hypocrisies in the North. She understood that black-only establishments and communities in the South thrived, and while this was not an argument in favor of segregation, it did affirm the importance of such places.

Hurston's thoughts on race were complex and not easily distilled to simplistic beliefs. Although she had many white friends, she was wary of liberalism and the condescension it often directed toward African Americans. She vehemently rejected the notion that whiteness or association with whites was what blacks most desired. Later in her life, she espoused ideas that were more in line with conservative or nationalistic thinking, though it is impossible to imagine that she would have embraced any such label. Recognizing the violence that underpinned white supremacy, she at times advocated more strident actions: "If some of us must die for human justice, then let us die.... A hundred Negroes killed in the streets of Washington right now could wipe out Jim Crow in the nation as far as the law is concerned and abate it at least 60% in actuality. If any of our leaders start something like that then I will be in it body and soul" (Kaplan 2003, 482, letter from Hurston to Cullen in 1943). She also repeatedly decried segregation in the military. While visiting the Signal Corps School in Florida, she was appalled by the conditions: "The Govt. was forced by pressure to grant this ONE AND ONLY S.C. for Negroes, and it is a mockery to all of us in the U.S.A. Not that the teachers are not good. They are. But the living conditions surrounding them, I mean this little jerk of a school without adequate living quarters, and the food and all is a scandal" (Kaplan 2003, 468, letter from Hurston to Claude and Etta Moten Barnett in 1942). Alerted to the situation by Hurston, Walter White sent the NAACP's special counsel to Florida, and after the charges were confirmed, William Gray, the college president, was put on notice by the War Department.

Hurston did not widely publicize her more radical ideas. The first edition of *Dust Tracks on a Road* presented a milder version of her views on contemporary issues. And despite the conflict over her remarks to the *World-Telegram*, her promotion of the book helped it find a broader audience. *The Saturday Review of Literature* and the Anisfield-Wolf Foundation awarded it the John Anisfield Award in Racial Relations. Hurston appeared on the cover of the *Saturday Review* and received $1,000. The prize money allowed Hurston to at last invest in her own home; characteristically, it was built to travel. In May, she bought a thirty-two-foot-long houseboat that she called *Wanago*, a blurring of the phrase "want to go." She anchored the boat at Howard Boat Works in Daytona Beach for a few months while she had it repainted and repaired. The boat was small for all her books and possessions, but it afforded her the solitude she wanted. It also provided her with a new stability and domestic focus. She began cooking more and staying in to explore her eclectic literary interests. She read widely, from books on Taoism to the philosophy of Benedict de Spinoza, as well as contemporary novels by Willa Cather and Sinclair Lewis.

Her writing of this period is primarily essayistic. For *The American Mercury*, she published "The 'Pet' Negro System," "Negroes Without Self-Pity," and "High John de Conquer," which described the importance of the figure High John in African American culture. She described High John as "our hope-bringer" who through humor and laughter found a way to cope with struggle and hardship. The essay had to be altered for publication in *The American Mercury* in order "to flatter the war effort," Hurston explained to Alain Locke, noting that "sometimes you have to give something to get something" (Kaplan 2003, 490, letter from Hurston to Locke in 1943). Rather than keep High John a figure of black folklore, Hurston introduced him as someone who could redeem all Americans in this troubled time of war: "You will know, then, that no matter how bad things look now, it will be worse for those who seek to oppress us. Even if your hair comes yellow, and your eyes are blue, John de Conquer will be working for you just the same" (Hurston 1943). "Negroes without Self-Pity" is a short account of Hurston's observations at a meeting of the Statewide Negro Defense Committee. She hailed the robust discussion in which a number of African Americans spoke about current race relations. This was in her estimation evidence of "a new, wholesome note in the black man's relation to his native America" (Hurston 1943).

"The 'Pet' Negro System" remains one of the most provocative of Hurston's essays. It explores the contradictions in Southern race relations in which whites may loudly oppose educational opportunities for African Americans yet express pride for "pet Negroes" who they know personally to be good, upstanding citizens. Channeling the thoughts of such white Southerners, Hurston writes, "If all Negroes were like them he wouldn't mind what advancement they made. But the rest of them, of course, lie like the cross-ties from New York to Key West. They steal things and get drunk. Too bad, but Negroes are like that" (Hurston 1979, 157). This disjuncture between the African Americans who whites treat almost as family and think of as exceptional stands in striking opposition to pervasive beliefs in black inferiority and criminality. And yet, Hurston argues, the same paradoxical psychology is at work in how blacks view whites. They too have "their white pets," often people who they identify as "quality" (Hurston 1979, 158). Hurston's description of Southern race relations suggests that the customary vitriol assumed between black and white is undermined by the depth of these personal relations. She does not claim that the pet Negro system applies to everyone, noting instead that this "web of feelings and mutual dependencies" has elevated a certain class of African Americans: "It isn't half as pretty as the ideal adjustment of theorizers, but it's a lot more real and durable, and a lot of black folk, I'm afraid, find it mighty cosy" (Hurston 1979, 157). Hurston's essay reveals the complexity of race relations in the South. African Americans could exploit white paternalism to their individual advantage while whites were often more intimately attached to their black workers and neighbors than they wanted to admit. These dynamics also highlight a major theme in Hurston's later reflections on race: the power of personal relationships to transform sweeping generalizations about other racial groups.

Though primarily residing in Daytona Beach, Hurston took the *Wanago* along the St. Johns and Halifax rivers and often visited friends in Eatonville, Sanford, and Winter Park. After purchasing a lot next to the local Baptist Church, Hurston was asked to help build a civic center in Eatonville. Hurston had noted that the acclaimed Hungerford School of her youth had transformed into "a sort of reformatory by the Negroes of the state" where "unmanageable children" are sent. She observed that without "any uplifting influence" the town "has sort of drifted" (Kaplan 2003, 497, letter from Hurston to Edwin Osgood Grover in 1943). This effort was coupled with her participation in Recreation in War, a program organized by Mary Holland, the wife of Florida Governor Spessard Holland. Holland was so charmed by Hurston that she thought her ideal to help entertain soldiers stationed throughout the state.

A February headline in the *Amsterdam News* announced that Hurston was to wed James Howell Pitts, a businessman from Cleveland. Although her relationship with Percy Punter had continued through her stay in California and beyond the publication of *Dust Tracks on a Road*, it appears that the affair had at last ended. It is not clear how Hurston met Pitts, who was originally from South Carolina and had a degree in pharmacy from Meharry Medical College. The wedding took place in January in Volusia County, Florida. Unlike her recent string of lovers, Pitts was older, forty-five to her fifty-three (though she claimed to be forty on the marriage license). Nonetheless, the marriage encountered the same problems as her earlier ones and ended shortly in divorce on October 31 of the same year. Though Hurston wrote to many friends and colleagues during this period, she never mentioned either her marriage or its breakup to them. However, in a 1957 letter to her nephew Everett, Hurston reflected, "Artistic people just don't go for much tying down even for the economic safety angle" (Kaplan 2003, 751, letter from Hurston to Hurston in 1957). Hurston never married again following this third divorce, perhaps having at last recognized the limitations it placed on her creative passions.

Hurston's marriage did nothing to alter her usual commitment to her work, a fact which no doubt hastened the relationship's demise. By the time the *Amsterdam News* ran the headline about her nuptials, she was already in New York, staying at the Hotel Theresa in Harlem and working with Dorothy Waring, the author of the book *American Defender* (1935), on a musical play called *Polk County*. Van Vechten privately wondered why Hurston would work with a writer of such little note as Waring, but it is possible she was more interested in the abilities of Waring's husband, Stephen Kelen-d'Oxylion, who produced plays on Broadway. Because *Polk County* includes material from "High John de Conquer," *Mules and Men*, and *Mule Bone*, Waring had little to add to its development. Their partnership was vexed from the start, and while some versions of the play list Waring as an author, others do not. Waring recalled wanting to incorporate a George Gershwin element to the music. Hurston curtly replied, "You don't know what the hell you're talking about" (Waring 1971, interview by Robert E. Hemenway on May 21). Once *Polk County* was completed, Hurston returned to the South. She spent a few days at Hampton Institute in Virginia to lecture and participate in a two-day event on cultural relations between the United States and Latin America. Upon her return to the Halifax River, she again settled into her solitude.

That fall, Hurston decided upon a new project after meeting Reginald Brett, an engineer who had spent years mining gold in Honduras. He was familiar with her anthropological work and suggested that she was an ideal researcher to explore the cultural roots of the country. Hurston was quickly persuaded to undertake the venture, though it would take considerable financial backing to complete. She wrote to Henry Allen Moe of the Guggenheim Foundation outlining her plans to collect material from the Paya Indians, Caribs, Mayans, and Zambu Indians. She was especially interested in learning about medicinal plants in the area, studying the architecture of the Mayan burial grounds, and visiting an ancient city that Brett had discovered. Moe explained that the Guggenheim Foundation only offered two years of support to scholars and Hurston had already received two fellowships. Though she was welcome to apply, he doubted that funding would be available to her. Hurston then appealed to Jane Belo, inviting her to accompany her to Honduras, but Belo remained noncommittal.

Hurston at last found some support from Fred Irvine, the Miami-based captain of the *Maridome*, who would become a good friend. Irvine offered to sail it for free if Hurston paid for new sails and some minor repairs to the twenty-seven-ton schooner. Born in England but raised in New York, Irvine lived off his late father's fortune and fancied himself a bohemian ladies' man. Though their relationship was always platonic, Hurston became a confidante; Irvine often came to her after the end of some disastrous affair. She privately wondered about the cause of his numerous romantic entanglements: "Maybe because he is a small guy and unsure of himself in other ways that he feels he must promote all those meanigless [sic] 'love' affairs to make him feel assured" (Kaplan 2003, 624, letter from Hurston to Burroughs Mitchell in 1950). Hurston listened to Irvine's heartaches but was wary of becoming too close to him.

Hurston sold her car and other belongings to finance the trip, vowing, "I am going no matter how I get there because I know that it is going to be epoch-making," and declaring, "I have never wanted to do ANYTHING so much as this piece of research" (Kaplan 2003, 507, letter from Hurston to Belo in 1944). Hurston tried to borrow a recording machine from the Library of Congress but learned that they were all being used for war-related activities. As she tried to find additional money to finance the trip, she worked on a new novel called *Road in the Wilderness* and published "My Most Humiliating Jim Crow Experience" in *The American Mercury*. In November, she went to New York to discuss a production of *Polk County*, but no one was willing to back the play. When she returned to Florida, she learned that her Guggenheim application had been denied. These frustrations exacerbated her observation of discontent around the country:

> These do be times that take all you have to scrape up a decent laugh or so. I do not refer to the battlefields, but to this enormous pest of hate that is rotting men's souls. When will people learn that you cannot quarantine hate? Once it gets loose in the world, it rides over all barriers and seeps under the doors and in the cracks of every house. I see it all around me every day. I am not talking of race hatred. Just hate. Everybody is at it. . . . Once it was just Germany and Japan and Italy. Now, it is our allies as well. (Kaplan 2003, 509, letter from Hurston to Benjamin Botkin in 1944)

Although Hurston derived some solace from a new boat, the *Sun Tan*, and the pleasures of Florida's natural beauty, she struggled to finish her novel and find support for her trip to Honduras. Early in 1945, she had a new bout of intestinal difficulties that led her to think "that I would kick the bucket" (Kaplan 2003, 523, letter from Hurston to Van Vechten in 1945). By the time she was well enough to write to Van Vechten, she was doing much better and hoped to convince him to join her in Honduras. Although she explained that she did "not ask you for financial reasons," Hurston still did not have the funds necessary for the expedition (Kaplan 2003, 524, letter from Hurston to Van Vechten in 1945). Her appeal to Van Vechten, who would hardly be caught tramping through the Central American jungle, may have reflected her desire to escape a country that was growing increasingly hostile to her voice. That summer she also wrote to Du Bois, noting that she always valued her freedom to "say what I want to," but lately "that is precious little at present, because publishers seem frightened, and cut every thing out that seems strong. I have come to the conclusion that for the most part, there is aan [sic] agreement among them to clamp on the lid" (Kaplan 2003, 520, letter from Hurston to Du Bois in 1945).

Earlier that year she published an essay for *The American Mercury* entitled "The Rise of the Begging Joints," which posed no threat to establishment ideas and mores, though it did rattle some African American readers. Exempting "Class A seats of learning" such as Howard, Fisk, Morgan, Tuskegee, Hampton, and others, Hurston attacked less prestigious black colleges that took advantage of African Americans eager for an education. Rather than offer a meaningful experience or degree to children of largely uneducated people, these institutions took their tuition dollars in exchange for little in the way of skills or knowledge. She scolded white donors who supported these "Begging Joints" rather than invest in schools with capable faculty and basic resources.

In the fall, Hurston submitted about two-thirds of her latest novel to Lippincott. Titled *Mrs. Doctor*, the book represented a significant departure from Hurston's previous work because it was "a serious one on the upper strata of Negro life." However, her publisher "decided that the American public was not ready for it yet" and returned it to her with no hope that it would ever be published in the future. Hurston responded by beginning a new novel, one that returned to Eatonville and included some material from *Mule Bone*. She described it as "a story about a village youth expelled from town by village politics going places, including Heaven and Hell and having adventures, and returning after seven years to achieve his childhood ambition of being a fireman on the railroad, and the town hero" (Kaplan 2003, 529, letter from Hurston to Van Vechten in 1945). Lippincott also passed on this manuscript, finding it sloppy and in need of extensive editing. Although Lippincott might have helped Hurston revise the manuscript into something publishable, he hoped for a novel as ready for the press as *Jonah's Gourd Vine* or *Their Eyes Were Watching God*. It is not clear if Lippincott was unable or unwilling to help Hurston organize her ideas. Either way, it does raise the provocative question of what Hurston might have produced had she worked with a more capable editor. With no advance money forthcoming from Lippincott, Hurston managed to pay her bills by doing freelance writing for magazines and submitting a few encyclopedia entries.

Though most writers find encyclopedic work uninteresting, Hurston described her entry, "The Negro in the United States," which ran from 1947 through 1954 in *Encyclopedia Americana*, as "the greatest honor that has come my way so far" (Kaplan 2003, 534, letter from Hurston to Katherine Tracy L'Engle in 1945). Her enthusiasm for the project stemmed from the fact that her essay would replace one written by W. E. B. Du Bois, whom Hurston privately referred to as Dr. Dubious. Hurston took this opportunity to extol Booker T. Washington, whom she felt Du Bois had unfairly maligned throughout his life. In Hurston's estimation, Du Bois had done little for the most impoverished African Americans. Hurston's entry differs from Du Bois's in significant ways. While Du Bois takes pains to describe the death and horrors wrought by the slave trade, Hurston attacks both Southern slaveholders and Northern carpetbaggers. She includes the historical detail that some free blacks held slaves and presents a common Southern perspective on emancipation: "What should have come to the Negro after a period of preparation, was thrust upon him while he was still in a state of unreadiness, leaving him not only maladjusted to his surroundings, but retarded in progress for generations" (Kaplan 2003, 442). She also offers a more expansive portrait of black arts than Du Bois. Additionally, for Funk & Wagnalls's 1946 edition of *The New International Year Book*, Hurston wrote an entry titled "Negroes," which included descriptions of African American accomplishments in education, religion, politics, sports, writing, and the military.

The December issue of *Negro Digest* published Hurston's most significant essay of the year, "Crazy for This Democracy." With the war over since September, Hurston was at last able to express some of her more controversial opinions. In the essay, she wonders if perhaps she misheard former President Roosevelt's description of the United States as being the "Arsenal of Democracy" as the "Ass-and-All of Democracy," since it "has shouldered the load of subjugating the dark world completely" (Hurston 1979, 166). She gushes over the idea of democracy but cautions, "The only thing that keeps me from pitching headlong into the thing is the presence of numerous Jim Crow laws on the statute books of the nation." She observes that Jim Crow is no American anomaly but the rule of law "in all colonial Africa, Asia, and the Netherlands East Indies" (Hurston 1979, 167). Such rampant segregation has profound psychological effects, as white children become convinced of their superiority while darker children accept their inferiority and understand "that competition is out of the question, and against all nature and God." She concludes with a forceful denunciation of such conditions: "I am for complete repeal of All Jim Crow Laws in the United States once and for all, and right now. For the benefit of this nation and as a precedent to the world" (Hurston 1979, 168). These ideas would come to be at odds with some of the positions she would take in the final years of her life.

Despite this impassioned essay, Hurston confided that she was "depressed and distressed by the state of the world" and lamented that "poor America is in an awful spiritual state!" (Kaplan 2003, 534–535, letter from Hurston to L'Engle in 1945). There was little in the new year to improve Hurston's mood. On January 9, 1946, her old friend and "favorite poet" Countee Cullen died (Kaplan 2003, 480, letter from Hurston to Cullen in 1943). He had collaborated with her on *Fire!!*, and they had launched their literary careers together when they both won prizes at the first *Opportunity* literary contest in 1925. Three months later, Hurston received news that Charlotte Mason had passed away at New York Hospital in Manhattan, where she had spent the last thirteen years of her life.

Godmother was ninety-one years old. These tragedies spurred Hurston to finalize her trip to Honduras, where she might lose herself in a new land and culture. Though she secured her passport and sold the *Sun Tan*, she still lacked the funds necessary for the trip. Instead, with a small royalty check from *Story* magazine, which planned to anthologize "The Gilded Six-Bits," Hurston went to New York in search of freelance work. She wrote several book reviews for the *New York Herald Tribune* and did some journalistic work for *The New York World-Telegram*. However, her most interesting pieces of this period were not accepted for publication. "The Lost Keys of Glory" took a satirical look at women in modern society, while "Back to the Middle Ages, Or How to Become a Peasant in the United States" offered a sharp critique of Communism.

These essays demonstrate Hurston's increasing interest in the political scene. That fall, she involved herself in the Harlem congressional campaign of Grant Reynolds, the Republican candidate looking to unseat Adam Clayton Powell Jr. A registered Republican, Hurston joined a number of celebrity supporters for Reynolds—a Florida native who also had been educated at Howard—including Etta Moten and the heavyweight boxing champion Joe Louis. Hurston worked with others in Reynolds's small office in Harlem, where she passed out pamphlets and occasionally wrote press releases for the campaign. However, her focus was primarily on convincing people in the arts and theater scene to support Reynolds. Although her candidate lost in November, she continued to engage in community work. From her room on West 124th Street in Harlem, she founded a "Block Mothers" plan in which local working mothers would take turns watching the neighborhood children for a day. The program included trips to parks, beaches, and other locations throughout the city. She also started a fund for children who could not afford the picnic lunch or transportation provided by the program. She explained her intention to a reporter from Barnard's alumnae magazine: "It's the old idea, trite but true, of helping people to help themselves that will be the only salvation of the Negro in this country. No one from the outside can do it for him" (Boyd 2003, 383).

Although Hurston remained active, she despaired over the atmosphere in New York. She avoided visiting her longtime friend Van Vechten because New York was

> too much of a basement to Hell to suite me. Everybody busy hating and speaking in either brazen lies or using just enough truth to season a lie up to make their viewpoint sound valid. Not hating anyone, I felt entirely out of place. I'm afraid that I got a little unbalanced. I got so that it was torture for me to go meet people, fearing the impact of all the national, class and race hate that I would have to listen to. (Kaplan 2003, 551, letter from Hurston to Van Vechten in 1947)

After her long sojourn in Florida, Hurston found that her true home was not in the bustle of the city but in the natural landscapes of her youth.

However, in the spring, Hurston grew hopeful about the possibilities of the city due to a meeting with Maxwell Perkins. Perkins was the editor of Marjorie Kinnan Rawlings, who'd helped set up the interview, but also of some of the greatest American writers of the twentieth century, including F. Scott Fitzgerald, Ernest Hemingway, and Thomas Wolfe. The editor at Charles Scribner's Sons, Perkins was instrumental in guiding *The Great Gatsby* (1925) and *The Sun Also Rises* (1926) to completion. Identifying him as "easily the greatest force in the literature of our times," Hurston was thrilled to meet him in April (Kaplan 2003, 552, letter from Hurston to Mitchell in 1947). After their second meeting, she had a book deal for her next novel and a $500 advance. Although she had worked with the J. B. Lippincott Company for over a decade, she hoped that Perkins would be able to advise her through new projects.

Before she began writing anew, she used the advance money to complete her now two-year-old dream to sail to Honduras. Despite the money she had invested in Fred Irvine's boat, he had lost interest in the trip. As a result, she booked passage alone on a commercial liner, aiming to travel to places almost completely unknown to the Western world. She started with the capital of Tegucigalpa and then moved on to the North Coast, where she settled in at the Hotel Cosenza in Puerto Cortés. There she began work on a new novel, which she sent to her literary agent at Scribner's. The office was delighted with her work but also informed her that Max Perkins had died suddenly at the age of sixty-two. She was reassigned to a new editor, Burroughs Mitchell, who sent her $500 after Hurston alerted him from Honduras that she was desperate for money: "A drab terror has settled upon me by reason of my situation, though possibly you can never know the feeling, never having been in a foreign country and finding yourself without" (Kaplan 2003, 553, letter from Hurston to Mitchell in 1947). Hurston had not received payment on some essays and, unable to communicate with her agent's office, had no one to turn to but her new editor.

Although Hurston planned on visiting a lost city in the mountains of Mosquita, she extended her stay at the Hotel Cosenza to work on her new novel. In early September, she sent the second half of the book and eagerly asked for feedback: "If you have made any notes, it would be a great favor to me if you would let me have them to work from. No use in having SCRIBNER'S for a publisher and not be helped by that justly celebrated editorial braids. I do want to grow along as a writer" (Kaplan 2003, 554, letter from Hurston to Mitchell in 1947). Within a few weeks, Mitchell sent extensive comments, and Hurston worked to incorporate them into her revision. She wrote detailed responses to him, clarifying her thoughts on a novel that focused on white rather than black Southerners. Her gratitude for his critique was substantial, as she noted, "You have helped me in so many ways, and I hope that you will continue where you see the script needs some attention. . . . Please remember that I am neither Moses nor any of the writing apostles. Nothing that I set down is sacred. Any word or sentence can be changed or even cut out. What we want is success, not my deification" (Kaplan 2003, 563, letter from Hurston to Mitchell in 1947).

After submitting a final draft of the novel, then called *So Said the Sea*, Hurston at last took to the Honduran field in the fall. She headed to the Mosquita rain forests but soon encountered an intense rainy season. She quipped, "Already I smell fishy, and another month or so of this weather, and I will be waving you a greeting with a fin" (Kaplan 2003, 564, letter from Hurston to Mitchell in 1947). The weather prevented her from continuing on into the interior of the country. Even in the cities, the lack of paved road made for unsteady transport. After eighteen inches of rain in three days, she was left to "gnaw finger-nails and do some articles from the inside of me" while watching the goings-on of her hotel (Kaplan 2003, 565, letter from Hurston to Mitchell in 1948). At the start of 1948, Mitchell asked Hurston to return to New York to discuss in person some additional revisions for her novel. With the $250 sent by her editor, she bought a ticket for the five-day trip back to the United States. She had been in Central America for almost ten months and joked, "Having been down here in the bush so many months, you might have to run me down and catch me and sort of tie me up in the shed until I get house-broke again. No telling what all I might do when I see all them houses" (Kaplan 2003, 569, letter from Hurston to Mitchell in 1948). Still, the time away had greatly refreshed her. As she wrote to a friend, "I shall always be grateful to Honduras, though for it has given me back myself. I am my old brash self again" (Kaplan 2003, 549, letter from Hurston to Perkins in 1947).

Hurston spent several weeks working with Mitchell on her new novel. She wavered on the title, considering *Good Morning, Sun* and *The Sign of the Sun* before settling on *Seraph on the Suwanee*. With the book slated for publication in October, she went to Rhinebeck to enjoy the summer with Constance Seabrook, wife of the author and explorer William Seabrook. In early September, Mitchell requested that she return to New York to begin planning the launch of her fourth novel. He was also eager to learn what else she was working on, no doubt anticipating a long and fruitful partnership ahead. Unfortunately, the darkest chapter in Hurston's life was about to begin.

9

Nightmare and Recovery

Less than a week after Burroughs Mitchell wrote to Hurston, she had settled into a new room on West 112th Street in Harlem. On the afternoon of September 13, 1948, she was startled by a knock at her door. Before her stood a New York City police detective with a warrant for her arrest. She was brought to Manhattan's Twenty-Fourth Precinct, where she was fingerprinted and charged with sodomizing three school-age boys. The allegations had been brought by the New York Society for the Prevention of Cruelty to Children. Detective Howard Clancy and Alexander Miller, an officer of the Children's Society, informed her that the charges had originated with Mayme Allen, her former landlady at 124th Street, where Hurston had been involved in the "Block Mothers" program. She had lived there from October 1946 to May 1947. However, according to the landlady, Hurston had molested her son for over a year, including during the time she had spent in Honduras. Two other boys had told similar stories of abuse.

The charges had no merit, and Hurston unequivocally denied them, even offering to take a lie detector test. She urged the police to review her passport, which proved that she had been in Honduras for most of the past year. There were also plenty of friends who could attest that upon her return to the United States, she'd spent the summer outside of Manhattan. Despite the obvious inconsistencies in the allegations, Hurston remained in jail for much of the day until Mitchell and attorney Louis Waldman arrived to negotiate her release. She spent the night at Mitchell's home.

The following day, Hurston was told by a judge that her bail was set at $1,500. She was reminded of her right to a preliminary hearing. In court, she stood before her former landlady and the woman's ten-year-old son, Billy. She could hardly remember the other boys, eleven-year-olds Bobby and Jerry. Hurston had laughed when she first learned that the allegations coincided with her time in Honduras, but the Children's Society then shifted their position to claim that the only fixed date named by the victims was August 15, 1948. Hurston's statement to the police had been used to benefit the prosecution and lend the initial accusations credibility in terms of the timeline outlined by the boys. Hurston was outraged by this maneuvering: "Horror of disbelief took me. I could not believe that a thing like that could be happening in the United States and least of all to me. It just could not be true! I must be having a nightmare" (Kaplan 2003, 571, letter from Hurston to Carl Van Vechten and Fania Marinoff in 1948).

Scribner's hired Waldman to represent Hurston. The publishing company capped his fees at $1,000 and allowed additional charges to be made to Hurston's open account. Like Hurston, Waldman was incredulous at the accusations and expected that she, in turn, might be able to sue the Children's Society. At her preliminary hearing on September 21, Hurston wore a dashing red scarf around her neck and listened to District Attorney Frank Hogan and Assistant District Attorney Edward Dunleavy present their evidence, which included nothing more than the testimony of the three boys.

Billy identified "Mrs. Hurston" to the court and stated that she had rented a room in his mother's Harlem apartment two years ago. He explained that every Saturday, he would meet Hurston at 4:30 in the afternoon in the basement of a building on 124th Street. Billy stated that in this location, Hurston inserted his genitalia into her mouth. She also did this to his friends, Bobby and Jerry, and then gave them fifty cents each. Billy stated that two other adults were involved in this abuse, a veteran of World War I who worked as a janitor in the building and a Puerto Rican woman who had four children and ran a local candy store. Hurston had never even heard of these individuals, known as "Rufus" and "Sally."

Hurston struggled to make sense of these baseless accusations. Although the other characters named in the allegations were strangers to her, she did remember Billy. He was a popular boy who was sometimes known for causing mischief. At one point while living in the 124th Street apartment, Hurston had suggested to Billy's mother that she seek help for him at Bellevue Hospital. She was concerned that he was emotionally troubled, and by the time the allegations were made, the boy was receiving treatment there.

Hurston was so shocked by the perverse descriptions offered by Billy that she made a small noise that the judge understood to be a laugh. He immediately asked her about this response, to which Hurston replied that she was not laughing. The judge suggested it might be nervousness, and Hurston agreed. Valerie Boyd reminds us that in *Mules and Men*, Hurston characterizes black laughter as having "a hundred meanings." It "may mean amusement, anger, grief, bewilderment, chagrin, curiosity, simple pleasure or any other of the known or undefined emotions" (Hurston 1935, 62). This was no moment of levity or hilarity for Hurston; it was the start of the greatest challenge of her life.

While Waldman cross-examined Billy, the boy confessed that he and the other boys sometimes went alone to the basement on Saturday afternoons and engaged in oral and anal sex with each other. During these episodes, no one coerced them; they participated willingly in these activities. With this admission, Waldman asked that the charges against Hurston be dropped, but while the judge acknowledged that the situation was unusual, he insisted that the case be tried before the grand jury.

The prosecutors charged Hurston and the janitor together. Grand jury proceedings began on September 30, when the boys as well as Alexander Miller testified along with a doctor, who stated that he found anal injury in two of the boys. On October 1, indictments were issued against both Hurston and the janitor. Ten days later, she was arraigned on three counts of sodomy, one count of assault in the second degree, and one count of impairing the morals of a child. She entered a plea of "not guilty."

Waldman was certain that the charges against Hurston would be dismissed. Under his advice, Scribner's went ahead with the October publication of *Seraph on the Suwanee*. Waldman reasoned that even if the indictment led to a trial, that process could take months if not longer. Moreover, children's cases were closed to the public, and therefore, no one beyond those involved in the proceedings would even know about the trial. Free on bail, Hurston could continue with her original plans to promote the book.

Scribner's was so confident in Waldman's assessment and in Hurston's literary talent that, days after the indictment, they gave her a $500 advance on her next novel. Reviews of *Seraph on the Suwanee* confirmed Scribner's faith in their newly acquired author. *The New York Herald Tribune* printed a glowing review of the novel, lauding Hurston's "astonishing, bewildering talent." The book upended narrative expectations: "Emotional, expository; meandering, unified; naïve, sophisticated; sympathetic, caustic; comic, tragic; lewd, chaste—one could go on indefinitely reiterating this novel's contradictions and still end helplessly with the adjective unique" (Hedden 1948). With three thousand copies quickly sold, another printing of two thousand was ordered.

As early as 1942, Hurston had described her "hopes of breaking that old silly rule about Negroes not writing about white people" (Kaplan 2003,

467, letter from Hurston to Van Vechten in 1942). It would take six years for Hurston to commit to this idea, producing in *Seraph on the Suwanee* a book focused entirely on the lives of poor whites who, through hard work and exploitation of their black help, manage to climb into the comfort and stability of the middle class. Hurston had long avoided direct confrontation with what she called "the Race Problem," noting, "I was and am thoroughly sick of the subject. My interest lies in what makes a man or a woman do such-and-so, regardless of his color" (Hurston 1942, 171). While Hurston does not address "the Race Problem" as it primarily affects African Americans, *Seraph on the Suwanee* is a book deeply about race and, in particular, what it means to be white in the South.

Although this shift in focus is initially surprising for an author so deeply committed to describing the contours of black folklife, Hurston was not alone among African American writers of the mid-twentieth century in writing specifically about the lives of white people. Richard Wright, Ann Petry, Chester Himes, and later, James Baldwin would all pen what have come to be known as white-life novels, that is, novels by African Americans centered almost exclusively on white characters. These postwar texts, from Petry's *Country Place* (1947) to Wright's *Savage Holiday* (1954), respond to key national and international developments. With the conclusion of World War II, a universalist vision in which all races were seen as equals took hold among Western intellectuals and scientists. To this end, the United Nations, founded in 1945, affirmed the common humanity of all people. The same year that *Seraph on the Suwanee* was published, President Harry Truman issued two executive orders banning segregation in the armed forces and guaranteeing fair employment practices in the civil service. These actions suggested the federal government's attempt to present a unified, egalitarian America in which race was increasingly irrelevant. Writing about the lives of whites in addition to the lives of blacks was one way for African American authors to exercise a new artistic freedom that affirmed a racially transcendent conception of humanity.

Hurston's interest in describing the marriage of Arvay and Jim Meserve, the main characters in *Seraph on the Suwanee*, may have been a bit more calculating. Hazel Carby suggests that Hurston wrote the novel in order to establish a relationship with Metro-Goldwyn-Mayer Pictures; she hoped that satisfied white executives would then finance a movie version (Hurston 1991). Frustrated with her earlier rejections by Lippincott and still fixated on traveling to Honduras, she may have shrewdly calculated that a book about white people would simply sell better. Despite focusing on white Southerners, Hurston did not abandon her distinctive language. Rather, in writing the book, she came to conclude that there was no unique "Negro dialect in the South" (Kaplan 2003, 559, letter from Hurston to

Mitchell in 1947). She admitted her disappointment in learning that African Americans are not responsible for the speech patterns of the South.

> About the idiom of the book, I too thought that when I went out to dwell among the poor white in Dixie Country that they were copying us. But I found their colorful speech so general that I began to see that it belonged to them. After my fit of jealousy cooled off, I realized that Negroes introduced into N. America spoke no English at all, and learned from the whites. Our sense of rhythm points it up a bit, but the expressions for the most part are English held over from the Colonial period. I began to read English literature and found much of the picture talk in there. The black minstrels of the past sold America on the notion that all colorful idioms originated with Negroes. Just stand around where poor whites work, or around the village stores of Saturday nights and listen and you will hear something. (Kaplan 2003, 577–578, Hurston to Marjorie Kinnan Rawlings and Norton Baskin in 1948)

Much of what Hurston describes here directly contradicts her previous statements on the distinctiveness of African American vernacular. The 1934 essay "Characteristics of Negro Expression" identifies as uniquely black the "rhythm" and "picture talk" that she now attributes to English literature. Such contradictory positions would become more obvious as Hurston's views on race and politics evolved with her age. It is also worth considering that these comments were made in a letter addressed to Rawlings, whose novel *The Yearling* was made into an Academy Award–winning movie starring Gregory Peck and distributed by MGM in 1946. Rawlings's achievements so neatly mimicked Hurston's own ambitions that it is possible Hurston wrote to her with the calculated design of ingratiating herself into an especially useful social circle.

Regardless of the origins of the idiom used in *Seraph on the Suwanee*, the book does not draw simplistic equivalences between white and black characters. This is not *Their Eyes Were Watching God* from the perspective of a white woman. In fact, the contrast between Janie's empowering journey and Arvay's increasing submission to her husband suggests how certain forms of whiteness can function as their own form of bondage. Ironically, as Arvay transforms from a "white cracker" into a middle-class "seraph," she sacrifices key freedoms. Jim's social power, however, only grows with his wealth.

Although Jim first appears as a charming suitor who promises to care for and protect Arvay, he rapes her before carrying her off to be married. Jim operates from the premise that by raping Arvay, he will become "the man she really wants" (Hurston 1948, 46). Rape will guarantee her desire for him as he becomes both Arvay's assailant and her savior from the social shame that will result if others know she has been violated. By both raping and marrying Arvay, Jim defines his commanding presence in the life they will share together. Unlike Janie, who has multiple lovers and finds lasting passion with Tea Cake, Arvay accepts whatever life puts before her and entirely abandons her dream to become a missionary once Jim enters her life. Jim defines her purpose as exclusively to please him, telling her, "Love and marry me and sleep with me. That's all I need you for. Your brains are not sufficient to help me with my work; you can't think with me" (Hurston 1948, 35). At no point does Arvay question Jim's judgment. Instead, she allows him to dictate all aspects of their lives, including decisions about their three children. Jim, meanwhile, works hard to elevate his family into a higher social class, though part of his success is due to his ability to manipulate the racial politics of the South. Though he appears to be a friend to certain African American characters, he uses his ease with them to maximize his own business opportunities.

If *Their Eyes Were Watching God* is a testament to one woman's determination to live by her own desires, *Seraph on the Suwanee* is the opposite: a portrait of how a woman is entrapped by marriage and loses herself in service to others. The novel concludes with Arvay reflecting that "just like she had not known Jim, she had known her own self even less" (Hurston 1948, 351). It is no surprise that Hurston admitted that Arvay was often a frustration to her; "I get sick of her at times myself," she wrote to Mitchell as she was completing the manuscript (Kaplan 2003, 557, letter from Hurston to Mitchell in 1947).

Additional reviews in outlets like *The New York Times* and *The Herald Tribune* lauded the book but pointed out some weaknesses in the characters. Black papers did not even bother to assess a novel whose subject matter was so far removed from the political demands of the day. Later African American critics savaged the book. Alice Walker dismissed it as "reactionary, static, shockingly misguided, and timid," while Mary Helen Washington spurned what she called "an awkward and contrived novel, as vacuous as a soap opera" (Hemenway 1977, xvi). Washington expressed what may have been the conclusion of many black readers of the time: "In abandoning the source of her unique esthetic—the black cultural tradition—she [Hurston] also submerged her power and creativity" (Washington 1979, 21). Although the novel has since received more generous readings from critics interested in examining its depiction of motherhood and marriage as well as its conception of whiteness, *Seraph on the Suwanee* remains the most contested of Hurston's four novels.

A week of good sales and strong reviews for her latest work was brought to an abrupt end when a reporter from *The New York Age* approached Hurston about the criminal charges brought against her. He had been alerted of the trial through a black court employee. "Hysterical and almost prostrate," Hurston rejected the accusations and asked why the testimony of an unstable child was valued over her own. She continued, "It smacks of an anti-Negro violation of one's civil rights" and warned, "If such injustice can happen to one who has prestige and contacts, then there can be absolutely no justice for 'the little people' of this community" (Chase 1948).

The same day that Hurston's reaction was printed in *The New York Age*, the Baltimore newspaper *The Afro-American* printed four separate headlines on its front page about Hurston's difficulties. First came, "Boys 10, Accuse Zora," followed by "Novelist Arrested in Morals Charge" and then two headlines that referred to lines from *Seraph on the Suwanee*: "Reviewer of Author's Latest Book Notes Character Is 'Hungry for Love'" and "Did She Want 'Knowing and Doing' Kind of Love?" During one of their discussions about their marriage, Jim tells Arvay, "I'm just as hungry as a dog for a knowing and a doing love" (Hurston 1948, 262). Though Hurston had little in common with domineering Jim Meserve, the paper framed his words as her perverse desire. A picture of Hurston with a sly smile and a low-cut dress accompanied the damning headlines.

The Afro-American's lurid account of the charges was distributed by the National Negro Press Association. Although less sensational headlines were used, the article was reprinted in newspapers across the country. Hurston was horrified by how the press handled the case. She was especially incensed that a black court employee was responsible for the media scandal: "That is the blow that knocked me loose from all that I have ever looked to and cherished" (Kaplan 2003, 571, letter from Hurston to Van Vechten and Marinoff in 1948). This betrayal, along with the response by *The Afro-American*, fostered a resentment against African Americans that lingered for many years.

Unable to face the public or reporters of any kind, Hurston ceased all promotional activities for *Seraph on the Suwanee*. She left Harlem for the Bronx, where she languished in a deep depression. "I care nothing for anything anymore," she wrote.

> My country has failed me utterly. My race has seen fit to destroy me without reason, and with the vilest tools conceived by man so far. A Society, eminently Christian, and supposedly devoted to super-decency has gone so far from it's [sic] announced purpose, not to protect children, but to exploit the gruesome fancies of a pathological case and do this thing to human decency. Please do not forget that this thing was not done in the South, but in the so-called liberal North. Where shall I look in this country for justice? (Kaplan 2003, 571–572, letter from Hurston to Van Vechten and Marinoff in 1948)

Many of her closest friends, including Fannie Hurst, Marjorie Kinnan Rawlings, and Carl Van Vechten, reached out to Hurston during this awful time. Even some of the women she had known when she lived on 124th Street came to her aid. She learned that the neighborhood was horrified by the situation and "various simple people have been running around trying to make themselves heard by officialdom, but they have no force, being ordinary colored people" (Kaplan 2003, 572, letter from Hurston to Van Vechten and Marinoff in 1948).

Hurston was so exhausted and sickened by the ordeal that she contemplated suicide: "All that I believed in has failed me. I have resolved to die. It will take a few days for me to set my affairs in order, and then I will go" (Kaplan 2003, 573, letter from Hurston to Van Vechten and Marinoff in 1948). She struggled through her depression, convinced that there were larger forces at work: "I believe in the unchangeable laws that govern the universe. Even if I am dead, the truth is bound to be known in time" (Kaplan 2003, 575, letter from Hurston to Van Vechten and Marinoff in 1948). The truth of Hurston's innocence would at last be known months later when all charges were dismissed, but until then she suffered through additional trials. In response to a reader's criticism of *The Afro-American*'s treatment of Hurston, the paper responded with an emphatic statement about how silence had allowed perversion to increase and only through publicity would it be possible to eradicate such disease. Hurston barely emerged from her residence in the Bronx through the end of the year.

The start of 1949 brought no relief for her. Instead, a man named Richard Rochester, whom Hurston later identified as "my enemy," made a series of false allegations about her. He contacted Scribner's, various black newspapers, and *The New York World-Telegram* columnist Helen Worden Erskine claiming that Hurston owed him money and was guilty of indecent exposure and using marijuana. In late January, he brought Hurston to municipal court, demanding that she pay $270.15 in outstanding debts. Hurston believed that Rochester was still angry about an earlier deal involving a friend of hers. Rochester had tried to sue this man for stealing his car and had enlisted Hurston to testify on his behalf, but she refused since she knew nothing about the transaction. Incensed by this response, Rochester had threatened her "with a nation-wide bath of filthy publicity" (Kaplan 2003, 579, letter from Hurston to Hurst in 1949).

Hurston and Waldman responded by telling *The New York Age* that with these false charges, Rochester aimed to vilify Hurston before her court date. They both considered the possibility that Rochester was at the root of the original molestation charge. Defeated in his civil suit, Rochester found no traction for pursuing his additional allegations. Despite this triumph, Hurston was beset by financial difficulties. Her advance from Scribner's was gone, and all royalties from *Seraph on the Suwanee* went directly to pay Waldman's fees. The bad publicity made it impossible for her to secure freelance work. After pawning her typewriter, she resorted to asking her friends for help. Fannie Hurst sent a check as soon as she received

Hurston's request, which began, "Please help me. You know that I can take it and would not cry out for help unless I was really desperate" (Kaplan 2003, 579, letter from Hurston to Hurst in 1949).

After studying the case closely, Waldman arranged a private meeting with District Attorney Frank Hogan. He submitted a copy of Hurston's passport, which demonstrated that she had been in Honduras when most of the crimes supposedly occurred, and he laid out the witnesses he had gathered to speak to her integrity and character. Hogan arranged for two deputy attorneys to investigate the matter thoroughly. These two men, Jack Cotton and Aloysius Melia, began by again interviewing the boys. In the presence of Children's Society officer Alexander Miller, the boys told the deputy attorneys that Hurston and the other defendants were innocent of the charges they had made. Billy explained that he had concocted the story to avoid telling his mother that he had been having sex with his friends. The others corroborated this version of events. Despite this admission, it is also possible that the case against Hurston originated with Billy's mother. Mayme Allen later confessed to two friends that she had caught Billy and Jerry engaging in sexual activity. She wanted to get rid of her son, especially since her lover strongly disliked the boy. Allen first attempted to send him to boarding school and then tried to have him committed. A biographer of Hurston's final decade, Virginia Lynn Moylan, suggests that Allen may have devised the allegations against Hurston to bolster her case for her son's commitment while neatly blaming another for his sexual activity (Moylan 2011).

In either case, with the new testimony of the boys, the district attorney recommended that the charges be dropped against Hurston and the janitor. His report chronicled the shifting statements of the boys and noted that the charges against the defendants were made soon after Billy's mother had beat him when she'd asked why he was acting oddly. The district attorney surmised that Billy's mother believed the charges since she was already annoyed by Hurston's suggestion that the boy needed psychological help. After reviewing the report, Judge Saul Streit determined that no trial was needed. He dismissed the charges against Hurston on March 14, 1949, and expunged her record. The same was done for the other defendant as well.

Following this decision, Mitchell wrote to Hurston with hearty congratulations and asked about her new novel. However, Hurston remained in virtual isolation. She wrote a book review for the *New York Herald Tribune* later in March but mostly kept to herself in her Bronx apartment. It took two months for Hurston to begin reaching out to friends again. She thanked them for their support and spoke of leaving New York once she had enough money. In September, she returned to Miami, where Fred Irvine had a new boat, *The Challenger*. Hurston joined the Englishman for a trip to the Bahamas, and they again revived the idea of sailing to Honduras.

Hurston settled back into the calm she had always enjoyed in her home state. She worked on her new novel, which she tentatively titled, *The Lives of Barney Turk*. Slowly, she began to heal from the terrible ordeal in New York; "I feel that I have come to myself at last. I can even endure [t]he sight of a Negro, which I thought once I could never do again" (Kaplan 2003, 621, letter from Hurston to Mitchell in 1950). Berthed on the MacArthur Causeway, *The Challenger* was an ideal place for Hurston to restore herself to peace and calm. Along the shore, she picked coconuts and visited a favorite sapodilla tree. Every evening she admired the colors of the sunset, telling Mitchell back in New York, "The show is changed every day, but every performance is superb" (Kaplan 2003, 622, letter from Hurston to Mitchell in 1950).

By the end of the year, Hurston was much improved. She wrote, "Day by day in every way I'm getting human again. I caught myself laughing fit to kill yesterday" (Kaplan 2003, 624, letter from Hurston to Mitchell in 1950). At the start of 1950, Hurston was nearly done with a complete manuscript of her new novel and had begun lecturing publicly again. Her friend Sara Creech invited her to Belle Glade to speak to the town's Inter-Racial Council. Founded by Creech and other progressives dedicated to improving local race relations two years earlier, the council was composed of fifteen black and fifteen white members. The group met once a month to assess the problems facing the area's black and migrant communities and develop solutions to them. Dressed in white linen, Hurston impressed the council with her insight and intelligence. Hurston was also in turn impressed by the work of the council, as it represented the kind of collaboration that she believed could produce lasting social change. In a letter shortly after her visit to Belle Glade, Hurston elaborated on such thoughts to Creech:

> I suppose that I should not be surprised at the steps you have taken, for never was I more surprised and delighted than when I spoke at Belle Glade and found your extraordinary inter-racial organization. It should be a model for the nation, and according to what I hear, you, Sara Creech are at the heart of it. This follows a conclusion that I reached some years ago from observation. That is, that the so-called Race Problem will be solved in the South and by Southerners. I have noted that when a Southerner becomes convinced, he goes all out for correcting the situation. (Kaplan 2003, 630, letter from Hurston to Creech in 1950)

Though she would later be criticized for her opposition to the Supreme Court ruling in *Brown v. Board of Education*, which outlawed segregated schools, Hurston's seeming conservatism was rooted in a belief that racial progress must develop gradually and organically from voluntary social interaction between whites and blacks. Creech, who would become one of Hurston's closest friends in the final decade of her life, exemplified the potential of the white South to rectify its own problems. A businesswoman and activist, Creech also founded an award-winning preschool called Wee Care for the children of migrant workers. However, her greatest accomplishment was the creation of Sara Lee, the first mass-market black doll.

Creech consulted closely with Hurston on the development of an African American doll that did not cater to stereotypes like the P & M Doll Company's Topsy, which featured exaggerated eyes and pickaninny braids. Creech had observed black girls playing with white dolls and discussed the difficulty of obtaining black dolls with her African American friends. These experiences—along with the infamous study by Kenneth and Mamie Clark, which demonstrated a marked preference among black children for white dolls—convinced her of the importance of producing a high-quality black doll for black children. Hurston, who had long decried colorism among the black community, vigorously supported Creech's efforts:

> Please allow me to say how pleased I am that you let me see the pictures of the Negro dolls that you plan to put on the market. They are exquisitely designed, and magnificently executed in model. The thing that pleased me most, Miss Creech was that you, a White girl, should have seen into our hearts so clearly, and sought to meet our longing for understanding of us as we really are, and not as some would have us. That you have not insulted us by a grotesque caricature of Negro children, but conceived something of real Negro beauty. These dolls are adorable. (Kaplan 2003, 629, letter from Hurston to Creech in 1950)

Hurston was so enthusiastic about Creech's work that she offered to show her models to a number of her most influential associates, including Charles S. Johnson, who had become the president of Fisk University, Morehouse College President Benjamin Hays, Mary McLeod Bethune, and Howard University President Mordecai Johnson. Creech found significant support from all of Hurston's contacts, including Van Vechten, who helped facilitate a detailed article on the doll's debut in the December 1951 issue of *Life* magazine.

Encouraged by Creech and other friends, Hurston spoke before a group of Dade County librarians and was questioned by one audience member about why all of her books except *Seraph on the Suwanee* were out of print. Despite this fact, her work was finding attention in other venues. Stetson Kennedy, Hurston's former supervisor at the Florida Writers' Project, relied on Hurston's research to write his social history of Florida, *Palmetto Country* (1942). Similarly, Benjamin A. Botkin, the previous director of the Federal Writers' Project's Folklore Division, published two folklore books that also highlighted Hurston's contributions to the field. Twenty-one of

> ## THE SARA LEE DOLL
>
> Produced by the Ideal Toy Company in the 1950s, the Sara Lee doll was the first mass-produced doll specifically made for African American children. White activist Sara Lee Creech was so troubled when she saw black girls playing with light-skinned dolls that she resolved to create a doll that would reflect their physical bodies. Creech's concern aligned with a series of studies conducted by Kenneth and Mamie Clark in the 1940s affirming that black children prefer to play with lighter-skinned dolls. These findings suggested that even at a young age, black children had assimilated negative social beliefs about their own race. The study was foundational to the argument against segregated schools as presented in the 1954 Supreme Court ruling in *Brown v. Board of Education*.
>
> Creech believed that a quality doll made to reflect African American children would help them feel more confident and proud of their racial identity. Creech found widespread support among a number of influential figures, including Eleanor Roosevelt, Ralph Bunche, and Mary McLeod Bethune. The sculptor Shelia Burlingame molded the first doll head. Creech eventually partnered with the Ideal Toy Company, and though the Sara Lee doll was heralded in *Time, Newsweek, Ebony,* and *Independent Woman*, it was not produced in the mass numbers Creech had hoped for. There was also some difficulty with the dye in the vinyl; it lost its color and seeped into the doll's clothing. Despite these setbacks, the Sara Lee doll was far ahead of its time. The next mass-produced black doll, Barbie's friend Christie, was not produced until 1968. Now dolls of all hues are widely available in stores across the nation.

her short pieces were included in *A Treasury of American Folklore* (1944), while *A Treasure of Southern Folklore* (1949) printed nine of them. Award-winning poet Carl Sandburg added Hurston's version of "Cold Rainy Day" to the latest edition of his collection of American songs, *New American Songbag* (1950).

In the fall of 1950, Hurston returned to New York for the first time since the molestation charges had been dismissed. While staying at a room on Harlem's West 131st Street, she reconnected with old friends like Van Vechten and Ethel Waters. Creech was also in New York to promote her Sara Lee doll, which had garnered the interest of Eleanor Roosevelt. While Hurston enjoyed her visits with Creech and other associates of the former first lady, the city stirred painful memories of the past. In November, she wrote a troubling letter to Charles S. Johnson suggesting that the reigning black intellectuals may have orchestrated her downfall through encouragement of the false molestation allegations: "Because I openly expressed my scorn of them, they got up what they took to be an unbeatably wonderful scheme to kill me off forever. Only these monumental 'intellectuals,' in their ecstasy, did not take the time to find out where I was when they stated the dates for things" (Kaplan 2003, 634, letter from Hurston to Johnson in 1950). Such unsubstantiated claims reflect a troubling paranoia that, while understandable given the horror of the charges she faced, suggest a weakened grip on reality.

By December, Hurston was ready to escape the cold of New York and return to the South. Creech had persuaded her to move to Belle Glade, but she refused her white friend's invitation to drive back together. Hurston was concerned that segregated hotels and restaurants would make the trip difficult for them both. Creech agreed to fly home while Hurston traveled alone, stopping first in Jacksonville to visit her brother John before arriving in Belle Glade at the end of the month. Though Creech invited Hurston to live with her and her mother, Mary, Hurston chose to rent a room at the Roof Garden Hotel. Though it had no cooking facilities or private bathroom, her room was close to the inviting Lake Okeechobee and only a few miles from Creech's home. While staying at the Roof Garden Hotel, Hurston adopted a black-and-white terrier named Spot and integrated herself among the locals. She had first visited Belle Glade in 1927 on one of her missions to collect folklore. Once comprising a few farms and stores, the town had grown to include a number of black-owned businesses, such as Houston's Drug Store, which hosted gossip sessions comparable to the ones in front of Joe Clarke's store in the Eatonville of Hurston's childhood. Though private, Hurston would occasionally stop at Maynor's Hair Salon or the local ice cream parlor. She enjoyed fishing in Lake Okeechobee and visiting the Seminole Indian Reservation. There she befriended Sally Tiger-Tail, the daughter of chief Billy Cyprus, who gifted her with various pieces of Seminole clothing.

Much of Hurston's time was spent with the Creeches. Sara took after her mother, who was also strongly independent and intelligent. Mary ran the city's first florist shop from the family home while her daughter operated her own insurance agency downtown. Hurston, along with Spot, often spent the day at the Creech home, talking and helping Mary with the flowers. She would occasionally stay for dinner, doing the cooking herself. The women feasted on Hurston's fried chicken, mashed potatoes, turnip greens, and sweet-potato pone, a custard dessert. Hurston also helped Sara paint the house. Mary sat on a chair outside to converse with the younger women, often attracting the interest of neighbors, who brought iced tea and their own chairs.

Hurston's admiration for both Creeches was deep. She considered Sara to be "a phenomena. Perhaps the foremost individual of the area for better race relations" and noted that Mary "is extraordinary too." Hurston was especially impressed that the Creeches were not of the Southern aristocracy but instead part of a population that had been historically marginalized. She observed, "When you think of the generations of individual talent among the poor whites that never got a hearing, it is truly tragic" (Kaplan 2003, 641, letter from Hurston to Carl Sandburg in 1951). Hurston's genuine affection and respect for the Creeches may explain the subject of the novel that she labored on during this time, *The Lives of Barney Turk*. Like *Seraph on the Suwanee*, its protagonist was also white. While many critics have lamented Hurston's interest in portraying white characters in her fiction, her relationship with the Creeches suggests that this shift was less about an abandonment of black culture than an increasing appreciation of her identity as a Southerner, irrespective of race. Moreover, by the 1950s, Hurston had become frustrated with other African Americans. In 1954, she wrote to a white friend that "Negroes, have played every vile trick upon me that can be imagined, without rhyme or reason except hating to see me reap any benefit from hard work.... I want no parts of them, and if somebody were to set up a nation of American Negroes, I would be the very first person NOT to go there" (Kaplan 2003, 709, letter from Hurston to William Bradford Huie in 1954). These sentiments reflect the scars of the 1948 scandal and demonstrate the tragic evolution of a writer who had previously dedicated her life to describing and understanding the contours of black life.

In February of 1950, Hurston sent Mitchell a complete copy of *The Lives of Barney Turk*. Mitchell found the manuscript less promising than all of her previous work and identified numerous weaknesses in its plot. Hurston agreed to implement the changes he suggested, but without an unequivocal acceptance of the book, she was left with no advance money to help pay her bills. Because she had dedicated all her time and energy to her new novel, she had not made any money on freelance work. Despite her wealth of good friends, Hurston was desperate for money.

At nearly sixty years old, she had no choice but to begin looking for work. She found a job as a maid for a couple living in Rivo Alto Island, an elite Miami suburb. Mr. and Mrs. Kenneth Burritt offered her $30 a week, plus room and board. Hurston had done such work when she was much younger, so the basic tasks were familiar to her, if far removed from the elite celebrity world she had occupied not so long ago. The Burritts showed no personal interest in their new domestic, who likely appeared little different from the other maids they had employed over the years. The only thing that distinguished Hurston was her name, which Mrs. Burritt came across one day in the latest issue of *The Saturday Evening Post*. The Alabama native was shocked to discover that her "girl" had published a story in the magazine, "The Conscience of the Court." She later explained,

It was a difficult few hours we spent after that. Servants are servants and must act accordingly unless the whole traditional relationship of employer and employee is to be endangered. But adjustments were called for in this case. I must say without reservation that Zora is one of the most cultured women I have ever met and surely one of the finest. (Lyons 1950)

Mrs. Burritt was so astounded by her maid's talents that the story quickly made the rounds. In March, James Lyons, a *Miami-Herald* reporter, appeared to investigate the situation. His headline read, "Famous Negro Author Working as Maid Here Just 'To Live A Little.'" Hurston stated that she had not taken the job out of financial necessity but rather because "you can only use your mind so long. Then you have to use your hands," adding, "A change of pace is good for everyone" (Lyons 1950). The article reported that Hurston intended to use her experiences as a maid to begin a national magazine for domestic workers. As with the disastrous *Afro-American* article, this one also received national attention. The story was reprinted in papers across the country. Lyons was commissioned to write a longer version for *The St. Louis Post-Dispatch*. Back in New York, *The Amsterdam News* published the headline "Famous Author Working as Maid for White Folks Down in Dixie!" and considered why she might have taken the job, noting with accuracy that despite her literary talents, she had never made much money. Hurston called it "one slam of a publicity do-dad." She had tried to avoid the media attention but could do little to stop the flood of interest. She acknowledged that at least "Miami is certainly Hurston-conscious," which had led to new interest in autographed copies of *Seraph on the Suwanee*. She confessed, "All I wanted was a little spending change when I took this job" (Kaplan 2003, 627, letter from Hurston to Mitchell in 1950).

There are multiple ironies at play in the fact that the story in *The Saturday Evening Post* that spurred this "publicity do-dad" was "The Conscience of the Court." Its main character, Laura Lee, is a devoted family servant who is charged with assault after trying to physically stop a man from collecting a debt from her employer. Although Laura Lee risks her freedom to protect the property of "Miz' Celestine," a white judge clears the charges against her. Hurston's stereotypical portrait of Laura Lee as a dutiful, self-sacrificing servant sharply contrasts with the far more nuanced black characters that populate her earlier fiction. However, Hemenway warns that "any analysis of 'Conscience of the Court' is complicated by Zora's admission that the story was heavily edited by the *Post*'s staff, and by the knowledge that she badly needed to sell the story" (Hemenway 1977, 327). Hurston certainly never harbored such fierce loyalty for the Burritts, though they may have been charmed by the thought that in a crisis their maid would act like Laura Lee. Instead, soon after the first article about Hurston appeared in *The Miami Herald*, she told the Burritts that she would be leaving their home. A number of ghostwriting offers had appeared along with the slew of publicity, offering the possibility that she could again make her living by writing.

Hurston's next published piece, "What White Publishers Won't Print," could not have been more different than the anodyne "The Conscience of the Court." The first line offers an apt description of how the Burritts would have first perceived their new maid: "I have been amazed by the Anglo-Saxon's lack of curiosity about the internal lives and emotions of the Negroes" (Hurston 1979, 169). Clearly inspired by her earlier experiences with Lippincott, Hurston rails against "the lack of literature about the higher emotions and love life of upper-class Negroes and the minorities in general." She blames this absence on a publishing industry that prioritizes profit over the exploration of complex subjectivities. Instead, stereotypes of African Americans that cater to comfortable notions of white superiority reign in literary texts. She asks for writing that explores "the average, struggling, non-morbid Negro" and affirms "that Negroes are no better nor no worse, and at times just as boring as everyone else" (Hurston 1979, 173).

Hurston also returned to politics during this time, taking a job in the campaign of George Smathers in the Florida Democratic Senate primary. This experience became the basis for an essay in the November issue of *The American Legion Magazine*. "I Saw Negro Votes Peddled" describes the buying and selling of black votes in the primary. Hurston claims such election rigging is not a thing of the past but that the injustices of Reconstruction continue on. Ignoring how black voter registration increased throughout the South once all-white primaries were challenged in the courts, Hurston focused only on negative behavior she witnessed such as the selling of votes for two dollars apiece. She decries this fraud and calls it an insult to the very premise of democracy. Although she calls out politicians for this deceit, she is especially distraught by the participation of African Americans: "It is positively astounding that any adult Negro could look upon the right to vote as a small thing, let alone regard this highest right in civilization in such a way as to put a price upon it" (Hurston 1950). Her characterization of African Americans as lacking both "integrity" and "brains" caused Lester Granger, the executive director of the NAACP, to challenge Hurston publicly. Other articles in *The Miami Herald* vigorously denied Hurston's account of vote peddling and championed the active political participation of African Americans.

Hurston's involvement in the Smathers campaign provided her with another opportunity; she was invited to ghostwrite a book for Smathers's father, the retired judge Frank Smathers. However, Hurston only stayed on the job for a few months. She acknowledged that "it did me good as an author for it gave me a better insight into human vanity." However, Smathers's entrenched prejudice made the position untenable, or as Hurston explained, "I could see at times that he could not accept the reality that a descendent of slaves could do something in an intellectual way that he could not." The judge was an inveterate patriarch whose chronic illness exacerbated his abusive tendencies. While he was accustomed to attacking his family members, Hurston stood firm: "I do not beat down easily, and we fought like tigers—from day to day, and I came to see that he loved it. He had met at last a foe worthy of his steel. I saw his wife and his two sons backing off him with bowed heads, but not your Topsy girl. I let him have it with both barrels time and time again" (Kaplan 2003, 630–631, letter from Hurston to Mitchell in 1950). At one point, the judge stuck his fingers in his ears to keep out Hurston's words. She not only kept talking but pulled his fingers out. Despite her boldness, the judge did not fire Hurston; instead, she left of her own will, exhausted by the entire family.

Hurston continued to work on her revision of *Barney Turk*, and after sending a new draft to Mitchell in September, she returned to New York. She gave the keynote address at a dinner for Ethel Waters and reunited with Van Vechten. However, by December she was ready to move on. She had no patience with the snow, and Florida beckoned with its eternal sun. The winter season also brought the disappointing news that Scribner's had rejected *Barney Turk*. Hurston had hoped she could build on the success of *Seraph on the Suwanee* with another story about a white protagonist, but Mitchell decided that the manuscript lacked her distinctive style and voice. He explained, "Somehow, the reader is not made to feel that what happens to Barney or what he does is important; the reader isn't taken right into the story, persuaded by it." He added, "There are of course wonderful flashes of writing—as there always are in anything you do. But they are not enough to make this a good piece of your work. It is a hard thing to have to say, but I must tell you that we think the publication of this book would be a disservice to you. We would not do well with it, we are sure of that, and your reputation would suffer" (Mitchell 1950, letter from Mitchell to Hurston on October 3). Mitchell's decision on the manuscript was so strong that he recommended she not revise it, but instead put it aside entirely. He suggested that it might be best to move on from fiction and focus on another volume of her autobiography.

Mitchell's rejection of *Barney Turk* left Hurston "with a year's work done for nothing, and me cold in hand. That is a Negro way of saying penniless. And I do mean penniless. God!" (Kaplan 2003, 647–648, letter from Hurston to Jean Parker Waterbury in 1951). She moved in with friends living in Belle Glade and began a series of new projects. She was desperate to sell something soon, as she was tired of "having to avoid folks who have made me loans so that I could eat and sleep. The humiliation is getting to be much too much for my self-respect, speaking from the inside of my soul" (Kaplan 2003, 648–649, letter from Hurston to Waterbury in 1951). Although Hurston would never publish another book, she did find hard-won satisfaction and peace in the final years of her life.

10

The Final Years

In January 1951, *The American Legion Magazine* approached Hurston about writing an article on the relationship between Communism and African Americans. Hurston had long harbored reservations about the Communist Party. Though she found some value in their ultimate goals, she was wary of their methods: "If I ever meet a Communist with a sense of humor, and a sentence he or she thought up him or herself, I will take the matter under serious consideration. Pooling material things is not so bad but if I have to quote and repeat the same identical phrases, down to the last stress on a syllable as everybody else, they can count me out of the Party" (Kaplan 2003, 501, letter from Hurston to Henry Allen Moe in 1944). Hurston expanded upon her doubts in the essay "Why the Negro Won't Buy Communism." She argued that Communists lured African Americans to their side with false promises when in fact "the plan was obviously to herd in the dumb black fools, and when the time arrived to use us up like so many worn-out undershirts and think nothing about it." The Communists succeeded only in "creating a permanent lower class" and in turn alienating African Americans because "the Negro is the most class-conscious individual in the United States." Comparing Communists to "soulless zombies," Hurston ended by noting that "we feel closer to the American white man than to any foreign Negro" and thus, as Americans, "we are confirmed in our springing impulses by the spirit that hovers this continent" (Hurston 1951).

The $600 Hurston received for the essay helped with her car payments and her adoring care of Spot. When the terrier went missing, Hurston was distraught: "I have almost been out of my head for the last two weeks" (Kaplan 2003, 639, letter from Hurston to Jean Parker Waterbury in 1951). She had developed a significant affection for the dog, and upon its return, Hurston doted on the dog: "I am very glad that I have come through to a calm balance again so that I can be of the best service to her, and also know just how she felt in those ten terrible days away from me. She is thin, because she had refused to eat, and I never saw such tragic eyes on anybody" (Kaplan 2003, 643, letter from Hurston to Waterbury in 1951). Spot inspired a short story that she sent to her agent along with a new novelette.

Although the Spot piece was rejected, her agent hoped that *The Golden Bench of God* would develop into a full-length novel. Hurston based it on the lives of the first female self-made American millionaire, C. J. Walker, who had made her fortune developing and selling beauty products for black women, and her daughter, A'Lelia, an associate of Hurston during the heyday of the Harlem Renaissance. Hurston was wary of committing herself to a novel after the failure of *Barney Turk*. Instead, she considered transforming it into a play or seeing it published another way: "I would pray that it get serialized in one of the big women's mags, but since I have paid no church dues in quite some time, Old Maker is under no obligation to me whatsoever." Though "the very mention of 'novel' gives me a shudder," Hurston agreed to continue work on it "as soon as I can get me some permanent place to live" (Kaplan 2003, 647–648, letter from Hurston to Waterbury in 1951). Jean Parker Waterbury, Hurston's agent, later admitted that her client's writing had deteriorated. She speculated that this was caused by "her deteriorating state of mind, health, and finances." The result was work characterized by "poor organization, lack of focus, and a tendency to degenerate into a diatribe of personal hate" (Moylan 2011, 85).

Once her payment from *The American Legion* arrived, Hurston moved into her own place and there "caught fire on the novel." She proclaimed that she felt "more confident about this story than anything I have done since THEIR EYES WERE WATCHING GOD" (Kaplan 2003, 649–650, letter from Hurston to Waterbury in 1951). However, her progress was cut short by illness. In March, she was struck by the flu. After not seeing her friend for over a week, Creech found her at the Roof Garden Hotel in an awful condition. Creech rushed Hurston to the hospital, where she stayed for nearly two weeks. "Never have I been so ill since I have been grown," she recollected (Kaplan 2003, 653, letter from Hurston to Waterbury in 1951). Back to health in the spring, Hurston returned to her novel, paying special attention to fleshing out the main characters. She had grand ambitions for the book, noting, "Never a truly indigenous Negro novel has been written so far. Punches have been pulled to 'keep things from the white folks' or angled politically, well to show our sufferings, rather than to tell a story as is. I have decided that the time has come to write truthfully from the inside. Imagine that no white audience is present to hear what is said" (Kaplan 2003, 655–656, letter from Hurston to Waterbury in 1951). Unfortunately, no manuscript of *The Golden Bench of God* survives.

In addition to working on her new manuscript, Hurston also approached *The Saturday Evening Post* about writing a profile of Ohio Senator Robert Taft, who was considering a run for the 1952 Republican presidential nomination. Though initially she "just want[ed] to take a good look at the man who might easily be our next prexy," she found "the more research I did on the man, the better I liked him" (Kaplan 2003, 656, 660, letter from Hurston to Waterbury in 1951). Published in December 1951, "A Negro Voter Sizes Up Taft" netted Hurston an impressive $1,000. Unfortunately, this price was not matched by much original thought. Hemenway observes that "it is the usual campaign rhetoric, full of praise and largely void of analysis" (Hemenway 1977, 335). In the essay, Hurston expresses her approval of Taft's work in the Senate; he opposed the poll tax while supporting the FEPC and local black politicians. Hurston suggests that he would be more vigilant in keeping out Communists than Dwight D. Eisenhower, who eventually won the Republican nomination.

Cleared of her debts from the payment by *The Saturday Evening Post*, Hurston took Spot and her belongings to Eau Gallie after a heartfelt goodbye from the Creeches. There she rented a house for five dollars a week, far less than what she'd paid in Belle Glade. Eau Gallie was a place Hurston had long wished to return to since it bore fond memories of happier years. She soon learned that the one-room house at the corner of Guava Avenue and Fifth Street that she'd occupied when she wrote *Mules and Men* was open. Although the neighborhood had changed significantly in the past twenty years, turning from black to white, Hurston seized on the chance to live there again and even hoped to buy the property. Her landlord, the mayor of the town, agreed to rent it provided that she work to improve the large yard. Hurston threw herself into its rehabilitation, writing:

> It looked like a jungle three weeks ago, and it took a strong heart and an eye on the future for me to move in when I arrived. . . . The grounds have great possibilities, and I really would love to own it. I still must remove tons of junk, old tin cans and bottles from the premises. Somehow, this one spot on earth feels like home to me. I have always intended to come back here. (Kaplan 2003, 663, letter from Hurston to Waterbury in 1951)

Hurston devoted herself to painting the house, tending the garden, and reviving the artesian well close to the house. She bought an icebox and furniture and paid her health and accident insurance for a year. Around her home, she chased cats away from the birds but kept the snakes because they killed rats. Though it was highly unusual for a black tenant to rent in a white neighborhood, as her landlord suspected, Hurston's efforts to beautify the land and her friendly disposition won over the neighbors. A local dairy even gave her a load of compost to help with her garden. She luxuriated in the natural beauty of her home and the hard work it required: "Living the kind of life for which I was made, strenuous and close to the soil, I am happier than I have been for at least ten years. I am up at five oclock and in bed around nine every night" (Kaplan 2003, 670). She even found that the physical labor led her to lose some of the weight she had put on in recent years. The only disruption came from the sky when aircraft heading to Patrick Air Force Base streamed by. But even such interruptions held wonder for Hurston: "It really is something to see something that looks like a silver barracuda tearing across the sky ahead of its own sound. As many as I have seen now, the thrill is still strong" (Kaplan 2003, 669–670, letter from Hurston to Burroughs Mitchell in 1951).

In early July, Hurston had a dream about her mother. It was one of only three dreams she'd ever had of Lucy Potts since her death almost fifty years earlier in 1904. Lucy appeared as an adolescent with a "serene and happy aura." Hurston remembered:

> She said nothing, just smiled and beamed on me, handed me a note written on the lined paper of a cheap tablet, and somehow was gone. I unfolded the note, written in lead pencil, and read, 'The hidden enmity will come out into the open now, but do not be afraid. Thank them for the insincere advice given with cheerfulness. Make the new arrangements suggested to you, and see yourself go to greater heights. (Kaplan 2003, 670, letter from Hurston to Waterbury in 1951)

The dream fortified Hurston for the news she would receive the following day: that Scribner's was rejecting *The Golden Bench of God* for publication. In his letter to Hurston, Mitchell explained that although he found the protagonist interesting, the manuscript read to him more like an extended short story than a developed novel. Unfortunately, he had no suggestions for revision. Hurston resolved to "[follow] the instructions of the dream, and shall answer pleasantly, but vague" (Kaplan 2003, 671, letter from Hurston to Waterbury in 1951). Mitchell urged her to reconsider writing a second volume of her autobiography, and after Lippincott also rejected *The Golden Bench of God*, she took the suggestion more seriously: "I am bunching my muscles for the leap" (Kaplan 2003, 676, letter from Hurston to Waterbury in 1951). We can only speculate what caused both publishers to pass on the manuscript. Hurston's writing skills may have deteriorated in her older age, or her move back to fiction focused on black life may not have been deemed of interest to white audiences. It is also possible that the 1948 scandal, though years past, may have been a factor in the decision of

Mitchell and Lippincott. Hurston's literary agent, Waterbury, also observed in retrospect that financial worries may have negatively impacted her work. She told Hemenway, "She could write like an angel and yet be absolutely sloppy when she was desperate for money . . . she would lose all sense of perspective and judgment, and just as long as there were words on a page she felt that she could get some cash for it" (Hemenway 1977, 341). Despite the negative reception *The Golden Bench* received from publishers, Hurston's passion and determination to write prevailed, even if less of her work received a wide audience.

During this time, she busied herself with other small writing projects. Spot had inspired a story that she was revising, and she considered a series of linked stories about various biblical figures, including Abraham, King Saul, Ham, and David. She was also "half through with a tongue-in-cheek exhortation to career women to return to the home lest we lose our ascendancy over men" and was considering an article called "Do Negroes Like Negroes?" in which she explored "the explosion from the center, driving us outward from each other" (Kaplan 2003, 674, letter from Hurston to Waterbury in 1951). With her finances still tenuous, Hurston learned that due to an estate dispute, she would not be able to purchase the house she was renting. However, since she lacked the money to buy, this news was hardly disappointing. Her landlord promised that she could continue renting as long as she liked.

None of her short pieces were ever published, and by the fall, she "ran out of groceries and had to hock my machine," meaning her typewriter. She had hoped to travel to New York to attend a tea hosted by Eleanor Roosevelt to decide on a skin color for the Sara Lee doll, but Hurston did not have enough money to make the trip. Although Creech would have paid for the visit, Hurston was too proud to accept such a gift. Even so, her spirits were positive and she affirmed that "keeping outdoors, raising a fine garden, both flowers and vegetables, has done me a world of good" (Kaplan 2003, 678, letter from Hurston to Waterbury in 1951). Her yard was so beautiful that tourists often came by to take pictures. Though her neighbors were aware that she had financial difficulties, Hurston generally refused help. A local white woman named Elizabeth Owen remembered that she once gifted Hurston with a box of typewriter paper but Hurston insisted on paying for it. On another occasion, Hurston cared for Owen's young daughter, Caroline, while she and her husband took a trip to Virginia. She would not accept payment for the favor but instead presented Owen with an inscribed copy of *Seraph on the Suwanee* that read, "To Mrs. Clifford Owen, a throne-angel in a robe of shining rainbows" (Moylan 2011, 90).

Toward the end of the year, however, Hurston's health declined precipitously. She described herself as having "been the victim of some kind of tropical virus that the doctors do not quite understand" and speculated that it may have been contracted from impure water in Honduras (Kaplan 2003, 682, letter from Hurston to Waterbury in 1951). The illness operated in cycles, leaving her so weak that she could barely lift a hand and with painful swelling in her groin and underarms. She was forced to stay in bed for days, until the illness subsided just as quickly as it had come on.

Once she recovered, she organized five folk concerts in the Eau Gallie area with the help of Owen. Locals learned of Hurston's history of putting on such productions and urged her to bring her experience to their stages. She organized a cast of local black children to perform a version of her original folk concert, *The Great Day*. The first concert was performed at a Melbourne High School Parent-Teacher Association meeting, with Hurston playing the bongo drum. The four concerts for whites and one for blacks helped cover her expenses, but she found that they took away from her writing time: "Too much work for too little money," she concluded (Kaplan 2003, 683, letter from Hurston to Waterbury in 1951). Her tight financial situation caused her to pass on a few invitations. She was asked to attend a debate between Taft and Eisenhower in Boston and to work on the Citizens for Taft Committee in New York. However, she had neither a winter coat nor the funds to travel North. Concerns about money also impeded her ability to write well. She confessed to a friend, "I try to get down to work but it is hard now when I worry about money." She continued to tinker with pieces about Spot, writing, "You have no idea how much animal psychology I have acquired," but nothing proved to be publishable (Kaplan 2003, 688, letter from Hurston to Waterbury in 1951). Hurston seems to have retreated so far into herself and the idyllic isolation of her home in Eau Gallie that she was no longer able to appeal to a broad audience.

She at last found some escape from her frustrations when *The Pittsburgh Courier*, a black newspaper with a national circulation, invited her to cover what Hurston would call "perhaps the most sensational trial ever held in the South" (Hurston 1952). Ruby McCollum, a thirty-seven-year-old mother and the wealthiest black woman in Live Oak, Florida, was tried for the murder of Dr. Clifford Leroy Adams, a prominent white doctor and state senator. Hurston described Adams as "a broad-shouldered six-footer with magnificence of body" (Hurston 1952). McCollum was married to Sam McCollum, who had made his fortune from bolita, a popular gambling game, but for years she had been sexually involved with Adams. After McCollum was arrested, her husband fled with their children but died of a heart attack when he arrived at the home of his mother-in-law. In addition to facing a charge of first-degree murder, McCollum was the subject of a $100,000 civil suit filed by Adams's widow. Although McCollum pleaded self-defense, the prosecutors portrayed her as a cold-blooded killer and argued for the death penalty. The case proved to be one of the most riveting trials in the history of Florida and garnered national coverage. As a result, it brought danger for a lone black woman like Hurston. Live Oak was known to be a central location of Ku Klux Klan activity, and locals were not just suspicious of but at times openly hostile to journalists and other outsiders.

Hurston's first account of the case appeared in the October 11 issue of the *Courier*. She described the courtroom and McCollum, who only spoke once to whisper something to her lawyer. Hurston noted that the audience members must have awaited the trial feeling their own worries vanish and lucky not to be in the defendant's shoes. Next to McCollum's troubles, Hurston's own financial concerns must have seemed inconsequential. In chronicling the story, Hurston was less concerned with the details of the case than with the life and character of Ruby McCollum. For her ten-part series, Hurston interviewed friends, relatives, neighbors, and even McCollum to better understand her motives. McCollum and Adams had begun their affair in 1948. They had one child together, and McCollum was pregnant at the time of the murder. McCollum claimed, however, that their relationship had not always been consensual, and in doing so became the first black woman to testify that a white man sexually abused her.

Throughout her coverage of the case, Hurston offered her own opinions on matters, though she framed them as the kind of conventional wisdom everyone should recognize: "Colored women ought to be proud to stick to their own men, and leave these white men alone. And more specially when they ought to know that white men ain't no trouble at all. They can't do nothing in bed but praise the Lord. Nothing to 'em at all" (Hemenway 1977). However, the trial soon revealed that the problem between McCollum and Adams was not simply one of race. Ruby worked as her husband's bookkeeper, keeping accounts not only of those who participated in bolita but also those state and local officials who were bribed to look the other way. Ruby explained that Adams had demanded payments from her, exacerbating their already fraught and at times violent relationship. The trial led to more public attention on the bolita racket, including the law enforcement officials, politicians, and businessmen who profited from the game. Another factor at play was that Adams had taken on a twenty-year-old white girlfriend. In recent months, he'd spent less time with Ruby, who in turn felt increasingly dependent on his attention. She became mentally unstable and three times was admitted to Brewster Hospital in Jacksonville for treatment.

Hurston portrayed McCollum in language that mimicked the awakening of her most famous protagonist, Janie Crawford from *Their Eyes Were Watching God*. Like Janie embarking on her quest for self-discovery, McCollum "was ready to set out on her journey to the big horizon." Hurston even went so far as to invoke the metaphor of the pear tree: McCollum "felt like a blossom on the bare limb of a pear tree in the spring ... opening her gifts to the world, but where was the bee for her blossom?" (Hurston 1953). Over the course of the trial, Hurston seemed to identify more and more with McCollum. She was especially irritated by the ways in which other African Americans treated Ruby, who was wealthier and better educated than most people in her community. Hurston found the local black gossip about Ruby cowardly and small-minded: "These local Colored people were, for the most part, little people, the kind of people irrespective of race, who have only the earth as their memorial. The sprig of hyssop was in their hands, and they were sprinkling the blood of the paschal lamb around their doorways so that the Angel of Death would pass over them" (Moylan 2011, 123). Hurston's comments resonate with her own disdain for the African Americans who betrayed her during the 1948 scandal. Just as she felt that the black courthouse clerk and the reporters at *The Afro-American* were quick to tear down her reputation, she felt that McCollum's social success fed local jealousy and spite.

Although the jury found McCollum guilty, Hurston ended her series with a more ambiguous pronouncement. Referring to McCollum, she wrote: "As she said, she does not know whether she did right or wrong, and neither does anyone else, including the sovereign State of Florida, in spite of the verdict" (Hurston 1953). Hurston found support for the cause of McCollum in the white journalist William Bradford Huie. Together they worked to save her from the electric chair. The case was appealed to the Florida Supreme Court, which declared McCollum insane. She was eventually sent to a mental institution, where she remained until her release in 1974. Huie embarked on a long investigation into additional components of the case following the trial. He learned that Adams had been a member of the Ku Klux Klan and was an often-careless physician who in some cases endangered the lives of his patients. Adams's concern for the poor was a ruse simply to garner support for his political ambitions. Hurston had initially planned to collaborate with Huie on what became his bestselling book, *Ruby McCollum: Woman in the Suwannee County Jail* (1956). They corresponded in detail about Huie's investigation, and Hurston offered considerable insight and counsel on his findings. Rather than complete this project with Huie, Hurston wrote a thirteen-page essay largely based on her previous writings for *The Pittsburgh Courier* on the trial. Huie's published volume proved so controversial that it was not sold in Florida because he feared the possibility of lawsuits. Hurston also considered writing with Huie a collection of short stories called *The Cracker Crop* about the adventures of a Southern white man named Cousin Mule who is always "stealing mules, making love to widder women, stealing good hound-dogs and lying magnificently" (Kaplan 2003, 712, letter from Hurston to Huie in 1954). The book was never completed.

Despite the rich insight of Hurston's coverage of the trial, *The Pittsburgh Courier* failed to compensate her for her work beyond the first payment of $200. She had to wait two days following the end of the trial before she received sufficient funds from the *Courier* to pay her way home. The trial had taxed Hurston both mentally and physically. The stress exacerbated her sinus and gallbladder problems, and she had no money to seek medical help. At long last, Hurston returned to Eau Gallie and was eager to settle into a permanent home.

Since buying the cottage was no longer an option, she looked elsewhere in the area and found an eight-acre tract close to the highway. She was given until the first week of March to come up with the $1,100 down payment. This amount was a stretch for Hurston, even with the $800 promised from *The Pittsburgh Courier*. She wrote to her ex-husband Herbert Sheen, who was now living in Los Angeles, to ask for a loan: "You know very well that I would not ask this favor of you if things were not terribly pressing. I can see something really big coming from this land deal" (Kaplan 2003, 691, letter from Hurston to Sheen in 1953). Although they were decades past their marriage, Hurston and Sheen maintained an intimate and caring correspondence. They never became lovers again, but many of Hurston's letters, especially those penned in her final years, attest to the depth of their decades-long relationship. She called him "the most loved man on earth," explaining "that does not mean that I hope or expect to thrust myself into your life except as a friend. I am with you to the end. Just something you can think about on a cloudy day when you might feel depressed" (Kaplan 2003, 697, letter from Hurston to Sheen in 1953).

Hurston had grand plans for the eight-acre tract in Eau Gallie. She intended to convert over half the area into a commercial orange grove, lease two acres for a white trailer park, and use the remaining section for her own home. Two real estate firms were also interested in the site. Eau Gallie, once a quiet village, was becoming an exciting place for new development due in part to its close proximity to Patrick Air Force Base and eventually the Kennedy Space Center in Cape Canaveral. Unfortunately, *The Pittsburgh Courier* fell through on the $800 Hurston was expecting, and as a result, she lost both the land she hoped to buy as well as her car.

In December 1953, Hurston learned that her friend Marjorie Kinnan Rawlings had died. Hurston took the news especially hard, as she explained to a friend, "first because I am deprived of the warmth of the association, and secondly because I feel that I failed her in her last extremity." Rawlings had been a stalwart friend during the worst of the 1948 scandal, and though Hurston knew she had been ill and had promised to visit, she never made the trip: "My car. [sic] like the old one-horse shay, just fell to pieces, and there I was with no transportation, and no means to replace it, and could not bear to admit to her lest she feel sorry for me" (Kaplan 2003, 728, letter from Hurston to Mary Holland in 1955). Rawlings's death was followed by that of Mary McLeod Bethune. Although Hurston had not been especially close to Bethune, it was another reminder of her own advancing age.

Despite her earlier setbacks in writing, Hurston dived into a new project on a subject that had long fascinated her: the biblical figure of King Herod. She spoke of the project with great enthusiasm in an interview that appeared in the August 1953 issue of *All-Florida Magazine*. As early as 1947, Hurston had described herself as eager to write this "whale of a story" (Kaplan 2003, 552, letter from Hurston to Carl Van Vechten in 1947). Much of Hurston's interest in the story of Herod, which ultimately occupied her for over fifteen years, stems from her fascination with the history of the Jewish people. She aimed to "show that instead of the Jewish people being a peculiarly evil and hard-headed race of people, doomed by God to suffer and be hated, that they were just people fighting for all those things which other people hold sacred and conducing to the rights and dignity of man" (Kaplan 2003, 530, letter from Hurston to Van Vechten in 1945). Hurston was astounded by the 3,000-year struggle of the Jews, and considering what she understood as the absence of direct testimony of their suffering, she wanted to bring to light their story. In her study of Jewish history, Hurston became especially intrigued by the life of Herod. She believed him to be a key figure in understanding the history of Western religion and enlightenment: "The LIFE OF HEROD THE GREAT is not really the story of a man, but of a movement which has ended up in Christianity on one hand, and as the basis of Western civilization on the other ... Herod is THE connecting personality between the old Judaism and Christianity" (Kaplan 2003, 665, letter from Hurston to Mitchell in 1951). Hurston also characterized Herod as supremely courageous, intelligent, and handsome, an ideal figure not just for the stage but also for Hollywood. One of her objectives was to rescue him from the conventional assumption that he was just a tyrant intent on killing the infant Jesus. She challenged the accuracy of the Gospels and claimed that legend had come to supplant the truth. There is, in fact, no historical evidence proving that Herod or anyone else ordered the slaughter of male infants. Instead, Hurston argued, Herod helped create an environment for Christianity to flourish by honoring the Essenes, a group that formed the early church.

Hurston wrote to Mitchell about this ambitious project, and he replied with warm enthusiasm. Through 1953 and 1954, Hurston dedicated herself to its research and writing, even as she continued to take assignments that helped pay her immediate expenses. She wrote the book not as straight history but rather with the sensitive eye of a fiction writer. She began the book with Herod at twenty-five, recently relishing the elevation of his father as governor of Judea by Caesar. Herod was in turn named the governor of Galilee and charged with bringing order to the strife in the region. Hurston imagines Herod marching into his new city: "He waved his right hand in salute to the cheering people, flashed his brilliant smile, drew his jewel-hilted sword and waved it above his head as he announced in a loud and convincing voice that the Lion of Judah sought his prey. The people went mad and cheered louder. That was their Herod!" (Moylan 2011, 100). By 1955, Hurston had two-thirds of the manuscript complete, and she wrote to former prime minister of England Winston Churchill to ask if he would write the book's introduction and provide commentary on the political significance of each chapter. Churchill politely replied that his health prevented him from accepting the task.

Hurston sent her lengthy manuscript to Mitchell in June. Though she attempted to shorten it, the story proved too unwieldly. The following month, he replied that despite her passion and knowledge, the book was not publishable: "There is a wealth of fine material here but somehow it has failed to flow in a clear narrative stream. We think the book would prove difficult reading for the layman" (Kaplan 2003, 742, letter from Mitchell to Hurston in 1955). Hurston responded with striking equanimity: "Please do not think that I feel badly about the rejection. I was astonished myself how easily I felt. Perhaps it is because I have such faith in the material and now my conviction that I can handle it. All is well" (Kaplan 2003, 742, letter from Hurston to Mitchell in 1955). Rather than being deterred by Mitchell's response, Hurston continued working on the book for the rest of her life. She did quibble with Mitchell's complaint that the manuscript lacked historical accuracy. Recognizing that her work challenged accepted views of the period, she defended her adherence to the facts and reminded him of the church's self-interested fictions.

As Hurston continued to research the life of Herod, she kept abreast of current events, and unsurprisingly, she had strong opinions on issues related to race. In August 1955, *The Orlando Sentinel* published a letter to the editor by Hurston under the headline "Court Order: Can't Make Races Mix." In response to the 1954 decision in *Brown v. Board of Education*, which ruled segregated schools to be unconstitutional, Hurston declared, "I regard the ruling of the U.S. Supreme Court as insulting rather than honoring my race." Hurston claimed that Florida's black schools were "in very good shape and on the improve." Her Eatonville education proved that white children had not been necessary to her academic success. She warned against "govt by fiat" and explained, "I can see no tragedy in being too dark to be invited to a white school social affair." Hurston was not against integration but rather objected to its forced institutionalization. She concluded the letter by suggesting an alternative way forward: "Growth from within. Ethical and cultural desegregation. It is a contradiction in terms to scream race pride and equality while at the same time spurning Negro teachers and self-association" (Hurston 1955).

The inflammatory letter, which, as Hemenway observed, "ignored the inescapable evidence that black schools were inadequately and unequally funded," was reprinted widely in Southern newspapers (Hemenway 1977, 336). Segregationists showered her with fan mail while civil rights leaders decried her regressive perspective. The letter is best understood as a reflection of Hurston's personal experiences rather than as a broad judgment on contemporary race relations. While her own elementary school offered a vibrant education, Eatonville was exceptional; it did not suffer from a lack of resources nor with comparison to adjacent white schools that teemed with educational opportunities. Hurston failed to untangle white student populations from the funding they brought.

She also firmly believed that forcible integration was the first step toward dangerous government overreach. Hurston confided to a friend that she was "astonished that my letter to The Orlando Sentinel has caused such a sensation over the whole United States." She continued by clarifying her position:

> I actually do feel insulted when a certain type of white person hastens to effuse to me how noble they are to grant me their presence . . . It is not that I have any race prejudice, for it is well known that I have numerous white friends, but they are friends, not merely some who seek to earn a spurious "merit" by patronizing Negroes, or by seeking political advancement through our votes. (Kaplan 2003, 743, letter from Hurston to Margrit de Sabloniére in 1955)

The ever-proud Hurston refused white condescension of any kind and demanded that cross-racial social interaction be born of genuine affection rather than governmental prescription.

Hurston was wary of pushing integration when whites continued to harbor such deep-seated racial prejudice. Although *Brown v. Board of Education* was a landmark decision that affirmed the basic values of the nation, as Hurston may well have anticipated, it did not lead to an integrated country. She was a proponent of more gradual change that came about through unforced personal interactions:

> It seems to me that it all comes back to the fundamental fact that general public opinion is not quite ready as yet to accept the descendants of slaves as equals as yet, and national and state executives have not the courage as yet to buck that public opinion. The next question before our house is, could an executive succeed in enforcing these things even if he tried? Maybe, yes, or maybe in a few years from now. God only knows the answer. (Kaplan 2003, 681, letter from Hurston to Helen Worden Erskine in 1951)

Hurston was not against integration; instead, she recognized the danger of mandating change that needed to be rooted in more progressive social exchange.

Hurston could not understand the decision of Autherine Lucy, a black student who was refused entrance to the all-white University of Alabama in 1952. Lucy endured threats of violence and public scorn as she fought for her right to attend the school through the courts. Hurston was puzzled that Lucy would not have simply opted for a quality education at Howard or another historically black college. Although both Hurston and Lucy were the first black women to attend their respective universities, Barnard had provided a welcoming environment; the school and its administrators had wanted Hurston to succeed. Reflecting upon Lucy's decision, Hurston wrote, "My nature would not permit me to go through what Authorine [sic] Lucy undertook. I could not bear to be so rejected. I am a sensitive soul, so I would rather go on to some school where I would be welcome" (Kaplan 2003, 747, letter from Hurston to De Sablonière in 1956). Such an observation reflects the profoundly personal nature of Hurston's positions on race. She tended to extrapolate from her individual experiences, often ignoring social conditions she did not know firsthand and dismissing the choices of others.

An unpublished essay entitled "The Enemy: A Unique Personal Experience," which Hurston wrote in early 1955, sheds light on the kind of relationship she sought to develop across racial divides. The essay focuses on Hurston's friendship with the Pindars, a white family with two children and elderly grandparents living close by. Hurston develops a strong attachment to seven-year-old Bobby, a "captivating child with heavy, curly dark hair, liquid dark eyes very thickly lashed, a graceful little boy and a winning grin" (Hurston 1955). The boy proves to be a budding raconteur and amuses Hurston with tales of his various adventures. Hurston recounts the family's struggles following the death of Grandpa Brown, who indulged his wife's every desire. Without her husband to wait upon her, the older woman becomes difficult and irritable. The Pindars ask Hurston to spend some time with her to ease her frustrations, but they eventually move the elderly Mrs. Brown to a nursing home, where she dies. While the adults are preoccupied with funeral arrangements, Hurston arrives to care for the children. Bobby immediately lashes out at her, accusing Hurston of taking Granny to the nursing home. Hurston holds the boy's wrists and listens to him until he falls sobbing into her arms. She understands that Bobby's anger is not about her, but reflective of his grief over the loss of his grandmother: "I kept telling him as gently as I knew how that he had nothing to blame himself for, but I knew that it would take at least twenty years to comprehend what I was saying . . . the real enemy was time. So I let him weep himself out and beat on my knee all he wanted to" (Hurston 1955). Throughout the essay, Hurston draws little attention to the racial difference between her and the Pindars. Their relationship is not defined by race but instead by the care and concern of affectionate neighbors.

The following year, Hurston was dismayed to learn that her house for the past five years had been sold. She was left "terribly distressed at the thought and necessity of stopping everything to pack up my numerous papers and books to find another location" (Kaplan 2003, 746, letter from Hurston to de Sabloniére in 1956). Amid this tumult, she tried to find copies of her books, now all out of print. Margrit de Sabloniére, a Dutch writer, had offered to translate her works. Although it was difficult to secure copies of now-classics like *Their Eyes Were Watching God* and *Mules and Men*, Hurston's legacy had not been forgotten. She often received requests to excerpt or anthologize portions of her writings, and numerous academics identified her as an important black author. In May, she received an award from Bethune-Cookman College for education and human relations.

Despite her abiding literary fame, Hurston still struggled to find steady work to pay her bills. Unlike many black writers of her time, Hurston was never offered a teaching position at a university. While Sterling Brown taught at Howard and Arna Bontemps at Fisk, Hurston had never cultivated the kind of relationships with administrative leaders that would have led to a comfortable old age among eager students. No doubt her gender and iconoclastic views also played a role in the absence of such an offer. Her lack of savings reflects the limited, piecemeal income she received throughout her life. Unlike her white peers, her advances were always in the hundreds, not the thousands, and she had no family wealth in terms of financial assets to rely upon. In general, she lived thinking about the demands of the moment and her immediate desires, not long-term goals of retirement and leisure. At the end of *Dust Tracks on a Road*, she reflected, "I don't know any more about the future than you do. I hope that it will be full of work, because I have come to know by experience that work is the nearest thing to happiness that I can find. No matter what else I have among the things that humans want, I go to pieces in a short while if I do not work" (Hurston 1942, 231). Despite Hurston's embrace of work as a guiding principle of her life, in her final years, her employment opportunities narrowed considerably and she was forced to take positions that did not cater to her strengths.

In June, Hurston began working at the Patrick Air Force Base in Cocoa as a librarian. The job was a poor fit from the start, as Hurston was tasked with overseeing the technical literature for Pan American World Airways. However, the $1.88-per-hour wage provided enough money for her to continue working on her King Herod project. Though she began renting a small house in Cocoa, she soon moved to a house trailer on Merritt Island, which offered a better writing environment. However, after almost a year at the Patrick Air Force Base, Hurston was fired. The work bored her, and she had trouble with some of her coworkers. Her supervisor told her that she was "too well educated for the job," but she suspected that the real cause of her dismissal was that she maintained friendly relations with someone who had reported on another employee (Kaplan 2003, 759, letter from Hurston to Holland in 1957). Rather than protest her termination with the department head, in typical grand fashion she wrote to Vice President Richard Nixon claiming that her firing was a violation of the Fair Employment Practices Act. Ultimately, she was disappointed to lose the steady income but relieved to be done with a workplace that from her perspective disparaged all Southerners.

Hurston considered writing an article called, "Take For Instance Spessard Holland," a profile of the former governor and current Florida senator that would demonstrate how the South had changed since the turn of the century. She explained to a friend that her experience at the technical library "pointed up to me the vast ignorance of that gang of latter-day carpet-baggers." To combat the stereotypes that defined Northern conceptions of the South, she wanted to highlight how southern lawmakers "see the problems, economic and sociological, and ponder them seriously and intelligently, seeking the answers infinitely more earnestly than the on-lookers from above the Mason-Dixon line" (Kaplan 2003, 762, letter from Hurston to Holland in 1957). Hurston was eager for solutions to the country's worsening race relations or what she called the "hate-filled, stinking mess" (Kaplan 2003, 764, letter from Hurston to Holland in 1957). However, she vehemently disagreed with the strategies of the NAACP. As she saw things, "they are working on the wrong end of the Negro. All their fights boil down to a matter of seats." For her, the issue was not about who could sit where on buses as suggested by the bus boycotts and sit-ins held all over the South. Championing an ethos of self-reliance, she offered a solution reminiscent of Booker T. Washington's ideals:

> I clamor that improvements should start on the other end. Let us learn more about a better, a higher and cleaner way of life and all other things will follow. Let us not concern ourselves so much about wherev [sic] we are going to sit, but rather what we are going to DO to contribute to the welfare of this nation. Be givers and not receivers only. That is the only answer, and eventually we will be driven to it whether we will or not. (Kaplan 2003, 757, letter from Hurston to Holland in 1957)

The article on Spessard Holland was never completed, as Hurston entered a more introspective stage of life. At sixty-six, she suffered from mild arthritis and high blood pressure. Though she continued working on the book she came to call *The Life of King Herod the Great*, she realized that it might never be finished. Reflecting on her life, she told Sheen,

> I have no sentimental involvements. I have no talent for business nor finance, but I do not mind that ... I am not materialistic. I do take a certain satisfaction in knowing that my writing [sic] are used in many of the great

universities both here and abroad, both literary and anthropological. If I happen to die without money, somebody will bury me, though I do not wish it to be that way. (Kaplan 2003, 755, letter from Hurston to Sheen in 1957)

She also looked past the rejections she had received, noting that she had "gone through a period that might appear outwardly unprofitable, but in reality extremely important." Success in the eyes of others was far less important than what she understood as her "phenominal [sic] growth as a creative artist" (Kaplan 2003, 755, letter from Hurston to Sheen in 1957).

A new writing opportunity led Hurston to move to Fort Pierce, eighty miles south of Merritt Island, at the end of 1957. C. E. Bolen, the owner of the black weekly *The Fort Pierce Chronicle*, offered her a part-time writing job. She penned a column called "Hoodoo and Black Magic" along with some articles about the area around Indian River. The following February, she was offered a job in the English department of Lincoln Park Academy, a black public high school. Though she had never taught at any level, she agreed to fill a recent vacancy and was given homeroom 10-C, considered to be the most troublesome in the school. Hurston was appalled that students brought knives and dice to class, and though she aimed to show them the importance of an education, difficulties arose with some of the other teachers. She noted, "My name as an author is too big to be tolerated, lest it gather to itself the 'glory' of the school here. I have met that before. But perhaps it is natural. The mediocre have no importance except through appointment. They feel invaded and defeated by the presence of creative folk among them" (Kaplan 2003, 766, letter from Hurston to Mitchell Ferguson in 1958). The principal of the school, Leroy C. Floyd, recognized that Hurston had been criticized by some of her coworkers, but he identified the problem as stemming from her lack of a Florida teaching certificate. Hurston left the school after there was a delay in receiving her transcript from Barnard, concluding, "I can live without teaching" (Kaplan 2003, 768, letter from Hurston to Ferguson in 1958).

Though Hurston did not last long at Lincoln Park Academy, her students remembered her fondly. Shirley Crawford, one of Hurston's English students, recalled that her unusual teacher often came to school in colorful clothes and large hats that sometimes generated mean comments from others. According to Marjorie Harrell, Hurston had an unorthodox teaching style: "Instead of using a textbook, she incorporated her grammar lessons with stories and fables about life. None of her students knew how famous Zora was, but they enjoyed her class. She would read stories from what I now realize were her own books, with great dramatic flair" (Moylan 2011, 155). Cleo Leathe, who taught social studies at Lincoln Park Academy, remembers that Hurston's health was clearly failing, but nonetheless, "she came to school every day and gave it her all" (Moylan 2011, 156).

During this time, Hurston rented a concrete-block house at 1734 School Court. Her landlord, Dr. C. C. Benton, was from an area close to Eatonville and had fond memories of her family. After learning that Hurston struggled on unemployment checks and her part-time wages from *The Fort Pierce Chronicle*, he let her occupy the house for free. The two-bedroom cottage included a bathroom, kitchen, and living space. Hurston decorated it with throw rugs and beanbag chairs. She lived frugally, using wooden fruit crates to form bookshelves and a writing table. Hurston had long given up her unique sartorial style, preferring plain, comfortable clothes. She drew little attention to herself though maintained friendly relations with her neighbors. Occasionally, she enjoyed jazz sessions held at the home of A. E. "Beanie" Backus, a local white landscape painter who supported a group of black landscape painters known as the Highwaymen. There she befriended white journalists Marjorie Silver and Ann Wilder. Silver recalls their initial meeting at her home: "The first afternoon Zora came over, was like she was digging in an archaeological site for something. After that, she blossomed out and was Zora" (Moylan 2011, 154). Silver remembers Hurston dining in a turban at her home and taking leftovers home to give to the neighboring black children.

Dr. Benton was one of the few people in the area who knew of Hurston's literary accomplishments. Well-educated and charmed by his neighbor, he became Hurston's personal physician. He often insisted that she eat Sunday dinner with him and his family, and together they could talk for hours. By this point in her life, Hurston had lost contact with most of her New York friends, including Van Vechten, Fannie Hurst, and Ethel Waters. Over eight years had passed since her last trip there. But Dr. Benton proved to be a devoted friend and engaging conversationalist. They spoke about art and current events, and he often checked in on her or brought her dinner from his home. His two daughters, Arlena and Margaret, also treated Hurston as an extended member of their family.

Hurston passed her days working on her King Herod book and tending to her year-round vegetable garden. Though her garden kept her busy, she had gained a considerable amount of weight. At over two hundred pounds, Hurston did little to improve her high blood pressure, preferring to dedicate herself to new writing projects. She wanted to write a series of articles on the migrant labor camps in Florida for *The Miami Herald*. Unfortunately, the editor found the first installment weak and refused to publish it. She also contacted a new press, the David McKay Company, about her King Herod book. The publisher expressed interest, but Hurston became seriously ill before she could send off the manuscript. In fact, her last letter, dated January 16, 1959, was written to Harper Brothers inquiring about interest in her book on King Herod. She explained, "One reason I approach you is because you will realize that any publisher who offers a life of Herod as it really was, and naturally different from the groundless legends which have been built up around his name has to have courage" (Kaplan 2003, 771, letter from Hurston to Harper Brothers Publishers in 1959). It is especially fitting that her final missive demonstrates her adamant commitment to her transgressive writing.

On September 19, Hurston was admitted to the Fort Pierce Memorial Hospital for hypertensive heart disease. This condition led to shortness of breath and fatigue, and though it was treatable, it could also be fatal. Hurston was released but instructed to lose weight and stop smoking. Dr. Benton continued to watch over Hurston, though he was increasingly concerned about her health. He urged her to contact her family, but she refused, insisting that she could take care of herself. On occasion, she had to call Dr. Benton to ask him to buy her groceries. By May, she'd applied to welfare for help buying her prescription drugs because she could no longer keep up with her articles for the *Chronicle*. The following month, she'd applied for food aid. In October, she returned to the hospital, having suffered a stroke. Two weeks later, she was transferred to the segregated Lincoln Park Nursing Home, which was run by the St. Lucie County Welfare Agency. Hurston did not want to go but was completely unable to care for herself. Dr. Benton and some other friends visited her. They noted that she had lost the ability to concentrate for any significant period of time. Wilder recalls that Hurston had a room in the basement that was somewhat gloomy: "Even though she was on the down track, you didn't really feel sorry for her, because she knew who she was, and that she might have to be on charity, but she knew her quality. It wasn't exactly pride, it was an inner self-confidence that never failed her" (Moylan 2011, 159).

Hurston's brother Clifford Joel also came to visit along with his wife, Mabel, and daughter, Vivian. Hurston told her family that she was fine and wanted to be at the nursing home. Her niece recalls how Clifford Joel brought her some gifts but she gave them all to the other patients. Then, on January 28, 1960, Hurston suffered another stroke. She was sent back to Fort Pierce Memorial Hospital but died en route. The conclusion of *Dust Tracks on a Road* suggests that Hurston had no regrets upon her death. She had experienced too much of life's wonders:

> When I get old, and my joints and bones tell me about it, I can sit around and write for myself, if for nobody else . . . Then when the sleeplessness of old age attacks me, I can have a likker bottle snug in my pantry and sip away and sleep. Get mellow and think kindly of the world. I think I can be like that because I have known the joy and pain of deep friendship. I have served and been served. I have made some good enemies for which I am not a bit sorry. I have loved unselfishly, and I have fondled hatred with the red-hot tongs of Hell. That's living. (Hurston 1942, 231)

The Percy S. Peek Funeral Home called Marjorie Silver, a friend of Hurston's and a local journalist, the following day. There wasn't enough money to bury her body. Silver described the situation in an article for *The Miami Herald*. The news was then picked up by national outlets, including *Time* magazine and *The New York Times*, which published their own obituaries. These initial accounts of her life all misidentified her birth date, listing her as young as fifty-two. She was in fact sixty-nine at the time of her death.

These reports inspired many to send money to Peek's Funeral Home. Lippincott and Scribner's both sent $100 each, and additional funds came from Hurst and Van Vechten. Teachers from Lincoln Park Academy also gathered donations, as did a group of Hurston's former students. The offerings totaled $661.87, still short of the $900 required for a proper burial. The undertaker donated the plot, and on February 7, Hurston was buried. Clifford and his wife attended the service in the mortuary's small chapel along with over a hundred people. Chairs had to be placed on the sidewalk to accommodate the crowd. So many floral arrangements arrived that the casket could hardly be seen. Hurston was dressed in pink, Silver recalled, commenting, "She would have been holding her sides laughing" (Boyd 2003, 433). After Rev. R. J. Cliffin of Mount Olive Baptist read a scripture and Rev. Wayman A. Jennings, the pastor of St. Paul AME, gave the eulogy, a choir from Lincoln Park Academy sang "Just a Closer Walk with Thee."

Hurston's body was then conveyed to Genessee Memorial Gardens, a segregated cemetery. There was not enough money for a headstone. Ironically, Hurston anticipated a solution to such a situation in a 1945 letter she sent to W. E. B. Du Bois. She proposed that he, as the "Dean of American Negro Artists," consider the construction of "a cemetery for the illustrious Negro dead." She suggested securing approximately one hundred acres in Florida, claiming that this selection was not due to her native bias but rather because it afforded trees and flowers of exceptional beauty that would remain green year-round. Instead of a chapel, she envisioned a meeting hall. "Let the Negro sculptors and painters decorate it with scenes from our own literature and life. Mythology and all." Funerals might also be held there. Hurston hoped to relocate the remains of important African American figures like Frederick Douglass and Nat Turner, though she acknowledged that Turner's "bones have long since gone to dust." These lofty goals were grounded in a more practical concern that had eerie resonance for her own death fifteen years later: "Let no Negro celebrity, no matter what financial condition they might be in at death, lie in inconspicuous forgetfulness. We must assume the responsibility of their graves being known and honored" (Kaplan 2003, 519, letter from Hurston to Du Bois in 1945).

Weeks after the funeral, Fannie Hurst wrote a short essay about Hurston for the *Yale University's Library Gazette*. Van Vechten had initially been approached for the job, but at eighty years old, he deferred. Hurst's tribute brought him to tears as he remembered his thoroughly original friend. Hurst wrote, "To life, to her people, she left a bequest of good writing and the memory of an iridescent personality of many colors" (Hurst 1960, 21). Though Hurst and Van Vechten longed to keep Hurston's memory and work alive, many of her papers were burned shortly after her funeral by people hired to clean out her belongings. Fortunately, Patrick Duval, a deputy with the St. Lucie County Sheriff's Department, happened to drive past Hurston's last home at 1734 School Court. He spotted smoke coming from the backyard and stopped to investigate. Aware of Hurston's accomplishments, Duval put out the fire with a garden hose and saved many of her papers. These documents, which included an incomplete manuscript of *The Life of Herod the Great*, were donated, as Hurston planned, to the Department of Rare Books and Manuscripts at the University of Florida in Gainesville. For years, they were largely ignored, until Robert E. Hemenway consulted them in the 1970s for what became the first biography of Hurston.

However, the resurrection of Hurston's literary legacy primarily belongs to Alice Walker, who in August 1973 visited Fort Pierce to honor the grave of the writer who had inspired so much of her own work. She found that the Genessee Memorial Gardens had become the Garden of Heavenly Rest, an abandoned graveyard covered in weeds. Walker identified what she believed to be Hurston's grave and there placed a simple gray

---

ALICE WALKER

Alice Walker is one of the premier African American novelists of the late twentieth century. The author of seven novels and other works, including collections of stories, poems, and essays, she has received the Pulitzer Prize in Fiction as well as the National Book Award. Novels such as *The Color Purple* (1982), *Possessing the Secret of Joy* (1992), *Meridian* (1976), and *The Third Life of Grange Copeland* (1970) are considered pioneering contributions to black feminist literature. Walker's bold exploration of female sexuality and pleasure as well as the damaging effects of violence and patriarchy offered a new language to discuss issues once largely taboo in the African American community. She coined the term "womanist" to describe her intersectional approach to feminism, which recognizes how systems of oppression like sexism, racism, and homophobia work in tandem. Much of Walker's later work, such as *Living By the Word* (1988) and *Anything We Love Can Be Saved: A Writer's Activism* (1997), reflects a greater concern with spirituality and the health of the earth. Consistent with the range of her writings, Walker remains a committed activist who champions human rights across the globe. However, her views have been controversial, especially her critical position on Israel, which she identifies as fostering a system of apartheid.

> **ZORA NEALE HURSTON FESTIVAL OF THE ARTS AND HUMANITIES**
>
> Established in 1990, the Zora Neale Hurston Festival of the Arts and Humanities, also known as ZORA! Festival, is a multiday intergenerational event involving public talks, museum exhibitions, theatrical performances, and educational programming. In 2019, the event celebrated its thirtieth anniversary and included talks by Alice Walker, Trudier Harris, Cheryl Wall, and Rollins College President Grant Cornwell. The festival takes place in Eatonville and the surrounding area of Orange County. The festival has three principal aims: to honor the life and legacy of Zora Neale Hurston, to celebrate the history of Eatonville, and to rejoice in the cultural contributions of the African diaspora. Each year, thousands of visitors attend the festival, which is organized by the Association to Preserve the Eatonville Community. Past speakers include Maya Angelou, Nikki Giovanni, Henry Louis Gates Jr., Sonia Sanchez, and Danny Glover. ZORA! Festival also includes a series of tours through geographic sites of notable significance to Hurston's life. The event tends to take place in either January or February.

headstone engraved with the words, "Zora Neale Hurston: A Genius of the South." This monument honors not only Hurston but her belief that a cemetery memorializes important figures of the past; in her letter to Du Bois urging him to consider the creation of a graveyard for African American celebrities, she wrote, "I think that the lack of such a tangible thing allows our people to forget, and their spirits evaporate" (Kaplan 2003, 520, letter from Hurston to Du Bois in 1945). Walker described her trip to Fort Pierce in a 1975 essay in *Ms.* magazine that inspired fresh enthusiasm for Hurston's work. That year, the Modern Language Association hosted its first session devoted to Hurston's writings. Hemenway's pioneering study, *Zora Neale Hurston: A Literary Biography*, came out two years later in 1977, and soon her most important works were reissued. With more than a million copies published, *Their Eyes Were Watching God* is now a staple of high school and college English classes, while Hurston's anthropological work has proved seminal to studies of black folklore.

Since 1989, Eatonville has hosted the Zora Neale Hurston Festival of the Arts and Humanities. Part academic conference, part street fair, the event attracts fans from all over the world. Hurston's books have been translated into a wide variety of languages, from Spanish to Japanese, German to Chinese. Her work is the subject of dissertations, college courses, critical essays, documentaries, and children's literature, and her name is on numerous libraries, schools, and museums. Hurston left behind a body of writing that will continue to inspire students and scholars. Her literary legacy reflects a life lived with bold vitality and boundless curiosity.

Why Zora Neale Hurston Matters

Zora Neale Hurston is often thought of as the foremother of African American writers like Alice Walker, Maya Angelou, and Toni Morrison. She is also frequently grouped with contemporaries like Langston Hughes, Richard Wright, and Nella Larsen. All these pillars of the African American literary canon share with Hurston an exquisite talent and vision. However, none of these major writers approach the fundamental singularity of Hurston's life, career, and work. There is perhaps no more pioneering author in the history of American letters than Zora Neale Hurston. She is quite simply incomparable.

Much of Hurston's originality lies in her vibrant, raucous voice. A stunning raconteur with a sly wit, Hurston charmed nearly everyone she met, from wealthy white patrons to poor turpentine workers, from voodoo priests to internationally acclaimed academics. She moved in social circles as diverse as the entire United States, befriending Native American chieftains, conservative politicians, transgressive bohemians, and respected pastors. These eclectic influences fueled an artist who was both deeply rooted in the African American South and transcendent of any single identity category. In her many travels, both within the United States and throughout the Caribbean, Hurston gathered stories and learned about cultural practices involving the broad African diaspora. This material deeply impacted her own creative voice, which melds an often-wry personal perspective with centuries-old collective wisdom. Nearly a century past Hurston's first anthropological expeditions, we must be mindful of how radical and at times dangerous it was for a lone black woman to inhabit such different social worlds. Though a native of Florida, a place she studied and lived in for years, Hurston was always eager to explore new facets of African American and African diasporic life. In this way, she represents both a fierce individuality and a deep commitment to cultural legacies. This somewhat paradoxical position led in her later life to politically conservative views, even as her younger self espoused beliefs more consistent with the burgeoning civil rights movement. Hurston was a writer who embraced change, allowing individual experiences as well as shifting social mores to influence her perspective on race, identity, art, and the future of the United States. This biography aims to explore how these elements impacted her creatively and produced a powerful series of texts that will continue to inspire readers for many years to come.

While most authors are primarily dedicated to a single narrative mode—fiction, poetry, drama, or essays—Hurston worked across a variety of genres. One theme that permeates her life is her refusal to be contained by a single idea, category, or expectation. It is no surprise, then, that although she is best known for her novels, she also wrote plays, a series of provocative essays, and groundbreaking anthropological texts that describe her experiences in the American South, Haiti, and Jamaica. Although we can clearly distinguish between Hurston's major fictional and academic work, much of her writing straddles these two forms. She penned many stories based on well-known folktales, and some of her most memorable lines are common expressions among black Southerners. While readers might assume that some of Hurston's most striking lines, such as "now you're cooking with gas" and "God don't eat okra," are born of her own imagination, they are frequently used phrases in African American vernacular. This observation does not lessen the force of Hurston's artistry but instead testifies to her close engagement with a powerful source of metaphorical and creative inspiration: the language of her childhood. One of her most appealing pieces, "The Eatonville Anthology," which takes its name from Hurston's self-identified hometown, defies any simplistic categorization as it merges Hurston's unique artistic vision with her cultural upbringing. Structured as a series of discrete reflections, the work includes amusing character descriptions and old folktales. This "anthology" is hardly comprehensive in its account of Eatonville life but instead offers an inside view on life in the town where Hurston was raised. And yet, the piece is not merely the transcription of an attentive listener; it is a reflection of an author who found profound artistry and insight in the community she loved.

Despite Hurston's rural roots and deep commitment to black folklife, she is most often associated with the Harlem Renaissance. Although she was a reliable and somewhat infamous figure at the rent parties and jazz cabarets that made Harlem the hottest destination in the 1920s, she published only a handful of pieces during the heyday of this literary movement. She worked closely with artists and intellectuals like Countee Cullen, Langston Hughes, and James Weldon Johnson to develop a new approach to African American cultural production. Together they sought to overturn the elitist expectations for black art set out by W. E. B. Du Bois, the reigning African American intellectual of the day. Du Bois believed that art must function as propaganda to call attention to the social and political plight of African Americans. By contrast, Hurston and a group she termed the "Niggerati" believed that creative freedom was paramount to the future of African American art and literature. Moreover, while Du Bois tended to favor Western forms, visual artists like Aaron Douglas and writers like Hughes affirmed that black art should celebrate what Hurston termed "the Negro farthest down" (Hemenway 1977, 107). A commitment to black folklife and creative freedom was foundational to *Fire!!*, the literary journal Hurston and her colleagues founded to challenge Du Bois's *The Crisis* and Charles S. Johnson's more sociologically oriented *Opportunity: A Journal of Negro Life*. Despite an editorial board loaded with talent, from Wallace Thurman to Gwendolyn Bennett, *Fire!!* was a financial failure and lasted only for a single issue. Hurston and her fellow editors were possessed of a bold vision but lacked the pragmatic smarts and marketing savvy to make *Fire!!* a viable investment. Nonetheless, *Fire!!* anticipated profound changes in how black art would be created and received in the early twentieth century. The elitist agenda of Du Bois had long since passed as Hurston and her friends pioneered new ways of understanding and producing black art.

Hurston was brought to national attention at the start of the Harlem Renaissance with her impressive showing at an awards dinner hosted by *Opportunity* editor Charles S. Johnson in 1925. Although Hurston did not win any first-place prizes, she took the most awards home. "Spunk" won second place in the short story category, and her play *Color Struck* won second place in drama. She also received two honorable mentions for the story "Black Death" and the play *Spears*. Hurston soon became a fixture of the Harlem scene. She opened her small apartment to writers and artists and delighted in the music, dance, art, and poetry of this important literary movement. Despite the excitement and energy surrounding Harlem in the 1920s, this period was a time of gestation for Hurston rather than the raw inspiration for her most important work. She also did not have the luxury to devote herself entirely to her writing because she had to support herself. Financial insecurity proved to be a lifelong challenge for Hurston and set her apart from many of her contemporaries, who could rely on higher profits from their publishing houses, a comfortable academic position, or a safety net of generational wealth. At every step in her life,

Hurston made her own way. This would be admirable for any writer, but for a black woman in the early twentieth century, it is especially impressive and required a good amount of creativity, performance, and humility. Hurston worked as a domestic worker, waitress, manicurist, and cashier, and in her final decade, when her manuscripts were no longer being accepted for publication, she returned to maid service, claiming with customary pride that she was doing research for a new project.

It is also no wonder that Hurston was not especially prolific during the Harlem Renaissance, because in addition to conspiring to get *Fire!!* off the ground and keeping up with the latest gossip surrounding such Harlem celebrities as Carl Van Vechten, Alain Locke, and Ethel Waters, she also attended Barnard University on a partial scholarship. Hurston took a full load of classes while also learning about the necessity of tennis whites among a student body far removed from rural Florida. Her interest in studying different cultures led her to take classes with Franz Boas, the father of American Anthropology. Soon she was measuring the heads of passersby in Harlem to test whether skull size was linked to race and intelligence. Boas and Hurston took to one another immediately, sharing a passion for exploring the nature of cultural differences and a light sense of humor. He recognized immediately that with her charm and familiarity with African American cultural practices, she would be an asset in the field. Before she even finished her BA, he sent her back to her home state to collect black folk material.

After some initial difficulties in explaining her purpose to people she had known as a child, Hurston managed to collect a veritable trove of songs, stories, dances, games, lullabies, religious practices, and superstitions. Hurston soon learned that she needed to drop her hard-won "Barnardese" to converse with migrant workers and rural townspeople. By holding "lying" contests in which locals were invited to tell their most outrageous and entertaining tales and sometimes indulging in a few "lies" herself, Hurston won the trust and admiration of many of the people she met in her travels. A chance encounter with Langston Hughes in the South led to a deepening of their relationship along with an introduction to his secret patron, Charlotte Mason. With the generous support of the wealthy New York widow, known to her many black protégés as Godmother, Hurston received fresh funds to continue her research. She eventually translated her folk material into a number of artistic productions. She organized a series of black folk concerts, variously titled *The Great Day* and *From Sun to Sun*, that showcased real black work songs and included elaborate dances from the Bahamas. But perhaps most importantly, Hurston eventually published *Mules and Men* (1935), her account of black folklore and voodoo practices in the United States. The book established Hurston as the premier expert in black folklife and opened numerous funding opportunities for her.

Even as Hurston's anthropological career was taking off, she continued to dedicate herself to her creative ambitions. The year before *Mules and Men* came out, she published *Jonah's Gourd Vine* (1934), a novel based on her parents' tumultuous but loving marriage. *Jonah's Gourd Vine* was nothing short of a revelation in the world of American letters. It showcased Hurston's signature mastery over black vernacular and heralded the appearance of a major creative talent. Hurston revealed the poetry in common African American expressions and a metaphorical depth that endowed complex existential and philosophical ideas with a vivid physicality. Long presented in literature by white Americans as a childlike, even primitive language, black vernacular in Hurston's hands became not the language of the uneducated masses but a dynamic idiom of a people long oppressed but ever resilient and insightful. The novel's stunning prose was matched by its nuanced presentation of John and Lucy Pearson, a couple who rise from sharecropping to become prominent members of their all-black town. Like Hurston's own father, the book's protagonist proves to be a brilliant preacher, but his able tongue is also his downfall, as he seduces numerous women. Lucy, devoted to John and their many children, tolerates his infidelities, knowing that John's roving eye reflects the insecurities of his impoverished upbringing and marriage to a woman whose wealthy family unequivocally rejected him.

Although Hurston's first novel won glowing reviews in major national outlets like *The New York Times Book Review*, it also began a long-standing conflict between Hurston and many of the leading black writers and intellectuals of her day. *The Crisis* called *Jonah's Gourd Vine* "a failure" and criticized the attention she paid to "a backward Negro people" (Burris 1934). By the end of the 1930s, Richard Wright and his school of protest fiction was ascendant. Where Wright argued that black writers have a responsibility to showcase the racial inequities that subjugate African Americans, Hurston insisted on making issues of discrimination secondary in her portrait of black life. Blackness was not to be defined by victimization and a history of oppression; instead, she reveled in its diversity and a way of life that celebrated humor, word play, story, song, and dance. Though Hurston certainly had artistic and intellectual allies throughout her life, including James Weldon Johnson and Countee Cullen among many others, her work stands alone in its embrace of black forms. There are simply no other novels that rival the kind of vernacular mastery evident in *Jonah's Gourd Vine* and, of course, her masterpiece, *Their Eyes Were Watching God* (1937).

Most people first encounter Zora Neale Hurston through her second novel, *Their Eyes Were Watching God*. Commonly taught in high school and college classrooms, it has become a modern classic, describing Janie Crawford's journey to self-discovery and her passionate romance with Tea

Cake. Readers discover a vernacular language rich in metaphor and philosophical insight and a natural world bursting with beauty and meaning. The novel's simple story belies a number of radical elements that distinguish it from what is typically assigned as core curriculum. Most obviously, *Their Eyes Were Watching God* operates within an all-black world. White characters are peripheral, and blackness is portrayed not as a tragic condition of oppression but as a vibrant, multifaceted identity. Although the book does not ignore the effects of racial inequality, it is also not premised upon the horrors of white supremacy. Instead, it celebrates and delights in the joys of African American life—the stories shared on the porch of Joe Starks's store, the pride of Eatonville, and the energetic, often stunning contours of its language. *Their Eyes Were Watching God* is also notable for its bold focus on a female protagonist. Unlike many of the best-known female characters in American literature, from *The Scarlet Letter*'s (1850) Hester Prynne to *The Awakening*'s (1899) Edna Pontellier, Janie is neither tragic nor long-suffering. Though she endures the slights and insults of two husbands, she at last finds a lasting love with the charming Tea Cake. Janie willingly leaves the wealth of her late second husband and the safety of her home to explore life among the "muck" with her exuberant and much younger lover.

At every turn in *Their Eyes Were Watching God*, Hurston surprises her readers with complex depictions and unexpected narrative moves. Though Tea Cake is clearly the love of Janie's life, he begins their marriage by abandoning her in order to gamble away her fortune. Later on, he beats her merely to prove to others that he can. What kind of romance countenances violence? If Janie is so independent, why doesn't she stand up to Tea Cake? Hurston supplies no easy answers to such questions. Instead, she leaves readers with troubling developments: Janie later kills Tea Cake after he is bitten by a rabid dog and tries to hurt her. Just as Janie remains conspicuously silent at her trial for the murder of her third husband, Hurston does not explain the nuances of her text. The book asks readers to reconcile often unsettling accounts of human nature. Does Nanny, Janie's grandmother, repeat the logic of slavery by forcing her young granddaughter to marry Logan, an older landowning farmer? Is this an act of love or bondage? Hurston celebrates Janie's empowerment, but is it only possible because her second husband Jody dies? Would she have remained his obedient wife if he had continued to live? These questions enliven a text that continues to fascinate readers. We find in the contradictions of the novel a true account of human nature, which is rarely consistent and predictable. Janie, like her creator, encompasses multitudes, and her identity is formed as much by the vicissitudes of life as by the choices she pursues.

While many novelists find difficulty moving past the subject matter of their first book, Hurston delighted in setting new challenges for herself in her fiction. Unlike Richard Wright, who repeats the themes and ideas of *Native Son* (1940) in *The Outsider* (1953) and "The Man Who Lived Underground (1969)," Hurston explored characters and settings far removed from John Pearson and Janie Crawford in her later novels. *Moses, Man of the Mountain* (1939), published two years later, retells the story of the biblical prophet in an African American context. Hurston presents her Moses as a reluctant hero who would rather commune with God and nature before he is called to rescue the Hebrews and lead them to the Promised Land. Although the novel makes no explicit mention of American race relations, it offers a canny critique of contemporary dynamics. Hurston was especially concerned with exploring the nature of freedom. She presents the emancipated Hebrews as eager both to follow and to complain about their new leader, Moses, rather than embrace the struggle of making their own choices. Toward the end of the novel, Moses concludes "that no man may make another free. Freedom was something internal" (Boyd 2003, 369). This was a sentiment consistent with Hurston's own understanding of the world. She refused to be bound by any single ideology or set of beliefs but always insisted on viewing life according to her own values.

Hurston's final novel, *Seraph on the Suwanee* (1948), was, like much of her previous work, embraced by white reviewers but scorned by black critics. Focused primarily on white Southerners, the book challenged what Hurston called "that old silly rule about Negroes not writing about white people" (Hemenway 1977, 308). The book is perhaps best read as a companion to *Their Eyes Were Watching God*, since the journey of its protagonist, Arvay Meserve, is so at odds with the empowerment and independence demonstrated by Janie Crawford. While Janie follows her passion for Tea Cake, Arvay submits to her husband, Jim. She discovers not so much a sense of self by the novel's end as an absence of self, recognizing that her entire purpose lies in serving Jim and their children. *Seraph on the Suwanee* also exemplifies Hurston's evolving understanding of race and racialized language. She presents Jim as fluent in African American vernacular, suggesting that linguistic elements she once identified as uniquely black are instead part of a broader Southern legacy. While many critics decry *Seraph on the Suwanee* as a betrayal of Hurston's commitment to black folklife, the novel deepens our understanding of how Hurston understood race relations and the country as a whole. Having written books that extol the beauties of the black community, Hurston looked to expand her literary landscape. Like *Moses, Man of the Mountain*, *Seraph on the Suwanee* challenges readers to understand new perspectives and ideas. The diversity of Hurston's work and her decidedly mixed critical reception has led Carla Kaplan to suggest that she "may be American literature's most controversial writer" (Kaplan 2003, 26). Even deep admirers of her writings like Alice

Walker have grave reservations about many of Hurston's texts. Such controversy, however, only reaffirms Hurston's hallmark contrariness. No doubt she would rather have readers argue about her than simply praise her talents.

Hurston's fictional accomplishments are more than sufficient to enter her into the pantheon of literary greats, but she followed up *Mules and Men* only three years later with a study of voodoo and other cultural practices from Jamaica and Haiti entitled *Tell My Horse* (1938). With funding from the Guggenheim Foundation, Hurston spent over a year collecting material on the two island nations. She apprenticed herself to multiple voodoo doctors, stayed with a mountain Maroon community descended from escaped slaves, and learned about various sexual practices. Though she had enough material for multiple volumes, her publisher insisted on a single monograph. *Tell My Horse*, like *Mules and Men*, continues to be a landmark study. Hurston had infiltrated communities that most Westerners knew nothing about. Her work, however, did little to demystify certain aspects of Caribbean culture. Her portrayal of voodoo beliefs, and in particular her writings on zombies, or the reanimated dead, allude to incidents that could not be easily explained. She was content to recognize and at times even embrace the mysteries that lie not just in various cultural practices but in humanity's basic relationship to the world.

While studying voodoo in New Orleans, where she encountered the complex system of voodoo beliefs for the first time, Hurston clearly departed from the objective observation approach practiced by leading anthropologists. Unlike Boas and others, Hurston was not satisfied to sit back and take notes on the rituals, dances, and customs she observed. Instead, she threw herself into the communities she studied. Footage of her travels in the South show her drumming on the bongos and singing along with excited church congregants. She styled herself as a "native" anthropologist, someone who in learning about a specific group came to adopt part of the practices she observed as her own. Though Hurston's literary achievements frequently overshadow her anthropological contributions, both are critical to understanding her legacy.

We might then understand her autobiography, *Dust Tracks on a Road* (1942), as a fusion of her artistic and anthropological aims. Here she takes her own life as the subject of study, applying her indelible perspective to her childhood home, family, teachers, and experiences. As many readers have noted, there is much of Hurston's life omitted from this text, making it less an autobiography than a selective memoir on topics she cared to discuss. For example, absent from the book is her deep friendship with Langston Hughes, which ended in anger and resentment over their collaboration on the play *Mule Bone*. Hurston also avoids significant mention of her love life, a subject that she was notoriously reticent about even with her closest friends. And though she surely must have experienced many instances of racism and sexism, here she presents herself as almost immune to such petty forms of discrimination. The book describes her fellow students at Barnard eagerly welcoming her into their social lives, though as the first black graduate of the college, Hurston must have encountered some resistance. Similarly, in reflecting on her job as a manicurist in Washington, D.C., Hurston presents both her race and gender as an asset. Because she was a black woman, her clients were more comfortable disclosing bits of gossip and political insights, for presumably she had no one to tell. Such a reversal of expectation is typical of Hurston, who tired of those people "always at my elbow reminding me that I am the granddaughter of slaves" (Hurston, "How It Feels," 1979, 153). She had little patience for "the sobbing school of Negrohood who hold that nature somehow has given them a low-down dirty deal and whose feelings are all hurt about it" (Hurston, "How It Feels," 1979, 153). Hurston claimed instead that those who might scorn her—on the basis of race, gender, or any such category—were only depriving themselves of her own brilliance.

Much of Hurston's self-confidence derives from her supportive and encouraging mother, as well as the example of her father, who came from what she called "regular hand-to-mouth folks. Didn't own pots to pee in, nor beds to push them under" (Hemenway 1977, 280). Despite his humble upbringing, John Hurston rose to become the mayor of Eatonville and a preacher so powerful he earned the nickname "God's Battle-Axe" (Boyd 2003, 26). Although Hurston was born in Notasulga, Alabama, not Eatonville, Florida, as she claimed, her identity is inseparable from the all-black town that she called home. Hurston's father moved the family there when she was still a toddler. The family of eight children thrived in a large two-story house that included a lush vegetable garden. Hurston attended the local Hungerford Industrial and Normal School, which emphasized self-reliance and achievement. In this vital, dynamic community, Hurston witnessed the full range of black life and saw that race was no impediment to happiness and success. All town institutions were run by African Americans, though none were of greater import to Hurston than Joe Clarke's store. There townspeople gathered on the front porch to discuss the latest gossip, share stories, tell folktales, and express themselves in the vernacular that would become the hallmark of Hurston's writings. In Eatonville, Hurston developed a sense of pride and self-determination that was at odds with a country where the lynching of African Americans was largely an unpunished crime and women had still not won the right to vote. And yet, Hurston entered the world convinced of her own brilliance, a fact that, given the country she was born into, was nothing short of a radical act.

Rather than focus on matters of discrimination, throughout *Dust Tracks on a Road*, Hurston presents herself as an almost mythical figure, a portrait borne out by many aspects of her life. As Darwin T. Turner noted in a foreword to the 1970 edition of *Mules and Men*, "Zora Neale Hurston herself should have been a character in a folktale. But an author would not dare create her. Readers and critics would denounce him for inventing an unbelievable person" (Turner 1970, n.p.). At times it is difficult to separate fact from the persona Hurston aimed to project. This is not to suggest that *Dust Tracks on a Road* is inaccurate but rather that like all first-person life narratives, it is subject to the selective memory and deliberate curation of its author. Moreover, it is essential to bear in mind that Hurston did not want to write the book. She had many close friends and intimates but often did not share with them key details about her life; no one, for example, seems to have known about her third and final marriage. Exposing all the struggles and triumphs of her life was inconsistent with a woman who lied to everyone about her age and was evasive about key years in her youth. Born in 1891, she passed as more than a decade younger for most of her life. Although this deception began as a way to take advantage of free educational opportunities, later it seems that Hurston learned that by projecting youth, she could more easily attract the mentorship of others.

Despite her reluctance to pen the book, *Dust Tracks on a Road* provides deep insight into much of Hurston's life and self-conception. Early in the book, she describes a series of visions that gripped her when she was a young child. She claims each of these vivid images eventually came to pass in her actual life and guided her through key milestones like the death of her mother and her first acquaintance with the influential Charlotte Mason. Is this true? Did Hurston have such power of premonition? While such visions may have appeared to her, they are most potent as affirming a life guided by a greater plan or direction. Hurston found meaning by creating such a life, presenting its major influences as fated.

While Hurston was routinely criticized by black intellectuals and civil rights leaders for not taking more progressive political positions, she was often constrained by her editors. *Dust Tracks on a Road* was published shortly after the United States entered the Second World War. Her editor at the time, Bertram Lippincott, was wary of including any material that might be construed as controversial or overtly political. Although recent editions of *Dust Tracks on a Road* are true to Hurston's original vision of the text, when it was first published, Lippincott insisted on excising chapters that vehemently denounced U.S. involvement overseas and the hypocrisies of purportedly Christian nations. The Hurston of "Seeing the World as It Is" is deeply concerned with contemporary politics and adamant about forging a nation true to its original values (Hurston 1942). Nonetheless, Hurston's political opinions did shift over time, and her overt critique of white supremacy in the 1930s eventually evolved into perspectives that were more difficult to understand. In her final years, she took a bold stance against the Supreme Court ruling in *Brown v. Board of Education*, the landmark case outlawing school segregation. Writing in *The Orlando Sentinel*, Hurston declared the ruling insulting to her race. Although Hurston was not against integration and in fact encouraged it broadly and in her personal life, she firmly objected to its forced institutionalization. She also rejected claims that black schools were inferior to white schools, a charge that may have been true in certain districts she knew well but was hardly consistent across the country. Her stance against *Brown v. Board of Education* alienated many civil rights leaders and won her fan mail from segregationists. Few, however, took the time to understand the roots of Hurston's bold position. She believed strongly that harmony between the races was only possible through voluntary personal relationships. Moreover, her later years were marked by a growing paranoia and fear of governmental intrusion. In 1948, Hurston was the victim of baseless allegations of child molestation. Although the charges were eventually cleared, she suffered greatly from negative media attention, especially from the black press.

Hurston never regained her footing either artistically or financially following the 1948 scandal. She continued to write and even completed a number of manuscripts, but none were accepted for publication. Instead, she took freelance work where she could. At times the assignments, such as ghostwriting a politician's memoir, were too tedious to bear, though other opportunities, such as her coverage of the Ruby McCollum trial, considered to be one of the most scandalous in all of Florida's state history, provided new avenues for her talent. Although she found good friends in her final years, Hurston's financial struggles made writing difficult. By the time of her death in a nursing home run by the county welfare agency, none of her books were in print and there wasn't enough money for a proper burial.

This shift from Harlem celebrity to anonymous grave speaks to the devastation wrought by the 1948 scandal but also to the lack of obvious heirs to Hurston's work. Where Richard Wright helped mentor Ralph Ellison and James Baldwin, securing in part his own legacy, there were no immediate black writers and scholars who took on her anthropological work or wrote anything comparable to *Their Eyes Were Watching God* or *Moses, Man of the Mountain*. It would take decades until Alice Walker went looking for black literary foremothers, found Hurston, and marked her grave. Now, every one of Hurston's books is in print and she is the subject of countless books, dissertations, essays, and other works. Most recently, her first complete manuscript, a book called *Barracoon* (2018) based on the life of Cudjo Lewis or Kossola, known as the last American survivor of the Middle Passage, was published to widespread acclaim. Readers and scholars are just catching up to Hurston. Though it is a cliché to describe any writer or artist as ahead of her time, the phrase is especially apt here. *Barracoon* is a book that could only be published in a time when historians have a broader understanding of the slave trade as not simply the result of European greed, but as a consequence of African complicity. Hurston may have been wary of offering testimony that indicts Africans as well as white slave traders during a time of entrenched segregation and questions about black inferiority. *Barracoon* is further evidence of the depth and range of Hurston's insight into black life and American history.

Hurston is a writer of astounding complexity, and yet much of the beauty of her writing is quite simple. In her 1928 essay "How It Feels to Be Colored Me," she offers her best assessment of her own identity:

> But in the main, I feel like a brown bag of miscellany propped against a wall. Against a wall in company with other bags, white, red, and yellow. Pour out the contents, and there is discovered a jumble of small things priceless and worthless. A first-water diamond, an empty spool, bits of broken glass, lengths of string, a key to a door long since crumbled away, a rusty knife-blade, old shoes saved for a road that never was and never will be, a nail bent under the weight of things too heavy for any nail, a dried flower or two, still a little fragrant. In your hand is the brown bag. On the ground before you is the jumble it held—so much like the jumble in the bags, could they be emptied, that all might be dumped in a single heap and the bags refilled without altering the content of any greatly. A bit of colored glass more or less would not matter. Perhaps that is how the Great Stuffer of Bags filled them in the first place—who knows? (Hurston 1979, 155)

Hurston's brown bag may have been randomly filled by the "Great Stuffer of Bags," but she knew to fill her life with people full of items different than her own. She celebrated difference as the very lifeblood of our country and yet knew as well that in the end we are all bags full of items both "priceless and worthless." This woman of paradox and opposition lived embracing how we are both different and the same.

Timeline

1891

Zora Neale Hurston is born on January 7 in Notasulga, Alabama, to John and Lucy Hurston.

1893

John Hurston moves his family to the all-black town of Eatonville, Florida, and becomes the pastor of Zion Hope Baptist Church.

1904

Lucy Hurston dies, leading to the disintegration of the family. Hurston is sent to the Florida Baptist Academy in Jacksonville.

1905

Hurston returns to her father's home, only to fight with Mattie Moge, her new stepmother.

1906–1911

Called the "Wander Years" by biographer Valerie Boyd, this time is marked by the absence of Hurston in the public record. Hurston was notably silent about this time in later accounts of her life.

1912

Hurston moves in with her older brother Robert in Nashville, Tennessee.

1917

After joining a Gilbert and Sullivan repertoire company, Hurston moves to Baltimore, Maryland. She begins attending the black prep school Morgan Academy, lying to school officials about her birth date.

1918

John Hurston dies. Hurston moves to Washington, D.C., and begins working as a waitress to finance her education at Howard Academy.

1919

Hurston receives her high school diploma from Howard Academy in May and begins college classes that fall.

1920

Hurston meets Herbert Arnold Sheen, whom she later marries.

1921

Hurston publishes her first short story, "John Redding Goes to Sea," in the Howard literary magazine, *Stylus*.

1923

Hurston stops taking classes at Howard due to financial difficulties.

1924

Hurston publishes the short story "Drenched in Light" in *Opportunity*.

1925

Hurston moves to New York City. She wins second-place awards for the short story "Spunk" and the play *Color Struck* in *Opportunity*'s literary contest.

She enrolls in Barnard College and begins corresponding with Fannie Hurst, who briefly hires Hurston as a secretary. She attends Barnard College and studies with Franz Boas.

1926

Hurston begins working with Franz Boas at Columbia University. With Langston Hughes, Wallace Thurman, and Bruce Nugent, Hurston publishes one issue of the magazine *Fire!!*. It includes Hurston's short story "Sweat." "The Eatonville Anthology" is published in the *Messenger*.

1927

Hurston first meets Mrs. Rufus Osgood Mason and signs a contract to collect black folklore in the South. She also receives a fellowship from Carter G. Woodson and marries Herbert Sheen.

1928

"How It Feels to Be Colored Me" is published in *The World Tomorrow*. Hurston receives a Bachelor of Arts degree from Barnard.

1929

Hurston interviews Cudjo Lewis, the last known survivor of the Atlantic slave Trade and begins drafting the manuscript *Barracoon*, which was posthumously published in 2018.

1930

Hurston writes the play *Mule Bone* with Langston Hughes.

1931
Hurston divorces Sheen and publishes "Hoodoo in America" in the *Journal of American Folklore*. She also breaks with Hughes over the authorship of *Mule Bone*.

1932
Hurston writes and helps produce the concert *The Great Day*, first performed on January 10 at the John Golden Theatre in New York. She begins work with colleagues at Rollins College in Winter Park, Florida, to organize a concert of African American music.

1933
Hurston publishes "The Gilded Six-Bits" in *Story* and helps produce *From Sun to Sun* at Rollins College. She also writes "The Fiery Chariot."

1934
Hurston publishes six essays in Nancy Cunard's anthology, *Negro*. *Jonah's Gourd Vine* is published by J. B. Lippincott. It is a Book-of-the-Month Club selection. *Singing Steel* is performed in Chicago. She also publishes "Race Cannot Become Great Until It Recognizes Its Talent" in the *Washington Tribune*.

1935
Mules and Men is published by J. B. Lippincott. Hurston joins the WPA Federal Theater Project as a "dramatic coach."

1936
Hurston receives a Guggenheim fellowship to study West Indian obeah practices. She spends the year in Haiti and Jamaica.

1937
Hurston writes *Their Eyes Were Watching God* in seven weeks while in Jamaica. The novel is published by J. B. Lippincott. She returns to Haiti on a renewed Guggenheim fellowship.

1938
Hurston writes *Tell My Horse: Voodoo and Life in Haiti and Jamaica*. It is published by J. B. Lippincott.

1939
Moses, Man of the Mountain is published by J. B. Lippincott. Hurston joins the Federal Writers' Project in Florida and receives an honorary doctor of letters degree from Morgan State college. She publishes "Now Take Noses" in *Cordially Yours*. She also marries Albert Price III.

1940
Hurston files for divorce from Price.

1941
Hurston writes *Dust Tracks on a Road: An Autobiography* and publishes "Cock Robin, Beale Street" in the *Southern Literary Messenger*. She begins working as a consultant at Paramount Pictures.

1942
Dust Tracks on a Road is published by J. B. Lippincott. Hurston also publishes "Story in Harlem Slang" in the *American Mercury* and a profile of Lawrence Silas in *The Saturday Evening Post*.

1943
Hurston receives Howard University's Distinguished Alumni Award and the Anisfield-Wolf Book Award in Race Relations for *Dust Tracks*. She also appears on the cover of *The Saturday Review*. "The 'Pet Negro' Syndrome" is published in the *American Mercury*. Her divorce from Price is granted.

1944
Hurston marries James Howell Pitts in January and divorces him in October. She publishes "My Most Humiliating Jim Crow Experience" in *Negro Digest*.

1945
Hurston writes *Mrs. Doctor*, but it is rejected by Lippincott. She publishes "The Rise of the Begging Joints" in the *American Mercury* and "Crazy for This Democracy" in the *Negro Digest*.

1947
Hurston travels to British Honduras, staying there until March of 1948. She writes *Seraph on the Suwanee*.

1948
Seraph on the Suwanee is published by Charles Scribner's Sons. Hurston is falsely accused of molesting a boy and is arrested.

1949
The molestation case is dismissed.

1950
Hurston publishes "Conscience of the Court" in *The Saturday Evening Post* and "I Saw Negro Votes Peddled" in *The American Legion*.

1951
Hurston publishes "Why the Negro Won't Buy Communism" in *The American Legion* magazine and "A Negro Voter Sizes Up Taft" in *The Saturday Evening Post*.

1952
Hurston is hired to write about the Ruby McCollum case for the *Pittsburgh Courier*.

1956
Hurston receives an award at Bethune-Cookman College and works as a librarian at Patrick Air Force Base in Florida.

1957–1959
Hurston writes a column for *The Fort Pierce Chronicle* on "Hoodoo and Black Magic."

1958
Hurston works as a substitute teacher at Lincoln Park Academy in Fort Pierce.

1959
After suffering a stroke, Hurston enters the St. Lucie County Welfare Home.

1960
On January 28, Hurston dies in the St. Lucie County Welfare Home and is buried in an unmarked grave in the Garden of Heavenly Rest in Fort Pierce.

1973
Alice Walker discovers and marks Hurston's grave.

1975
Walker publishes "In Search of Zora Neale Hurston" in *Ms.*

2018
Hurston's previously unpublished story of the life of Cudjo Lewis, *Barracoon: The Story of the Last "Black Cargo,"* is posthumously published by Amistad.

Bibliography

Bass, George Houston, and Henry Louis Gates Jr., eds. *Mule Bone: A Comedy of Negro Life by Langston Hughes and Zora Neale Hurston.* New York: HarperCollins, 1991.

Boas, Franz. Franz Boas to Otto Klineberg, November 25, 1929. Franz Boas Papers, American Philosophical Society.

Bontemps, Arna. Arna Bontemps to Langston Hughes, November 24, 1939. In *Arna Bontemps–Langston Hughes Letters, 1925–1967,* edited by Charles H. Nichols, 44. New York: Paragon House, 1990.

Bontemps, Arna. Interview by Robert E. Hemenway, November 1970. Robert E. Hemenway Personal Papers, University of Kansas.

Bontemps, Arna. Interview by Robert E. Hemenway, December 18, 1970. Robert E. Hemenway Personal Papers, University of Kansas.

Bordelon, Pamela. "New Tracks on *Dust Tracks*: Toward a Reassessment of the Life of Zora Neale Hurston." *African American Review* 31, no. 1 (Spring 1997): 5–21.

Bordelon, Pamela. "Zora Neale Hurston: A Biographical Essay." In *Go Gator and the Muddy Water: Writings by Zora Neale Hurston from the Federal Writers' Project,* edited by Pamela Bordelon, 16. New York: W. W. Norton, 1999.

Boyd, Valerie. *Wrapped in Rainbows: The Life of Zora Neale Hurston.* New York: Scribner, 2003.

Burris, Andrew. "Review of Jonah's Gourd Vine." *The Crisis,* June 3, 1934.

Chase, Bill. "Noted Novelist Denies She 'Abused' 10-Year-Old Boy." *The New York Age,* October 23, 1948.

Diouf, Sylviane A. *Dreams of Africa in Alabama: The Slave Ship Clotilda and the Story of the Last Africans Brought to America.* New York: Oxford University Press, 2007.

Du Bois, W. E. B. "The Talented Tenth." In *The Norton Anthology of African American Literature*, 3rd ed., vol. 1, edited by Henry Louis Gates Jr. and Valerie A. Smith, 1057. New York: W. W. Norton, 2014.

Ellison, Ralph. "Recent Negro Fiction." *New Masses*, August 5, 1941.

Gilbert, Douglas. "When Negro Succeeds, South Is Proud, Zora Hurston Says." *The New York World-Telegram*, February 1, 1943.

Hall, Lynda Marion. *Social Rituals and the Verbal Art of Zora Neale Hurston*. Washington, D.C.: Howard University Press, 1996.

Hedden, Worth Tuttle. "Turpentine and Moonshine." *New York Herald Tribune Weekly Book Review*, October 10, 1948.

Hemenway, Robert E. *Zora Neale Hurston: A Literary Biography*. Urbana: University of Illinois Press, 1977.

Holt, Hamilton. *The Life Stories of Undistinguished Americans as Told by Themselves*. New York: Routledge, 2000.

Howard University. *The Bison*. Howard University Yearbooks, 1923. https://dh.howard.edu/bison_yearbooks/103.

Huggins, Nathan Irvin. *Harlem Renaissance*. New York: Oxford University Press, 1971.

Hughes, Langston. *The Big Sea: An Autobiography* (1940). London: Pluto, 1986.

Hughes, Langston. Langston Hughes to Carl Van Vechten, January 16, 1931. Hurston Papers, Yale.

Hughes, Langston. Langston Hughes to Louise Thompson, February 7, 1931. Alain Locke Papers, Howard University.

Hughes, Langston. Langston Hughes to Zora Neale Hurston, January 19, 1931. Alain Locke Papers, Howard University.

Hughes, Langston. "The Negro Artist and the Racial Mountain." In *The Norton Anthology of African American Literature*, 3rd ed., vol. 1, edited by Henry Louis Gates Jr. and Valerie A. Smith, 1320–1324. New York: W. W. Norton, 2014.

Hurst, Fannie. "Zora Neale Hurston: A Personality Sketch." *Yale University Library Gazette* 35 (July 1960): 17–22.

Hurston, Zora Neale. "Art and Such." In *Go Gator and the Muddy Water: Writings by Zora Neale Hurston from the Federal Writers' Project*, edited by Pamela Bordelon, 142. New York: W. W. Norton, 1999.

Hurston, Zora Neale. *Barracoon: The Story of the Last "Black Cargo."* Edited by Deborah G. Plant. New York: Amistad, 2018.

Hurston, Zora Neale. "Characteristics of Negro Expression." In *The Norton Anthology of African American Literature*, 3rd ed., vol. 1, edited by Henry Louis Gates Jr. and Valerie A. Smith, 1050–1062. New York: W. W. Norton, 2014.

Hurston, Zora Neale. "The Chick with One Hen." Unpublished essay, early 1938. James Weldon Johnson Correspondence, Yale University.

Hurston, Zora Neale. *The Complete Stories.* Introduction by Henry Louis Gates Jr. and Sieglinde Lemke. New York: HarperCollins, 1995.

Hurston, Zora Neale. "Court Order: Can't Make Races Mix." Letter to the Editor, *The Orlando Sentinel,* August 1955.

Hurston, Zora Neale. "Crazy for This Democracy." In *I Love Myself When I Am Laughing . . . And Then Again When I Am Looking Mean and Impressive,* edited by Alice Walker, 166. New York: The Feminist Press, 1979.

Hurston, Zora Neale. "Cudjo's Own Story of the Last African Slaver." *The Journal of Negro History* 12, no. 4 (October 1927): 648–663.

Hurston, Zora Neale. *Dust Tracks on a Road.* Philadelphia: J. B. Lippincott, 1942. Reprinted, with restored text and foreword by Maya Angelou, New York: Harper Perennial, 1996.

Hurston, Zora Neale. "The Enemy: A Unique Personal Experience" (1955), 1, Zora Neale Hurston Papers, Special and Area Studies Collections, George A. Smathers Libraries, University of Florida, Gainesville.

Hurston, Zora Neale. Fellowship application to the Julius Rosenwald Fund, December 14, 1934, Fisk University.

Hurston, Zora Neale. *Go Gator and Muddy the Water: Writings by Zora Neale Hurston from the Federal Writers' Project.* Edited and with a biographical essay by Pamela Bordelon. New York: W. W. Norton, 1999.

Hurston, Zora Neale. "High John de Conquer." *The American Mercury,* October 1943.

Hurston, Zora Neale. "Home." Unpublished poem from the Hurston Collection at the Schomburg Center for Research in Black Culture, New York City.

Hurston, Zora Neale. "Hoodoo in America." *Journal of American Folklore* 44, no. 174 (October–December 1931): 317–418.

Hurston, Zora Neale. "How It Feels to Be Colored Me." In *I Love Myself When I Am Laughing . . . And Then Again When I Am Looking Mean and Impressive,* edited by Alice Walker, 152–153. New York: The Feminist Press, 1979.

Hurston, Zora Neale. *I Love Myself When I Am Laughing . . . and Then Again When I Am Looking Mean and Impressive.* Edited by Alice Walker, introduction by Mary Helen Washington. New York: The Feminist Press, 1979.

Hurston, Zora Neale. "I Saw Negro Votes Peddled." *The American Legion Magazine* 49 (November 1950): 13, 54–60.

Hurston, Zora Neale. *Jonah's Gourd Vine.* Philadelphia: J. B. Lippincott, 1934. Reprinted, with a foreword by Rita Dove, New York: Harper Perennial, 1990.

Hurston, Zora Neale. "The Life Story of Mrs. Ruby J. McCollum!" *The Pittsburgh Courier,* March 14, 1953.

Hurston, Zora Neale. *Moses, Man of the Mountain*. Philadelphia: J. B. Lippincott, 1939. Reprinted, with a foreword by Deborah E. McDowell, New York: Harper Perennial, 1991.

Hurston, Zora Neale. "Mourner's Bench, Communist Line: Why the Negro Won't Buy Communism." *The American Legion Magazine* 50 (June 1951): 14–15, 55–60.

Hurston, Zora Neale. *Mules and Men*. Philadelphia: J. B. Lippincott, 1935. Reprinted with a foreword by Arnold Rampersad, New York: Harper Perennial, 1990.

Hurston, Zora Neale. "My Most Humiliating Jim Crow Experience." In *I Love Myself When I Am Laughing... And Then Again When I Am Looking Mean and Impressive*, edited by Alice Walker, 163. New York: The Feminist Press, 1979.

Hurston, Zora Neale. "Negroes without Self-Pity." *The American Mercury*, November 1943.

Hurston, Zora Neale. "The 'Pet' Negro System." In *I Love Myself When I Am Laughing... And Then Again When I Am Looking Mean and Impressive*, edited by Alice Walker, 157. New York: The Feminist Press, 1979.

Hurston, Zora Neale. "Race Cannot Become Great Until It Recognizes Its Talent." *Washington Tribune*, December 29, 1934.

Hurston, Zora Neale. "Ruby McCollum Fights for Life." *The Pittsburgh Courier*, November 22, 1952.

Hurston, Zora Neale. *Seraph on the Suwanee*. New York: Charles Scribner's Sons, 1948. Reprinted, with a foreword by Hazel V. Carby and afterword by Henry Louis Gates Jr., New York: Harper Perennial, 1991.

Hurston, Zora Neale. "Stories of Conflict." *The Saturday Review of Literature*, April 2, 1938.

Hurston, Zora Neale. *Tell My Horse: Voodoo and Life in Haiti and Jamaica*. Philadelphia: J. B. Lippincott, 1938. Reprinted, with a foreword by Ishmael Reed, New York: Harper Perennial, 1990.

Hurston, Zora Neale. *Their Eyes Were Watching God*. Philadelphia: J. B. Lippincott, 1937. Reprinted, with a foreword by Mary Helen Washington, New York: Harper Perennial, 1990.

Hurston, Zora Neale. "What White Publishers Won't Print." In *I Love Myself When I Am Laughing... And Then Again When I Am Looking Mean and Impressive*, edited by Alice Walker, 169. New York: The Feminist Press, 1979.

Hurston, Zora Neale. "Who Has Not Felt the Fire." Untitled poem, dated April 21, 1919. Hurston Collection at the Schomburg Center for Research in Black Culture, New York City.

Hurston, Zora Neale. "You Don't Know Us Negroes." Unpublished essay written for *The American Mercury*, 1934. Manuscript Division, Library of Congress.

Hurston, Zora Neale. Zora Neale Hurston to Albert Price, October 2, 1942. The Kinsey Collection: The Personal Treasures of Bernard & Shirley Kinsey, Norton Museum of Art, West Palm Beach, Florida.

Hurston, Zora Neale. "Zora's Revealing Story of Ruby's First Day at Court." *The Pittsburgh Courier*, October 11, 1952.

Hurston, Zora Neale, and Langston Hughes. *Mule Bone: A Comedy of Negro Life*. Edited and with introductions by George Houston Bass and Henry Louis Gates Jr. New York: Harper Perennial, 1991.

Hurston, Zora Neale, and Charlotte Mason. Contractual agreement signed December 8, 1927. Alain Locke Papers, Howard University.

Jones, Jacqueline. *Labor of Love, Labor of Sorrow: Black Women, Work and the Family, from Slavery to the Present*. New York: Vintage, 1986.

Jordan, June. "On Richard Wright and Zora Neale Hurston: Notes toward a Balancing of Love and Hatred." *Black World* 23, no. 10 (August 1974): 4–8.

Kaplan, Carla, ed. *Zora Neale Hurston: A Life in Letters*. New York: Anchor Books, 2003.

Kennedy, Stetson. "Working with Zora." In *All about Zora*, edited by Alice Morgan Grant. Winter Park, FL: Four-G Publishers, 1991.

Lewis, David Levering. *When Harlem Was in Vogue*. New York: Vintage Books, 1979.

Lippincott, Joshua Ballinger. J. B. Lippincott to E. O. Grover, February 5, 1934. Zora Neale Hurston Collection, University of Florida.

Locke, Alain. "Dry Fields and Green Pastures." *Opportunity*, January 1940.

Locke, Alain. Untitled review. *Opportunity*, January 1938, 1057. New York: W. W. Norton, 2014.

Louis Gates, Henry, Jr. "A Tragedy of Negro Life." In *Mule Bone: A Comedy of Negro Life*, edited by George Houston Bass and Henry Louis Gates Jr., 5. New York: First Perennial, 1991.

Lyons, James. "Famous Negro Author Working as Maid Here Just 'to Live a Little.' " *Miami Herald*, March 27, 1950.

Lyons, James. "Successful Author Working as a Maid." *St. Louis Post-Dispatch Sunday Magazine*, April 24, 1950.

Mason, Charlotte. Charlotte Mason to Zora Neale Hurston, draft of letter headed "Zora," January 15, 1931. Alain Locke Papers, Howard University.

McDougal, Sally. "Author Plans to Upbraid Own Race: Zora Hurston Denies There Is 'Tragedy' in Being Negro." *The New York World-Telegram*, February 6, 1935.

Miller, May. Interview notes, April 29, 1971. Robert E. Hemenway Personal Papers, University of Kansas.

Mitchell, Burroughs. Burroughs Mitchell to Zora Neale Hurston, July 21, 1955. Scribner Archives, Princeton University.

Mitchell, Burroughs. Burroughs Mitchell to Zora Neale Hurston, October 3, 1950. Scribner Archives, Princeton University.

Moylan, Virginia Lynn. *Zora Neale Hurston's Final Decade*. Gainesville: University Press of Florida, 2011.

Nichols, Charles H., ed. *Arna Bontemps-Langston Hughes Letters, 1925–1967*. New York: Paragon House, 1990.

Nugent, Richard Bruce. Interview by Robert E. Hemenway, May 1970. Robert E. Hemenway Personal Papers, University of Kansas.

Otey, Frank M. *Eatonville, Florida: A Brief History of One of America's First Freedman's Towns*. Winter Park, FL: Four-G Publishers, 1989.

Rampersad, Arnold. "Foreword." *Mules and Men*, by Zora Neale Hurston, xv–xxiii. New York: First Harper Perennial Modern Classics, 2008.

Rampersad, Arnold. *The Life of Langston Hughes, Volume 1: 1920–1941—I, Too, Sing America*. New York: Oxford University Press, 1988.

Sheen, Herbert. Interview by Robert E. Hemenway. Robert E. Hemenway Personal Papers, University of Kansas.

Thurman, Wallace. *Infants of the Spring*. New York: Dover, 2013.

Tomkins, Lucille. Untitled review. *The New York Times Book Review*, September 26, 1937.

Turner, Darwin T. "Introduction." *Mules and Men*, by Zora Neale Hurston, 6–15. New York: Harper, 1970.

Wallace, Margaret. "Real Negro People." *The New York Times Book Review*, May 6, 1934.

Waring, Dorothy. Interview by Robert E. Hemenway, May 21, 1971. Robert E. Hemenway Personal Papers, University of Kansas.

Washington, Mary Helen. "Zora Neale Hurston: A Woman Half in Shadow." In *I Love Myself When I Am Laughing ... And Then Again When I Am Looking Mean and Impressive*, edited by Alice Walker, 21. New York: The Feminist Press, 1979.

Watson, Steven. *The Harlem Renaissance: Hub of African-American Culture, 1920–1930*. New York: Pantheon Books, 1995.

Wilkins, Roy. "The Watchtower." *Amsterdam News*, February 27, 1943.

Wright, Richard. "Between Laughter and Tears." *New Masses*, October 5, 1937.

Wright, Richard. "Blueprint for Negro Writing." In *The Norton Anthology of African American Literature*, 3rd ed., vol. 2, edited by Henry Louis Gates Jr. and Valerie A. Smith, 125–132. New York: W. W. Norton, 2014.

"Zora Hurston Denies Saying Race Better Off in South." *Atlanta Daily World*, March 3, 1943.

Index

Italicized entries indicate material in sidebars

"Academic Nightmare, An" (Hurston), 31
Africa Town, 83, *84*
African diaspora, 2, *187*, 189, 190
age, Hurston's, 1, 20, 22, 37, 122, 125–126, 133, 140, 198
All de Live Long Day (Hurston), 96
All-Florida Magazine, 176
American Legion, 164, 167
American Mercury, 132, 136, 139, 142
anthropology, 41–42, 48–49, 58, 100, 100–101, 141, 187, 189, 190, 192, 196; Gullah people, 127–129; Hurston's research expeditions, American South, 51–57, 60–71, 102–103, 121–122, 127–129; Hurston's research expeditions, Bahamas, 68–69; Hurston's research expeditions, Caribbean, 105–109; Hurston's research expeditions, Florida recording expedition, 121–122; Hurston's research expeditions, Honduras, 147; Maroon groups, 107, *107*; turpentine workers, 121–122. *See also Mules and Men; Tell My Horse*
Appassionata (Hurst), 39
"Art and Such" (Hurston), 115, 120

"Back to the Middle Ages, Or How to Become a Peasant in the United States" (Hurston), 145
Bahamas, 68–69, 70, 75, 192; Bahamian culture, 68–69; Fire Dance, 89, 91, 121
Baldwin, James, 1, 100, *130*, 199
Baltimore, Maryland, 21–22, 24
Barnard College, 36–41, 46, 61, 64, 134, 179, 192; "Barnardese," 52–53, 192, 197
Barnicle, Mary Elizabeth, 102–103
Barracoon (Hurston), 60n, 83–87, 199
Belle Glade, Florida, 102–103, 158, 161, 165
Belo, Jane, 127–129, 141
Bennett, Gwendolyn, 33, 42, 44, 191
Benton, Dr. C. C., 183, 184
Bethune, Mary McLeod, *76*, 97, 176
Bethune-Cookman College, 97, 180
black art, 43, 44, 63, 100, 113, 115, 130, 191. *See also* black theater
black church, the, *19*, 35, 120, 128
"Black Death" (Hurston), 35, 191
black theater, 2–43, 63, 88, 93, 103, 105, 123
Black Writers' Guild, 33
blackness, 5, 34, 42, 193, 194

213

"Blueprint for Negro Writing" (Wright), 113
Boas, Franz, 33, 41–42, 51–52, 57, 67, 69, 71, 96–97, 99, 100–101, 103–104, 192, 196
"Bone of Contention, The" (Hurston), 73
Bontemps, Arna, 36, 126, 180
Boyd, Valerie, 15, 16, 18, 21, 22, 25, 57, 59, 86–87, 101, 115, 122–123, 151
Breedlove, Sarah. *See* Walker, C. J.
Bronx, 155, 156, 157
Brown, Sterling, 29, 35, 104, 114, 118, 180
Brown v. Board of Education, 2, *30*, 158, *160*, 177, 178, 199

California, 130–131
Cane (Toomer), 55, *56*
Caribbean. *See* Haiti; Jamaica
Carl Van Vechten Gallery, 68
carpetbaggers, 144, 181
Challenge, 99
"Chapter from the Book of Life, A" (Hurston), 31
"Characteristics of Negro Expression" (Hurston), 97, 153
Chicago, Illinois, 99–100
"Chick with One Hen, The" (Hurston), 114
Churchill, Winston, 177
civil rights movement, 3, *19*, *76*, 190
Clarke, Joe, 5, 48. *See also* Joe Clarke's porch
Class, 152, 153–154, 162, 167; in Haiti, 120; in Jamaica, 106–107
"Cock Robin Beale Street" (Hurston), 130
Color Struck (Hurston), 35, 46, 47
Columbia University, 41, 69, 100, 101
Communism, 135, 145, 167, 169
"Conscience of the Court" (Hurston), 162–163
"Court Order: Can't Make Races Mix" (Hurston), 177–178

"Crazy for This Democracy" (Hurston), 144
Creech, Sara, 158–159, 160, *160*, 161–162, 168
Crisis, 29, *30*, 33, 43, 55, *68*, 98, 191, 193
Cross Creek (Rawlings), 132
"Cudjo's Own Story of the Last African Slaver" (Hurston), 56–57
Cullen, Countee, 33, 35, 40, 62, 144, 191, 193

"Dance Songs and Tales from the Bahamas" (Hurston), 75
David McKay Company, 183
Davis, John P., 44, 46
Daytona Beach, Florida, 138, 140
De Possum's Tail Hairs (Hurston), 96
death, Hurston's, 184, 199; burial, 185; funeral, 185; obituaries, 185–186; papers burned, 186; unmarked grave, 185, 186–187, 199
dialect. *See* vernacular
domestic work, 17, 20–21, 162–164, 192
Douglas, Aaron, 42, 44, 46, 58, 59, 68, 191
"Drenched in Light" (Hurston), 32–33
Du Bois, W. E. B., 29, *30*, 42–43, 45, 46, 96, 100, 118, 142, 143–144, 185, 191
Durham, North Carolina, 123
Dust Tracks on a Road, 130, 131, 133–136, 138, 180, 184, 196–198; omitted chapters, 134–135, 198; as selective memoir, 134, 196–198

Eatonville, Florida, 1–6, *2*, 92–93, 94, 115, 119, 140, 187, 190, 197; Hurston's research in, 52–53, 102–103; and Hurston's writing, 11, 28, 30, 48–49, 73–74, 79, 94, 110–112, 124, 133, 143, 194. *See also* "Eatonville Anthology, The"; Joe Clarke's porch
"Eatonville Anthology, The" (Hurston), 48–49, 61, 63, 190

Eau Gallie, Florida, 68, 169–170, 172, 175
education, Hurston's, 17, 21; college, 27–32, 36–41, 61; elementary, 10, 177; graduate, 100–101, 105; high school, 1, 14–15, 22, 23–25, 26–27
education, Hurston's views on, 142–143, 177–179
Egypt, Ophelia Settle, 29
Ellison, Ralph, 125, 199
Embree, Edwin, 100, 101
encyclopedic writings, Hurston's, 143–144
"Enemy: A Unique Personal Experience, The" (Hurston), 179

Fast and Furious, 88–89
Fauset, Jessie, 33, 55
Federal Writers' Project (FWP), *103*, 117–118, 120, 121–122, 159; Alsberg, Henry, 118; Corse, Carita Dogget, 117–118, 121; *Florida Negro*, 117, 118, 120; Hurston's writing, anthologized, 159–160. *See also Go Gator and Muddy the Water*
feminism, 1, 112, *186*
Fiery Chariot, The (Hurston), 91, 94
film industry, 152–153
financial difficulties, 41, 76–77, 87, 90, 91, 92, 93, 95, 146, 156–157, 162, 165–166, 172, 175, 180, 191–192, 199
Fire!!, 44–45, 46, 65, 191, 192
"The Fire and the Cloud" (Hurston), 99
Florida Baptist Academy, 14–15
Florida Normal and Industrial College, 131–132
folk concerts, 89–94, 95, 99, 121, 172, 192. *See also From Sun to Sun; Great Day, The; In the Beginning; Singing Steel*
folklore, 11, 38, 42, 48, 69, 93, 94, 95, 97, 103, 105, 112, 120, 121, 139, 187, 192
Fort Moosa, 56
Fort Pierce, 182–184, 186
Fort Pierce Chronicle, 182, 184

Frazier, E. Franklin, 33, 35
From Sun to Sun, 91–94, 95, 192. *See also Great Day, The; In the Beginning; Singing Steel*

Gilbert and Sullivan repertoire company, 20–21, 35
"Gilded Six-Bits, The" (Hurston), 94–95, 144
Gildersleeve, Virginia, 37, 39, 41
Gilpin Players, 78, 79, 80
"Glossary of Harlem Slang" (Hurston), 133
"Go Gator and Muddy the Water" (Hurston), 120
Go Gator and Muddy the Water: Writings by Zora Neale Hurston from the Federal Writers' Project, 118
Godmother. *See* Mason, Charlotte
Golden Bench of God, The (Hurston), 168–169, 170–171
Great Day, The, 90–91, 102, 172, 192. *See also From Sun to Sun; In the Beginning; Singing Steel*
Great Depression, 71, 76, *76*, 86, 91, 101, *103*
Great Migration, *76*
Green, Paul, 123, 127, 128–129
Grime, Angelina, 29
Grover, Edwin Osgood, 92, 136
Guggenheim fellowship, 96–97, 105, 108, 109, 117, 141, 142, 196
Gullah, 127–129, *128*

Haiti, 42, 65, 101, 106, 108–110, 114, 115, 120, 190, 196; Hurston's voodoo research in, 108–109
Harlem, 34–35, 40, 41, 42, 43, 45–46, 76, 101, 132–133, 140, 145, 149, 160, 191; Hurston's research in, 41–42, 192
Harlem Renaissance, 2, 33–34, 43–47, 49, 51, *68*, *76*, 83, 168, 190–191, 192
Harper Brothers, 183

health problems, 21–22, 87–88, 92, 93, 110, 130, 131, 142, 168, 171–172, 175, 181, 182, 183, 184
Hemenway, Robert E., 1, 36, 41, 57, 81, 134, 163, 169, 171, 178, 186, 187; *Zora Neale Hurston: A Literary Biography*, 187
Herskovits, Melville, 33, 101, 107
"High John de Conquer" (Hurston), 139, 141
Historic Sketches of the Old South (Roche), 57
Hollywood, 131
Holmes, Dwight O. W., 23, 26
Honduras, 141–142, 144, 146, 149, 150, 152, 157, 158
hoodoo. *See* voodoo
"How It Feels to Be Colored Me" (Hurston), 34, 53, 64, 200
Howard Academy, 27
Howard University, 25–27, *26*, 28–32, 137, 179; archive, 87; Greek life, 29, 32
"The Hue and Cry about Howard University" (Hurston), 38
Hughes, Bernice, 24, 25
Hughes, Langston, 33, 35, 40, 42, 43, 44, 45, 46, 55–56, 57, 59, 60, 61–63, 64, 69, 70, 98, 101, 119, 133, 191, 192, 196; collaboration with Hurston on *Mule Bone*, 73–81; feud with Hurston, 74–81
Huie, William Bradford, 174
Hurst, Fannie, 35, 38–40, 41, 62, 87, 96, 98, 105, 113, 155, 156–157, 183, 185
Hurston, Benjamin Franklin, 6, 54
Hurston, Bob (Hezekiah Robert), 4, 6, 14, 17, 18–20, 25, 54; daughter Wilhelmina, 119; daughter Winifred, 119, 122
Hurston, Clifford Joel, 6, 54, 184, 185
Hurston, Everett Edward, 6, 14, 15, 46, 54
Hurston, John, 3–5, 6–9, 11, 13–14, 15, 16, 17–18, 25, 31, 95, 97–98, 193, 197

Hurston, John Cornelius, 4, 10, 16, 17, 52, 54, 161
Hurston, Lucy Ann (Potts), 3–4, 6, 8–9, 11, 13–14, 31, 170, 197, 198
Hurston, Mattie (Moge), 15, 16, 17–18, 25, 31
Hurston, Richard William, 4, 14, 17, 54
Hurston, Sarah Emmeline, 4, 6–7, 15, 22, 54, 94

"I Saw Negro Votes Peddled" (Hurston), 164
Imitation of Life (Hurst), 38
In the Beginning, 89. *See also From Sun to Sun*; *Great Day, The*; *Singing Steel*
Infants of the Spring (Thurman), 48
Irvine, Fred, 141, 146, 157

J. B. Lippincott Company. *See* Lippincott, Bertram
Jacksonville, Florida, 14–15, 17, 51, 52, 68, 117, 122, 161
Jamaica, 106–108, 114, 115, 120, 190, 196; colorism, 106–107; Maroon groups, 107, *107*, 196; misogyny, 106–107
Jelliffe, Rowena, 78, 79, 80
Jelliffe, Russell, 78, 79, 80
Jim Crow laws, 6, *7*, 136–138, 144. *See also* race relations, segregation
Joe Clarke's porch, 10–11, 28, 35, 42, 47, 48, 52, 63, 161, 197; as Joe Starks's porch in *Their Eyes Were Watching God*, 110, 111, 194
John de Conqueror (Hurston), 127, 129
"John Redding Goes to Sea," 30–31, 32, 94
Johnson, Charles S., 32, 33–34, 35, 36, 83, 99, 191
Johnson, Georgia Douglas, 29
Johnson, James Weldon, 29, 33, 34, 35, 45, 83, 96, 114, 119, *119*, 191, 193
Jonah's Gourd Vine (Hurston), 25, 93, 95–96, 97–98, 99, 193
Journal of Negro History, 51, 56
Jungle Scandals, 88–89

Kaplan, Carla, 2, 53, 97, 105, 127; *Zora Neale Hurston: A Life in Letters*, 2, 127
Kossola. *See* Lewis, Cudjo
Krigwa Players, 42
Ku Klux Klan, 173, 174

Lewis, Cudjo, 54, 60, 60n, 70, 83–87, 199
Life of Herod the Great, The (Hurston), 176–177, 180, 181, 183–184, 185
Lincoln Park Academy, 182, 185
Lippincott, Bertram, 95–96, 98, 99, 109, 123, 129–130, 131, 134, 143, 152, 164, 170–171, 185, 198
Little Negro Theater, 42–43
Live Oak, Florida, 172–173
Lives of Barney Turk (Hurston), 158, 162, 165, 168
Locke, Alain, 29, 33, 35, 57, 59, 60, 62, 65, 70, 83, 90, 92, 114–115, 125, 136, 192
Lomax, Alan, 102–103
"The Lost Keys of Glory" (Hurston), 145
Loughman, Florida, 61–63

Magazine, Alabama, 63
"Magnolia Flower" (Hurston), 38
marriage, in Hurston's writing, 48, 94–95, 95, 111, 112, 153–154, 193
marriages, Hurston's: to Pitts, 140, 198; to Price, 122–123; to Sheen, 54, 88
Marshall, Thurgood, 30
Mason, Charlotte, 55, 57–59, 60, 61–62, 64–65, 67, 69–71, 74, 75, 76, 77, 79, 80, 87, 89, 90, 91–93, 94, 105, 133, 136, 144–145, 192, 198
McCollum, Ruby. *See* Ruby McCollum trial
McKay, Claude, 33, 59
Memphis, Tennessee, 20, 25, 54
Mencken, H. L., 33
Mershon, Katherine Edson, 130–131
Messenger, 33, 38, 48
Meyer, Annie Nathan, 36–37, 39, 40, 41, 53, 62

Miller, Mae, 25–26, 29, 35–36
Mis-Education of the Negro, The (Woodson), 52
Mitchell, Burroughs, 146–147, 149, 162, 165, 170–171, 177
Modern Language Association, 187
Moe, Henry Allen, 141
molestation charges, 149–151, 154–157, 199; allegations recanted, 157; charges dismissed, 156, 157; Hurston's racial resentment over, 155, 160–161, 162, 174; Hurston's resulting depression, 155–156; preliminary hearing, 150–151; press coverage, 154–155, 156, 199
Morgan Academy, 23–25
Morgan College (Morgan University), 23, 25
Moses legend, 105, 123–125, 195; in Caribbean, 124
Moses, Man of the Mountain, 123–125, 136, 195, 199
Moten, Etta, 130, 145
Mrs. Doctor (Hurston), 143
Mule Bone (Hurston and Hughes), 55, 73–76, 78–81, 141, 143
Mules and Men (Hurston), 66, 87, 93, 97, 99, 103–105, 120, 141, 170, 180, 192, 196
"Muttsy" (Hurston), 47–48
"My Most Humiliating Jim Crow Experience" (Hurston), 87–88, 142
"My People, My People!" (Hurston), 119

NAACP (National Association for the Advancement of Colored People), 29, *30*, 33, 45, *77*, *119*, 138, 164, 181
name, Hurston's, 4
Nashville, Tennessee, 18–19, 99
Native Son (Wright), 129, *130*, 131, 195
Negro (ed. Nancy Cunard), 97
"Negro Artist and the Racial Mountain, The" (Hughes), 43, *56n*
Negro Digest, 144

"A Negro Voter Sizes Up Taft"
  (Hurston), 169
Negro World, 31
"Negroes Without Self-Pity"
  (Hurston), 139
"Negrotarians," 37, 39, 40, 57
New Negro, The (ed. Locke), 38, 62, *68*
New Negro movement, 39
New Orleans, 65–67, 69, 71, 196
New York Herald Tribune, 145, 157
New York World-Telegram, 113, 145, 156
Nigger Heaven (Van Vechten), 45–46
"Niggerati," 42, 43–44, 45, 191
North Carolina College of Negroes, 123, 126–127; drama program, 123, 127
Notasulga, Alabama, 1, 3
Nugent, Richard Bruce, 29, 42, 44–45, 46, 48

obeah, 69, 105. *See also* voodoo
Ocoee massacre, 118
O'Neill, Eugene, 33, 35
Opportunity, 32, 33, *68*, 114, 191; awards, 35–36, 47, 191
Orlando Sentinel, 177, 199
Owen, Elizabeth, 171, 172

Parsons, Elsie Clews, 51
Perkins, Maxwell, 146
"The 'Pet' Negro System" (Hurston), 139
Pickens, William, 24, 25
Pitts, James Howell, 140
Pittsburgh Courier, 172, 173, 174, 175
plagiarism, 57
poetry, Hurston's: early poems, 28; "Journey's End," 31; "Night," 31; "O Night," 30; "Passion," 31
political views, Hurston's, 135, 144, 145, 158–159, 164, 169, 177–179, 190, 198–199
Polk County (Hurston and Waring), 141, 142
Porgy and Bess, 89, *90*

"Possum or Pig?" (Hurston), 48
Potts, Lucy Ann. *See* Hurston, Lucy Ann (Potts)
Potts, Sarah, 11
Price, Albert, III, 122–123, 126
protest fiction, 113, *130*, 193
Punter, Percival McGuire, 102–103, 105–106, 108, 112, 114, 123, 129, 140

"Race Cannot Become Great Until It Recognizes Its Talent" (Hurston), 100
race relations, 6, 9, 33, 132, 135–138, 139–140, 158–159; colorism, 106, 125, 159; "feather-bed resistance," 104–105; Hurston's views on, 20, 21, 53, 100, 104–105, 115, 131, 135, 136–138, 139–140, 144, 158–159, 161–162, 177–179, 181, 193, 195, 197, 198–199; in Hurston's work, 95, 113, 124–125, 130, 135–136, 152, 193, 194, 195; in literature, 115, 164, 193; segregation, 117–118, 136–138, 138, 144, 152, 177–179, 199; white supremacy, 2, 53, 135, 137, 138, 144, 194, 197; after World War II, 152
racial essentialism, 1, 41, 58; primitivism, 58–59
Rawlings, Marjorie Kinnan, 132, 146, 153, 155, 175–176
rent parties, 34–35, 190
Reynolds, Grant, 145
"Rise of the Begging Joints, The" (Hurston), 142–143
"Ritualistic Expression from the Lips of Communicants of the Seventh Day Church of God" (Hurston), 128
Road in the Wilderness (Hurston), 142
Robert Hungerford Industrial and Normal School, 9–10, 140, 197
Robeson, Paul, 35, 45, 98
Roche, Emma Langdon, 57
Rochester, Richard, 156
Rollins College, 92, 96, 97, 136

Roosevelt, Eleanor, *160*, 171
Rosenwald fellowship, 99–100, 101
Ruby McCollum trial, 172–174; Hurston's coverage, 173–175, 199

"Sanctified Church, The" (Hurston), 120
Sanford, Florida, 17, 95, 96, 140
Sara Lee doll, 159–160, *160*, 171
Saturday Evening Post, 133, 136, 162, 163, 169
Saturday Review of Literature, 113, 115, 138
Savage, Augusta, 42
Scribner's, 146, 150, 165, 170, 185. *See also* Mitchell, Burroughs; Perkins, Maxwell
Seraph on the Suwanee (Hurston), 131, 147, 151–154, 155, 156, 163, 165, 195
Sheen, Herbert Arnold, 28–29, 31, 35, 54, 55, 59–60, 88, 175
Shepard, James E., 123, 126, 127
Silas, Lawrence, 133
Silver, Marjorie, 183, 185
Singing Steel, 99. *See also From Sun to Sun*; *Great Day, The*; *In the Beginning*
Slavery, *19*, 60, 65, *76*, 83–86, 107, *107*, 115, 128, *128*, 143–144, 194, 199–200
Smathers, Frank, 164–165
Smathers, George, 164
Smith, Bessie, 43, 45, 55–56
Southern Literary Messenger, 130
Spears (Hurston), 35, 191
Spokesman, 38
Spot (Hurston's dog), 161; writing inspired by, 168, 171, 172
"Spunk" (Hurston), 32, 35, 38, 88, 191
Story, 94, 95, 115, 144
"Story in Harlem Slang" (Hurston), 132–133
Stylus, 29, 30, 32
"Sweat" (Hurston), 46, 47, 48, 94

Tell My Horse (Hurston), 87, 106, 108, 114, 120–121, 196
Their Eyes Were Watching God (Hurston), 108–114, 125, 131, 153, 173–174, 180, 187, 193–194, 195, 199; film adaptation, 131
There Is Confusion (Fauset), 33
Thompson, Louise, 70, 74, 75, 76, 78, 79, 80
Thurman, Wallace, 42, 44–47, 48, 65, 70, 101, 191
Toomer, Jean, 29, 33, 55, *56*
Turner, Lorenzo Dow, 29–30, 99
Twentieth Century American Authors, 136

Uncle Tom's Children (Wright), 115–116
University of Florida Department of Rare Books and Manuscripts, 186
University of North Carolina, Chapel Hill, 123, 127
unpublished late work, 171, 179, 183

Van Vechten, Carl, 35, 37, 39, 41, 45–46, 62, 78, 119, 136, 142, 155, 159, 160, 165, 183, 185, 185–186, 192; reactions to Hurston's work, 96, 98, 123. *See also* Carl Van Vechten Gallery
vernacular, 28, 31, 48, 83, 85, 97, 98, 104, 110, 125, 190, 193, 194, 197; white Southern, 152–153, 195
visions, 11–12, 14, 16, 21, 54, 58, 133, 198
voodoo, 56, 65–67, 101, 103, 106, 108, 120, 126, 182, 192, 196; in *Moses, Man of the Mountain*, 124; practitioner, Dieu Donnez St. Leger, 109; practitioner, Father Joe Watson, 66; practitioner, Kitty Brown, 66; practitioner, Luke Turner, 66–67; practitioner, Marie Leveau, 65
Voodoo Gods (Hurston). *See Tell My Horse* (Hurston)

Waldman, Louis, 149, 150, 151, 156
Walker, Alice, 56, 134, 154, 186–187, *186*, *187*, 195–196, 199
Walker, C. J., 68, 76, *77*, 168
Waring, Dorothy, 140–141
Washington, Booker T., 10, 55, 143, 181
Washington, D. C., 26–28
Washington Tribune, 100
Waterbury, Jean Parker, 168, 171
Waters, Ethel, 130, 131, 160, 165, 183, 192
Watkins, Mary Jane, 24
West, Dorothy, 56, 99
"What White Publishers Won't Print" (Hurston), 164
White, Walter, 45, 138
white-life novels, 152
Whiteness, 4, 9, 21, 138; and class, 152, 153–154, 162; in Hurston's fiction, 152–154, 162, 195

"Why the Negro Won't Buy Communism" (Hurston), 167
Wilkins, Roy, 137
Woodson, Carter G., 51, *52*, 56, 57
World Tomorrow, 64
World War II, 131, 137, 139, 142, 144, 198
WPA (Work Projects Administration), 103, *103*, 121. *See also* Federal Writers' Project
Wright, Richard, 1, 55, 113, 115–116, 129, *130*, 193, 195, 199

"You Don't Know Us Negroes" (Hurston), 100

zombies, 108, 109, 120, 196
Zora Neale Hurston Festival of the Arts and Humanities, 2, 187, *187*
Zora Neale Hurston Museum of Fine Arts, 2
Zora Neale Hurston Trail, 2

About the Author

Stephanie Li holds the Susan D. Gubar Chair in Literature at Indiana University. Her teaching interests include racial representation, gender politics, and theories of resistance in nineteenth- to twenty-first-century American and African American literature. She is author of five books, including *Playing in the White: Black Writers, White Subjects* and *Pan-African American Literature: Signifyin(g) Immigrants in the Twenty-First Century*. Her work has appeared in *American Literature, Callaloo, SAQ*, and various essay collections. She has guest edited special issues of *American Literary History* and *Black Camera*.

www.ingramcontent.com/pod-product-compliance
Lightning Source LLC
Chambersburg PA
CBHW060951230426
43665CB00015B/2149